Knowing the Poor

The International Library of Phenomenology and Moral Sciences

Editor: John O'Neill, *York University, Toronto*

The Library will publish original and translated works guided by an analytical interest in the foundations of human culture and the moral sciences. It is intended to foster phenomenological, hermeneutical and ethnomethodological studies in the social sciences, art and literature.

BRYAN S. GREEN

Knowing the Poor
A Case-study in Textual Reality Construction

Routledge & Kegan Paul
London, Boston, Melbourne and Henley

First published in 1983
by Routledge & Kegan Paul Plc
39 Store Street, London WC1E 7DD,
9 Park Street, Boston, Mass. 02108, USA,
296 Beaconsfield Parade, Middle Park,
Melbourne, 3206, Australia, and
Broadway House, Newtown Road,
Henley-on-Thames, Oxon RG9 1EN
Printed in Great Britain by
Hartnoll Print, Bodmin, Cornwall

Library of Congress Cataloging in Publication Data
Green, Bryan S.R.
Knowing the poor.
(The International library of phenomenology and
moral sciences)
Includes index.
1. Sociology-Research. 2. Ethnomethodology.
3. Semiotics. 4. Community. 5. Poor-Canada-
Case studies. 6. Poor laws-Canada-Case studies.
I. Title. II. Series.
HM48.G73 1982 301'.072 82-16489
ISBN 0-7100-9282-2

For my

Mother, Father and

Anna and Stuart

CONTENTS

PREFACE

This study is part of a developing body of sociological work which seeks to examine knowledge and reality as social phenomena by asking how 'knowledge' and 'reality' are constituted in the course of specific communicative practices. Much of the intellectual inspiration for the work has been provided by ethnomethodology (not least in its stubborn determination to explore the grainy details of specific materials rather than take flight in conceptual pyrotechnics). A difference appears, however, in that whereas ethnomethodology has programmatically focussed on situated interaction and speech, the present work takes writing as its theoretical object, treating it as a distinct locus of what Harold Garfinkel calls accounting devices.

With this shift of attention a new investigative constellation has begun to appear, combining the ethnomethodological interest in knowing as a practical social accomplishment with the topical concerns of inquiries like semiology, linguistic structuralism, hermeneutics and textual analysis. The integrating theme of such investigation is how reading-writing procedures are constitutive of (a) thoughtful relationships to knowledge objects; (b) interactive relationships to real objects; and (c) trans-individual, trans-temporal communities composed of definite combinations of those relationships. The latter may be scientific, literary, intellectual, religious, political or whatever. The decisive research requirement is that they be formatively dependent upon definite reading-writing practices for their existence as communities.

While the concept of community ensures the sociological character of inquiries into reading and writing formats, their analytic thrust is towards the constitutive principles, structural features, semiotic processes present in some particular sample of writing, conceived as part of a genre. I believe that the concept of genre, or something like it, is essential, firstly, to make a written artefact analysable; and, secondly, to provide a counterpart at the textual level of the sociological concept of community boundaries, thereby defending inquiries from the danger of degenerating into purely technical, linguistic analyses.

I will not attempt to document the developing body of work referred to above but I would like to acknowledge some immediate debts.

The general idea of examining Royal Commission Reports as case-studies in social reality construction was suggested to me

in supervising a doctoral thesis by Beng-Haut Chua (Reflexive
writing and reading of social policy-related reports, York
University, Toronto, 1976), which dealt with the 1965 Canadian
Royal Commission on Bilingualism and Biculturalism.

The concept of writing as a social phenomenon researchable
within the ethnomethodological frame of reference was further
opened up for me by another graduate student, Kenneth
Morrison. Specifically through his work on how introductory
sociology texts achieve pedagogic events through determinate
organizations of reading (K. Morrison, Readers' work: devices
for achieving pedagogic events in textual materials for readers
as novices to sociology, Ph.D. dissertation, York University,
Toronto, 1976). Morrison subsequently took up the question
of how sociology texts compose social objects in and as organizations of reading (in papers presented to the Canadian Sociology
Association Meeting, Fredericton, New Brunswick, 1977, and to
the Ninth World Congress of Sociology, Uppsala, Sweden, 1978).
Since then his interest has focussed on the demonstrative exhi-
bition of knowledge claims in scientific writing.

Behind these direct influences, and still within my institutional
setting, there is the work of Professor John O'Neill who has,
since around 1973, been cultivating an interest in writing as a
social phenomenon, beginning with the formats of introductory
sociology texts, continuing through an analysis of Montaigne's
'Essays' and currently proceeding as an investigation of the
writing procedures of science. This has yielded conference
papers on The social organization of texts (Session on Ethnomethodology, Ninth World Congress of Sociology, Uppsala,
Sweden, 1978) and Historians' artefacts: some production issues
in ethnohistory (International Conference on Practical Reasoning and Discourse Processes, St Hugh's College, Oxford
University, 1979); an article, The literary production of natural
and social science inquiry ('Canadian Journal of Sociology',
Spring, 1981); and a book, 'Essaying Montaigne: A Study of the
Renaissance Institution of Writing and Reading' (Routledge &
Kegan Paul, 1982).

Elsewhere, scholars like Dorothy Smith (an especially significant influence on the present study), Digby Anderson, Michael
Lynch, Karim and Dietrick Knorr, Steve Woolgar, Bruno Latour,
and S. Nigel Gilbert have in various ways sought to develop
the general area of inquiry to which I wish to add. (See, for
examples, two recent issues of 'Philosophy of the Social
Sciences', vol. II, nos 2 and 3, 1981.)

INTRODUCTION

In 1832 William IV appointed a Commission, chaired by Charles
Blomfield, Bishop of London, to make 'a diligent and full inquiry
into the practical operation of the Laws for the Relief of the
Poor in England and Wales, and into the manner in which those
laws are administered, and to report whether any and what
alterations, amendments, or improvements may be beneficially
made in the said laws, or in the manner of administering them'.[1]
In March 1834, a general report, assembled hastily to meet a
legislative deadline and penned predominantly by Edwin Chadwick, one of twenty-six Assistant Commissioners recruited as
on-the-spot inquirers, was submitted to the Cabinet. Five
months later its main recommendations were enacted as the
Poor Law Amendment Act and structured the treatment of the
poor through the rest of the century. The report is one of
three texts forming the materials of this analysis and which we
intend to treat as case-studies in the construction of knowable
social reality on paper. The other two texts were published in
1909 as the Majority and Minority Reports of a Royal Commission
appointed in 1905 to inquire into 'the working of the laws relating to the relief of poor persons in the United Kingdom and
into the various means which have been adopted outside of the
Poor Laws for meeting distress arising from want of employment,
particularly during periods of severe industrial depression'.[2]
Due perhaps to the ambivalent bifurcation of the Report into
Majority and Minority sections the Commission proved legislatively
barren. Whereas, however, the Minority Report has been incorporated into historical lore as 'one of the great milestones on the
road towards the Welfare State',[3] the Majority Report is mossed
with neglect. Having said this, it must be admitted that the
notability of the reports for substantive historical narration is
a matter of relative indifference to us in the light of our interest
in them as constitutive achievements. Within this light the following obvious and substantively trivial features stand out as
significant: that the Reports are written texts; that they
represent social reality as something externally there for further
seeing and acting; and that this representation is redeemable
through reading.
    Following the ethnomethodological project of making taken-for-
grantedness an occasion for inquiry, I wish to maintain the attitude that the representation of social reality in and as factual
reportage is a noteworthy accomplishment calling for a response
to the question, How is it possible? The question draws us to

1

a search for the constitutive features of a text essential to its redemption as factual reportage in the course of reading. Reading-writing is conceived as a primary social process, primary, that is, for what I will call the textual construction of social reality, and not as a mere technical competence. In other words, the aspiration here is to theorize the texts as reports rather than inquire into what they report on. To adopt the latter course would be to fall immediately into the reality frame of each report itself and so preclude any interrogation of what it is as opposed to what it talks about. Since, as will be argued subsequently, it is precisely the power of a text to captivate a reader in its content, to achieve constitutive innocence, which is the achievement of factual reportage, our theoretical aspiration can only be realized as a persistent struggle against this power. In order to thematize the struggle, transforming it from an inquirer's difficulty to an analytic resource, I will rely upon a concept of literal reading drawn against a background notion of emancipatory reading. At this point it is sufficient to note that any non-literal method of reading texts can be judged as more or less emancipatory according to its capacity for resisting capture in content and keeping the question of constitutive achievement open. Our search for the essential features of textual reality construction is thus inextricably linked to a quest for emancipatory reading procedures since only through the tensed resistance of the latter can the movement of inquiry demanded by the former be maintained.[4]

THE POLITICAL SIGNIFICANCE OF THE REPORTS

The concept of the Poor Law Reports as exemplars of textual reality construction indicates but does not yet fully reveal their interest for us. They are, in their methods of knowing social problems and adequate solutions, highly significant as political documents.

Textual reality construction is to be understood as a basic but unthought foundation of modern regimes of collective control. As such it is of crucial importance both for political analysis and social critique. At the heart of our inquiry is an anticipated connection between the project of an emancipatory metareading and the emancipatory intent of critical theory to open all self-formative constraints to rational reflection. (That intent is not, of course, to dissolve all collective constraint – which would be infantile wish-fulfilment – but to distinguish necessary limits from arbitrary impositions.) Something of the connection can be seen in the following proposition, which emerged as a central thesis of the inquiry in the course of grappling with the materials. It states that the textual construction of social reality, i.e. the production of reality effects on paper through literal reading, depends upon a methodical

negation of the constitutive features of situated reality construction (i.e. the interactional production of social reality in speaking-hearing).

It would be premature at this point to rush into the task of
explicating the proposition. I introduce it here to mark out in
advance a place of interplay between the interests noted above.
The place itself is further described in the following propositions:

1 Abstractions like the state, modern government and national
administration are visible to us as the authoritative imposition
of documentary reality[5] upon situated reality: the subordination of the latter to the former is the experiential indicator
whereby anyone can see that the state is acting or administration being done. Without it no one would know.

2 The historical development of modern government is synonymous with the progressive subordination of situated to documentary reality. The familiar sociological concepts of bureaucratization and rationalization are glosses on this basic process.

3 An important element in the rationalization of Western European societies has been the use of official inquiries to diagnose
problems. In England, Royal Commissions of Inquiry form a
salient sub-category of devices for societal self-reflection.

As a matter of historical and political interest it is worth
recalling that the Royal Commission of Inquiry, like empirical
sociology, was a nineteenth century invention. In Finer's words
'it is a legislative device barely met with before 1832. By 1849
more than 100 had been set up, and every major piece of legislation between 1832 and 1871 was ushered in by this type of
inquiry.'[6] It seems then that the call for disinterested knowledge of social facts coincided in England with a dramatic increase
in the scale and scope of government: one which has been
marked by historians as the Age of Reform. There seems to have
been an intent to positively reform society in accordance with
an informed knowledge of it which animated politicians as it
had already animated Comtean positivists and Benthamite
Utilitarians. Common to all these is the visionary project of
shaping social life according to categorical schemata. From our
perspective the Age of Reform was a dramatic and cumulative
increase in the invention and application of legislative categories:
a radical strengthening of the documentary mode of reality
construction. A re-forming of social reality in that mode. Proper
analysis of the process must await explication of the key concepts defining it. We can, however, remark upon some of the
more obvious ways in which it has entered public and academic
awareness.

Symptomatic concerns about documents
First, there are right-wing sensitivities to the growth of
officialdom and the regulative impositions of paperwork through
which it operates. A casual culling of editorials and articles

over two years included these specimens from British news-
papers:
(a) An article in the 'Daily Telegraph', 16 September 1976,
discussing the 1975 annual report of the Supplementary Benefits
Commission which detailed the problems it faced in giving
special assistance to 'poor people' whose needs were not adequately met by regular pensions and allowances.[7] Given the
indeterminacy of the Commission's legislative warrant, it is not
surprising, the report says, to find that officials were being
forced to exercise 'discretionary powers' based upon moral
judgements of individual claims. The article notes: 'With the
best of intentions, it had been assumed that exceptional situations could be dealt with in a uniform way.' When situated
contingencies challenged the assumption, the response was to
multiply official guidelines and instructional aids. The report
itself comments: 'These are so long, so complex and so frequently amended that officials themselves often find them very difficult to understand.' Subsequently, I will analyse this kind of
phenomenon, bureaucracy, as the endless task of pursuing
categorical closure on situated reality: or, in political (i.e.
evaluative) terms, as the incurable pathology of textual reality
construction in its translatory movement from written to concrete repression of situated reality construction. (An editorial,
in the same issue of the 'Daily Telegraph', used the same
report in making this mordant comment: 'It is hard to believe,
but officialdom itself is apparently beginning to sense that,
like some malignancy, it is outgrowing the ability of the host
body – the rest of us – to sustain it.')
(b) In 1976 there appeared a book by David Galloway analysing
the growth of public spending in Britain since the 1950s.[8] A
commentary in the 'Daily Telegraph', 14 October, heralded it
as 'a tract for the times' linking 'the explosion of State spending' to Britain's economic woes and endorsing Galloway's call
for a negative income tax system whereby welfare state services
like health, education and housing could be returned to the
market choice nexus. My interest here is in the word revolutionary which is used to describe Galloway's solutions. I would
argue that attempts to dismantle welfare-statism warrant the
term not in striking against the vested interests of an entrenched
bureaucracy but in attempting to reassert the claims of
situated over documentary reality construction. Genuinely
revolutionary change, as Marx teaches us, is an epistemological
event – a change of consciousness.
(c) At the level of the popular press, the 25 January 1977
edition of the 'Daily Mail' provides a specimen article headed
'Leaflet Lunacy'. Allowing for its sensational style,[9] the article
reflects thematic concerns resonant with my political interest.
Announcing a campaign 'to put an end to the tyranny of the
Leaflet', a full range of medical, gastronomic and catastrophic
metaphor is brought to bear on the problem: the National
Health Service is paralysed by a disease called 'leafletitis';

leaflets breed like germs until there are enough now 'to fill every warehouse in the land with the vast ballast of bureaucratic self-perpetuation'; every day 'new and unpalatable ingredients are added to this thick, monstrous minestrone cooked up by the bureaucrats'; leaflets pour down like 'a tidal wave' or 'an avalanche'; the individual citizen is caught in a mass of forms described as 'the world's biggest paper power pyramid'. The analytic value of rhetoric is notoriously small but I would argue that it can have diagnostic value as the symptom of an objective situation calling for analysis, especially the rhetoric of the popular press. Its popularity depends upon word play with pre-existing emotions whose widely shared nature points to tensions in the structuring of social life.

The preceding samples of mass media commentary suggest that the extension of documentary reality construction has entered contemporary consciousness as a problem of quantitative growth in paperwork as bureaucratic (especially government) activities have expanded. Given a definition of the problem as one of size and complexity, it follows that the appropriate solutions are limitation and simplification. The same definition and solutions are found in a second sign of the process: the problems of librarians and bibliographers in keeping pace with the output of government publications.

The Foreword to a recent American guide to government publications tells the story:

> The expansion of government at all levels ... has resulted in increasing government influence on the life of each citizen. Concomitant with this development is the proliferation of published directives, regulations, reports, technical studies, and other informational issuances in such volume that no one engaged in a business or profession, no financial tycoon, educator, researcher, farmer, housewife, welfare recipient, or unemployed person can function without some reference to government publications.... The present work, designed to provide the prospective user as well as the trained researcher and librarian with a guide to the maze, is a direct descendant of the Childs essay (J. Childs, 'Government documentary publications in the United States and elsewhere', 1927). The extent to which the mass of published material has grown is underscored by the contrasting physical size of the two publications: Childs' was a 78 page pamphlet containing approximately 400 entries whereas this book of over 400 pages cites more than 3000 titles.[10]

What is most worrisome then is the sheer volume of information which has to be monitored. The problem is that of keeping track so as to permit comprehensive search and retrieval operations. The appropriate response, it follows, is to devise more efficient tracking techniques and draw better maps of the

territory. It is worth noting that the book begins by listing
some bibliographies of bibliographies, at which point it appears
as a map of maps of maps.[11] My intent, however, is not to
satirize bibliographic labours but to argue that if the problem
of documentary reality construction is construed as one of
volume and mass – whether through terms like information
explosion or metaphors of deluge and avalanche – it appears as
a management and control problem soluble within the given
framework of documentary reality construction itself. In this
case, the perception of the problem as one of a repressive tension between two ways of formulating social life is precluded;
the political interest is dissolved in technical-administrative
discourse.

At first sight this would not seem to be true of a third way
in which the process has surfaced, namely a concern over
personal records as devices making individuals available for
inspection, examination, evaluation, treatment and sanction by
agents of normative order and public policy. Since the same
topic emerges directly from the substantive contents of the
Poor Law Reports, full consideration of it will be postponed.
We can, however, mark its outlines through discussion of a
collection of readings on record-keeping edited by Stanton
Wheeler.[12] We address the same questions to Wheeler's collection
as to any concerned account of documentary reality construction. How is the process presented as problematic? What is said
to be concerning about it? Are these ways of presenting the
problem adequate to preserve it as a political tension between
forms of social life? Or does the tension initiating the discussion evaporate in the course of its being done (as in rhetorical
letting off steam in heated mass media fulminations)?

Wheeler's introductory essay begins promisingly with the
observation that 'a file or dossier is likely to attain a legitimacy
and authority lacking in more informal types of communication'.[13]
I would like to read this as a direct reference to the domination
of documentary over situated reality construction. But is this
what Wheeler has in mind? He gives four good reasons for this
attainment of authority by 'paper traces of one's career and
existence'. The first three are performance, transferability and
composite flexibility. The transient events of personal life are
given a durable form so that anyone can look again at an objectified existence which transcends the person named in it. This
file-being can be copied, multiplied and circulated in expanded
or contracted form. Traces of various activities and statuses
can be combined to form a composite being greater than the
sum of its parts: a knowledge object whose validity and reliability is greater than the person corresponding to it. In
Durkheimean terms we could say that the file makes a personal
existence into a social fact. The paper traces outlast, dominate
and verify the identity of the person they contain.

Wheeler's fourth source of file authority is called 'faceless-
ness'. The fact that a file is removed from personal authorship

allows it to adopt the form of an oracle; an anonymous form
through which the voice of truth is relayed. Clearly, this idea
can be linked to the observation that the passive voice is the
grammatical hallmark of texts which aspire to let the facts
speak for themselves. I find Wheeler's ideas highly instructive
as suggestions answering to some of the concerns presented
previously: we will encounter them again in discussing the
documentary method of knowing the individual, and in analysing constitutive innocence as the achievement of factual reportage. At this point, however, I wish to concentrate on Wheeler's
extended display of what is concerning about file authority,
this being the major part of his essay.

Wheeler finds the significance of the topic in a risk of an
imbalance between 'the need for information on individuals as
a means of rational decision-making about them, and the often
contrasting needs and rights of the individuals themselves'.[14]
His aim is to assemble descriptive accounts of what goes on in
particular organizational locales (schools, universities, credit
bureaux, corporations, welfare agencies, etc.) as a preparation
for controlling the record-keeping process. This book is defined
as applied social science directed towards a social problem
which, like most others, consists of the unanticipated costs of
a self-evidently necessary activity as it extends in scope. In
this particular case the costs are recognized as threats to
privacy and to democratic rights of access and consultation.
The problem of record-keeping has now been placed inside two
unexamined assumptions: first the empiricist assumption that
the process is open to look-and-see reporting in organizational
locales, i.e. that observation is a practical but not a theoretical
problem; secondly, that record-keeping is a useful, necessary
phenomenon, problematic only when it exceeds limits adequately
defined by liberal-democratic rights. The useful negative lesson
here is that Wheeler cannot possibly pose radical questions to
record-keeping (either politically or theoretically radical) from
within this ideological set. The critical incapacity of the position
emerges clearly in subsequent statements:

> The single most important factor leading to the emergence
> of concern for record-keeping systems is the computer and
> the possibilities it presents not only for the extremely rapid
> and efficient processing of huge amounts of information on
> people, but for the sharing of information from a variety of
> sources.[15]

Let us suppose that computer extensions of record-keeping
possibilities did bring them to light as a problem. What compels
the conclusion that limitations on that which has only pointed
to the problem (i.e. scope and extent) will resolve the problem
itself? Only the equation of the problem of record-keeping with
extension beyond some normal, beneficial and definable limits
whose inscription in law will bring the solution. The limits

appear behind Wheeler's concluding list of policy issues: What kinds of information does any given organization really need? How can we ensure it is accurate? Does the organization have an effective and rational policy on confidentiality? Are there procedures ensuring that individuals know about their records and how they are used? Are there review procedures where accuracy or validity is challenged? Does the organization have continuous appraisal mechanisms to ensure conformity to procedures?

A revealing addition follows the list:

> If a reasoned response to these policy issues is forthcoming, it should help to prevent an irrational revolt against record-keeping and to protect the positive functions record-keeping serves for any modern society. It should not be impossible, in a society such as ours, to arrive at a reasoned and appropriate balance between the need for information as a basis for rational decision-making, and the need for controls over the amount and quality of information, as well as the use which is made of it.[16]

Record-keeping then is so intimately bound up with the preservation of a modern society like ours that any deep questioning of it is a questioning of a society like ours and therefore irrational. A form of Luddite childishness! Wheeler's ideological set places an arbitrary restriction on what can be rationally interesting about records. If documentary reality construction is thought of in terms of the compilation, use, access, review of information, where the problem is in the process, the system, the procedures, as organizational phenomena, then we cannot ask how documentary reality is accomplished as an epistemological question but only as questions of role, organization and technique: Who does record-keeping, where, when, by what methods, with what consequences? In this way the constitutive work of recording would be as effectively hidden in inquiry as in its own practice, and in both cases because hiding the work grounds the factual authority of referential statements.

Consider, for example, the question of how ability records are done in schools. An article in Wheeler's collection[17] describes types of educational records and their relationship to changing conceptions of what education draws from or puts into children, to variations in the scale and scope of educational systems, to demands placed by employers, parents and government agents. In short, it is a straightforward structural-functional description spiced with 'ethical-legal issues' of the kind reviewed by Wheeler. Within this, as in any empiricist frame, the response to how ability testing is done is an account of what is in the measuring instruments, the rationales legitimating their design and use, and the procedures for administering them.

A response alert to ability testing as a practical situated

accomplishment through which ability is constituted as a describable matter of fact for anyone who wants to know will look quite different. Compare, for example, Kenneth Leiter's ethnomethodological analysis of procedures for placing children in a 'mature' or an 'immature' kindergarten class.[18] In his own terminology, Leiter is concerned with the practices used by teachers 'to accomplish and sustain the factual properties of the students as social objects'.[19] More specifically, how were maturity and immaturity accomplished as factual properties of the children in this particular setting?

Initially, it was through performance in a screening interview with a teacher. The teacher begins with certain materials – a development test and list of standard questions about self and family – plus the project of completing an interview recognizable as such in being done and for subsequent purposes. Successful completion will allow the child's responses to be reasonably and reliably read as signs of an inner property called maturity. The interview makes maturity an observable matter of fact for the record. This assumes, of course, that the responses were fully determined by the property and merely recorded by the teacher. Leiter's analysis of the interviews as interactional accomplishments points up features glossed by that assumption. First, the work of producing an interview required the teacher to elicit responses decidably sufficient for the task at hand. Leading questions, contextual information, gratuitous interpretations of what might or must have been meant were used to remedy gaps, silences and cryptic responses, not only to fill the sheet but also to provide a continuous feed-back definition for the teacher of what was going on adequate to sustain a sense that what was happening was the accomplishment of a screening interview. Second, the teacher relied upon 'scenic attributes' of the child (size, sex and exact age specified to month) in order to evaluate performance as more or less mature. Classification, then, depended upon the ad hoc application of unexplicated normative models by teachers in the course of interviewing. It was not objectively given by the responses because the responses were not given in that way by the children. Leiter usefully marks a decisive difference between constitutive and empiricist inquiry into records: the former alert to the accomplishment of that objective reality which the latter unreflectively studies as something given.

CONCLUSION

We must now complete the introductory task of showing how Royal Commission reports in general, and these in particular, are germane to our interests. Within the context of English society, Commission inquiries are numerically minor contributions to the vast political task, undertaken by standing and ad hoc committees, advisory councils, research agencies, task

forces, review bodies and the like, whereby the state of the
nation and all its parts are made matters of reviewable fact on
paper.[20] However, they do have certain claims to special attention for my purposes:

1 Royal Commissions of Inquiry are conscious attempts to
formulate problematic social situations as stable knowledge
objects: 'The first duty of an investigating body is to present
reliable information upon a disputed subject. Then, in reporting
its proposals, the Commission must not only provide a *reasonable* solution about which the ebb and flow of political controversy may *centre*, but also narrow within *definable limits* the
area of such controversy.'[21] The accomplishment of epistemological weightiness against mere opinion is their primary aim.

2 Inquiry reports are doubly charged with sociological interest.
First, that of the substantive topic (e.g. poverty) they refer
to and, secondly, their status as politically salient exercises
in reality construction. The fact that they routinely contain
explicit self-understandings of method and procedure makes
them particularly stimulating as case-studies in the knowledgeable organization of society.

3 Available reports span a formative period marked as crucial
for understanding contemporary society by conventional sociological concepts like modernization and bureaucratization. Moreover, they include recurrent treatments of ostensibly the same
topics across the period. Poverty is one of these. We might hope
then through analysing repeated reports on the same topic to
detect historical variations in methods of reality construction
as well as invariant constitutive features within them.

Enough now has been said by way of introduction. We turn
next to the task of grounding and explicating our key concepts
and major propositions.

CHAPTER 1

The concept of textual reality construction

THE KANTIAN LEGACY

Impatient observers at the frontier of scientific sociology, gnawed with doubt at its failure to progress, have scanned the horizon in search of a Copernican revolution heralding the advent of sociology's Newton, unaware that the ground was shifting beneath their feet. They can be relieved of their watch by this simple message. Social theory has found its Copernicus. His name is Kant. But there will be no Newton because we are not doing that kind of thing.

Richard Bernstein has described the radical restructuring of social theory in terms of three convergent challenges from European philosophy to the Anglo-Saxon conception of a naturalistic social science.[1] They are analytic philosophy (especially Wittgensteinean language analysis); phenomenology, including Husserl, Schutz and their ethnomethodological heirs and, finally, critical theory, that potent blend of Marxist, Hegelian and Freudian thought brewed up by the Frankfurt School. The epistemological prong of this concerted attack on positivism and empiricism has as its sharp spearhead the Kantian proposition that all knowledge, even 'raw' sensory data, bears the ineradicable mediating imprint of the knower. There are, of course, strong differences between constructionist theories in the identification of mediatory structures and processes. For Kant, mediation of knowable experience is accomplished through a transcendental 'I' endowed with deep form-yielding and discriminatory capacities called respectively the faculties of sensibility and understanding. For Marx, mediation is grounded in social labour as the process in which nature is appropriated for human use. For Habermas, there are three knowledge-constitutive interests (in instrumental control, communicative competence and self-emancipation) rooted in three facts of human being: the fact of corporal being, giving a certain relationship to the world as environment; the fact of linguistic being, giving a certain relationship to others as communicants; and the fact of reflective consciousness (we might say dialectical being), giving a certain relationship to self as possibility. Behind such differences, however, is a significant communality: the abandonment of copy and correspondence theories of truth.[2] The constructionist view dissolves faith in the ultimate authority of observables to establish truth claims, and negates the assumption that properly composed minds through neutral language

11

will, like tranquil pools, reflect the objective reality of things. My interest in being able to question such assumptions is not given, however, by their status as warrants for naturalistic social inquiry but by the fact that they are embedded in the Poor Law Reports as overt statements of what is going on; in ethnomethodological terms, as indexicals of the enterprise. The point to be considered is not that they are offered as rationales or justifications but that they effectively operate to produce reality and knowledge effects in the course of reading. Moreover, that they tend to do so against the will or intent of the reader to suspend them. (The topic of literal and emancipatory reading is pre-figured here but would take us ahead of our discussion.)

Kant does not refer to reality and knowledge effects but points toward them through seeking the enabling conditions of human knowledge in whatever makes possible the experience of objects or, ultimately, the experience of somethingness as a standing against consciousness.[3] The judgemental activities of thought (identifying, distinguishing, connecting), depend upon a primordial I-it structure of experience, a linkage Kant calls the objective unity of apperception, giving in advance something to think about. Thought is a determining movement of conceptualization across the indeterminate something given by spatial-temporal sensibility. The positive lesson for our purpose is that the problem of knowledge effects can only be solved within the context of showing how reality effects occur.

Beyond this, however, our interests call for a distancing from Kant's work. Firstly, because his project of establishing the outermost limits of knowability, the absolute boundary between sense and nonsense, necessarily anticipates a single constitutive realm within which knowledge and reality effects can be produced. By suspending Kant's legislative concern and his commitment to natural science as the exemplar of human knowledge, one is freed from this preconception. Secondly, Kant's formulation of the constitutive medium as an I-it structure leaves the social theorist in an intolerable dilemma. Either he must see Kant's inquiry as a psychologically oriented, empirical investigation of cognitive processes, thus completely misinterpreting it,[4] or retain the axiomatic assumption of a transcendental 'I' which is disembodied and is not locatable in social interaction or historical process. The latter choice delivers the constructionist problem into the hands of transcendental philosophy, the former abandons it altogether by a return to empiricism. The erasure of Kant's formulation in subsequent critique is to be welcomed; not, however, as leaving a blank space but in clearing a site for social theorizing on knowledge and reality effects.[5]

My initial working assumption is that constitutive realms can fruitfully be thought of as analogous to game rules and grammars in that they establish possibilities of determinate being and accountable knowing for whatever and whoever enters their structure. Whoever enters a structure does so as the kind of communicant posited by its rules of possibility or, as I prefer to say, its constitutive features. Whatever enters becomes something within certain ontological and epistemological conditions. Propelling a ball through three white sticks with one's foot is to do nothing in particular unless it occurs within the constitutive jurisdiction of soccer rules, in which case, by reference to a definite structuring of time (the act must happen in game time), of space (it must happen within these pitch and goal lines), and contingency (offside rules, fouling rules, etc.), it becomes an objectively significant event: scoring a goal. I do not want to say that a list of game rules, an official handbook, would fit my intended usage of textual reality construction but a newspaper report of a game, relying on them to produce an orderly meaningful account of what happened, would do so. It is important, however, to notice its difference from a factual inquiry report. Whereas a sports report can rely upon a predefined code (the game rules) as that which the details document, a factual report on something like poverty has no such security. This is so even where legislation on the matter, such as the poor laws, already exists because the undertaking is to test the sufficiency of such laws against a reality brought to view beyond them. A sports report celebrates the re-enactment of an unproblematic code, hence its ritualist aspect; the counterpart in social reality reporting would be an executive memorandum on the routine administration of regulations in some organizational locale. The task of inquiries, however – that which makes them inquiries – is not to celebrate a code but to repair or generate one from the facts of a situation. If it is accepted that the facts, that is the errors, blemishes, defects, faults, possibilities, promises of a situation, cannot give themselves to blank staring but only to a purposive relevance structure projected ahead of inquiry as a precondition for encounter with particulars as evidence; if it is further accepted that a sense of factual encounter can only be sustained through preserving constitutive innocence, then every inquiry will bear the imprint of its essential constitutive features without being able to name them. A written report cannot discourse on anything beyond its own boundaries. The claim to do so is the error of objectivism and the triumph of inquiry. Social inquiries with a practical intent bear upon an infinite variety of substantive topics but every inquiry recommends the same thing through the detail: namely, its essential conditions of knowledge and reality production. Subsequently, we will demonstrate this through the detail of the 1834 and 1909 Poor Law Reports. Meanwhile, further comment is required on constitutive realms.

DOCUMENTARY REALITY CONSTRUCTION

The project developed in its early stages what seemed a clear distinction between documentary and situated reality construction. A strong influence at this time was Dorothy Smith's paper on the social construction of documentary reality.[6] I was vaguely uneasy about the inversion of my own formula - the documentary construction of social reality - but was not forced to confront it until exploration of the ethnomethodological literature showed that they were talking about documents in the context of situated reality construction. Where then was the clear distinction of the beginning? Eventually, I was led to reformulate the original distinction, and locate documents (including files, folders and dossiers) as boundary phenomena between the primary realms of textual and situated reality construction. To see what this means it is necessary to review the sources of disquiet.

A useful starting point is Garfinkel's definition of the documentary method as a sense-making activity:

> The documentary method consists essentially in the retro-spective-prospective reading of a present occurrence so as to maintain the constancy of the object as a sensible thing through temporal and circumstantial alterations in its actual appearances.... The documentary method occurs as a feature of situations of incomplete information in which effective actions nevertheless must be taken, matters of fact decided, and interpretations made. The method would seem to be an intimate part of a social process wherein a body of knowledge must be assembled and made available for legitimate use despite the fact that the situations it purports to describe (1) are, in the calculatable sense of the term, unknown; (2) are in their actual and intended logical structures essentially vague; (3) are modified, elaborated, extended, if not indeed created by the fact and manner of being addressed.[7]

This might well be taken as a precise description of what the Poor Law Commissioners and their investigators were faced with and what they did in using parish records, soliciting written evidence, collecting questionnaire responses, interviewing poor law administrators and so on, to make pauperism a stable knowledge object. Examination of the documentary method would focus attention on the situated accomplishment of inquiry involving an historical reconstruction of what those men did in their assembly work, but it would ignore the textual representation of that work as a report for reading. Garfinkel is talking about the documentary method as a handling device for actors caught up in the on-the-spot hurry and scurry of situated reality construction. Actual documents are seen as resources for achieving reality and knowledge effects in the course of interaction, not as written texts. Within this concept

one could also examine the use of the Poor Law Reports as
resources for Parliamentary debating and administrative enactment; again, however, their analytic status as texts would be
missed.

The point is readily confirmed by looking at ethnomethodological studies of the documentary method in formal organizations. Don Zimmerman, for example, tells how officials in a
public welfare agency went about the task of displaying eligibility in an applicant as objective and factual grounds for
taking administrative action.[8] His main point is that the processing of applicants' stories of need is done in such a way as to
routinely leave signs of proper procedure, i.e. procedure
proper to authoritative processing as opposed, say, to free
invention, personal bias or malicious distortion. Documents play
a crucial role in this:

> The work of using documents to reconstruct particular
> events consists of treating the document as a normal event
> within a determinate order of activities characterizable in
> terms of typical motives (e.g. 'getting the job done'),
> typical sequences of action (e.g. bureaucratic routines)
> and typical products (e.g. completed documents).[9]

Garfinkel initially observed the documentary method in the
operations of a psychiatric clinic.[10] His observations arose from
involvement in a research project using clinic records to study
the selection process through which applicant cohorts were
narrowed down to treatment groups. The research design
required that a 'clinical career form' for each person be compiled from application forms and case folder contents. Unfortunately, as is so often the case, they lacked sufficient detail and
continuity for the task. Pondering the typicality of 'bad' records
in social research (and it is relevant here to note the distress
of the 1834 Poor Law Commissioners over bad parish records),
Garfinkel proposes that their gaps and incompletions are aspects
of their suitability for organizational practices. Records compiled
by members in getting their work done necessarily become
troubles for researchers in doing their work. Why should this
be so? Because any case folder, file, dossier is readable in two
ways; either as a full representation of all transactions, open
to anyone caring to know regardless of the identity of the
reader or his interest in reading it, or as evidence that organizational responsibility (ethical, legal, technical, etc.) has been
discharged adequate to the various occasions when particularly
interested parties might check. The first reading seeks the
document as an 'actuarial record':

> The prototype of an actuarial record would be a record of
> installment payments.... A standardized terminology and
> a standardized set of grammatical rules govern not only
> possible contents, but govern as well the way a 'record' of

past transactions is to be assembled. Something like a
standardized reading is possible that enjoys considerable
reliability among readers of the record ... a reader's
claim to competent readership is decidable by him and
others while disregarding particular characteristics of
the reader, his transactions with the record, or his interests in reading it.[11]

The second reading seeks the document, in the case of the
clinic at least, as the record of a therapeutic contract between
patient and clinical personnel displayable as such for other
doctors, for lawyers, funding agencies, public watch-dogs,
as the occasion demands:

> In their occasionality, folder documents are very much like
> utterances in a conversation with an unknown audience
> which, because it already knows what might be talked about,
> is capable of reading hints ....Thus the folder contents,
> much less than revealing an order of interaction presuppose
> an understanding of that order for a correct reading.[12]

We might say then that the context of sense for a 'contractual
record' is a situated use involving interested parties. It is
adequate to all practical purposes of reconstructing the normative orderliness of the organization. Since the purposes can
and do vary, the meaning of folder contents must be variable:

> Documents in the case-folder had the further feature that
> what they could be read to be really talking about did not
> remain and was not required to remain identical in meaning
> over the various occasions of their use. Both actually and
> by intent, their meanings are variable with respect to cir-
> cumstances.[13]

We could well use Garfinkel's distinction between actuarial
and contractual records (or is it between ways of reading
records?) to suggest that one constitutive feature of textual
reality construction is the methodical negation of circumstantial
dependence of meaning, so that the content stands objectively
against a merely technical ability to read. This would be possible, however, only by bringing the question of constitutive
features of the text to his discussion, for it is not given there.
Garfinkel does not invite us to stay at the difference he has
marked, or to explore the inner horizons of documents as constitutive accomplishments in writing, because his sight is
firmly fixed on situated accomplishments. This is the ethnomethodological bias, its founding problematic, which predeter-
mines the significance of documents as one of usage for situated
reality construction. Within these bounds our topic can only be
glimpsed in passing.
We move, finally, in Dorothy Smith's analysis of documentary

reality, to a formulation very close to the present project.
Indeed, she explicitly identifies our inquiry as a kind of blank
space within her own. Smith argues that the production of an
account and its reading:

> are distinguished in the first place because at the point at
> which the account is put into its final form it enters what
> I shall call 'document time'. This is that crucial point at
> which much if not every trace of what has gone into the
> making of the account is obliterated and what remains is
> only the text which aims at being read as 'what actually
> happened' ....In reading back, therefore, the interpretive
> procedure bypasses the processes which produced the
> account.... From the rupture which occurs where the
> document enters document time, different methods of inquiry
> are required and different though related methodological
> problems arise. The relationship of sociologist to text is
> then as reader. The situation of reading and the interpre-
> tive work involved are a distinct and special practice which
> cannot be elaborated here. I emphasize, however, that a
> documentary reality is fully constituted only in the comple-
> tion of *both* phases.[14]

Why then hesitate to step into this space? Why insist that 'the
documentary construction of social reality' is importantly different from 'the social construction of documentary reality',
so important that it demands preservation in a third term,
'the textual construction of social reality'? Is it any more than
academic quibbling? To show that something more is at stake
I must recall Smith's account of the non-reading phase. Beginning with the observation that our knowledge of modern society
depends largely on documentary evidence, she proceeds to a
Marxian bracketing of the word knowledge by showing that
documentary reality is produced through and for administrative,
managerial and similar social practices. The traces of this productive work are, however, expunged in the finished products.
The parallel with Marx's analysis of commodity production and
false consciousness hardly requires comment. Smith concludes:

> Our 'knowledge' is thus ideological in the sense that this
> social organization [of documentary reality] preserves con-
> ceptions and means of description which represents the
> world as it is for those who rule it, rather than as it is for
> those who are ruled.[15]

I have two basic reservations:
1 Smith conceives reading as the consummatory phase of a
single productive process in the course of which concrete experiences are lifted out of their lived contexts and worked up to
the status of documentary artefacts suitable for organizational
use. Thus live births are transformed into registered births;

fragmentary particulars are transformed by defence lawyers
into clients' stories; a person's words and actions are used to
construct 'the patient' in psychiatric practice. The analysis,
using the metaphor of manufacturing, describes a stage-by-
stage transformation at the end of which originary experiences
are presented unrecognizably to reading as facts. Smith provides a box-and-arrow diagram to represent the total process.
Within this conceptual set a text would be analysed by showing
what the production workers did along the line. Showing what
they did would be accomplished through before/after, input/
output comparisons marking the emergence of the product.
Their work would appear in the difference they made to the
materials, especially to the relatively raw material of situated
experience. My difficulty here is that I cannot attend to the
constitutive power of a text to draw the reader into its own
realm of reality and, at the same time, attend to reading as the
end phase of a production process which extends beyond reading. An analysis guided by an external concept of text production is always looking outside the text, either backwards
towards previous materials or sideways to the interests, motives
and organized practices of knowledge workers. Treating a text
reductively as a manufactured object precludes attention to it
as a constitutive realm. Smith's incorporation of production and
reading into a single process called the social construction of
documentary reality is an open invitation to such reductionism.
My inversion of terms helps to break them apart but even this is
inadequate unless it is understood that the construction phase
which Smith concentrates on is not something separate from
reading but only expresses another method of reading on her
part, one which can be referred to as a sociology of knowledge
reading. In so far as a concept of emancipation emerges from
Smith's discussion it takes the form of recovering bypassed
production work behind the text - a Marxian dissolution of false
consciousness. My objection is that a claim to see events behind
the text poses its own form of bypassing, forgetting itself as
a method of reading. The emancipatory interest cannot be
satisfied in this way.
2 Although Smith does not elaborate the reading situation, her
references to it are accompanied by terms like 'interpretive
work' and 'knower's method', suggesting that she sees reading
as another instance of what ethnomethodologists call sense-
making practices.[16] This kind of formulation threatens a
relapse into methodological individualism whereby an active
subject confronts a passive object and uses his interpretive
capacities to make sense of it. If reader and text are seen in
this way then we cannot possibly attend to the constitutive
power of a text to formulate the reader it requires. The subject-
object separation completely inhibits our enterprise.
    Let us return now, as a conclusion, to the conception of
documents and documentary reality as something between situated and textual reality construction. My first observation is

that the difference between these realms is not to be found in
the presence or absence of documents (files, records, etc.)
since they are found in both, but in the confinement of textual
reality construction to the constitutive medium of reading-writing. My second observation is that documentary reality construction is the return of textual reality construction to situated
reality construction as a 'demand' for conformity to its own
constitutive principles. This return is synonymous with administration. The difference between the two realms not only calls
for but grounds the very possibility of bureaucratic practice.
This translatory movement of administrative imposition must,
however, be strictly separated from that negation of situated
reality construction occurring within a text as an essential
feature of factual reportage. It is to this topic that we now
turn.

THE NEGATION OF SITUATED REALITY IN FACTUAL REPORTAGE

It has already been proposed that situated reality construction
and textual reality construction are separate realms for producing knowledge and reality effects, also that the achievement
of such effects in the latter depends upon a methodical negation
of the constitutive features of the former, placing them in a
relationship of tense repression. To this we now add the
further claim that methodical negation occurs in textual reality
construction as a contrastive separation of elements which in
situated reality construction are fused together. At a readily
accessible level, I think, for example, of the is-ought, parti-
cular-abstract separations which famously vexed Max Weber.
Every text presenting itself as a representation of social reality
will include references to at least these separations (say as
discussions of precaution against bias, sensitivity over description versus prescription, the operationalization of concepts,
the representative adequacy of particular data) and these will
serve readers as indexical signs that the work under way is
that of reproducing an external reality. The work is attributed
only to the investigation behind the writing, however, and
not at all to the writing in being read, which is what factual
inquiry must effectively come to. In Garfinkel's terminology,
the self-reported research work of factual inquiries is a gloss
on the separative work of the text whereby it not only takes the
place of situated particulars but does so as their essential
truth, there for the reading. Every factual social report moves
from a displacement of situated reality towards its replacement
by textual orderliness (towards that form of rational accountability), but in unremarked ways. This does not mean, however,
that they are in any sense unremarkable. Movement across any
significant boundary must leave traces in that which moves.
An objective social report moves across a boundary having a

moral and an epistemological significance. Correspondingly, we can detect symptomatic marks of uneasy conscience as well as marks of transformatory knowledge work in texts in this genre. The former can be seen in thematic sensitivities which recur in social science writing; the latter in the typical turns (or tropes) through which writing composes a report. Further consideration of these points, especially the second, will help bring the topic of textual reality construction into clearer and closer focus.

Thematic sensitivities in social science
Scientific social inquiry looks forward to a progressive perfection of knowledge by applying formal criteria for evaluating measurement methods, data-processing techniques, theory construction and the explanatory adequacy of hypotheses. Application of the criteria enforces a strong departure and conspicuous distancing from ordinary language and its contents even though they must still be relied upon to provide topics, collect data, organize research work and legitimate the enterprise. Scientific social inquiry is thus placed in a radically ambivalent relationship to situated reality construction: negating it, as a condition for doing, and being seen to do, inquiry on paper, while depending on it in the practice of research. If this is so - if social science must deny its roots in order to appropriate them as data for analysis - we would expect its practitioners to display symptoms of repression. These occur at an explicit level as the misgivings of field researchers that they may somehow have behaved improperly in making a scientific report of lived experience, that they may have robbed situated reality of its richness and diversity or somehow betrayed the people they have spoken to or lived with. An extreme, and instructive, case of researcher sensitivity is provided in an article by Brian Lee.[17] Lee, a lecturer in English at a college in north-east England, lived and worked for two years in a nearby village, resolving to use the experience to satisfy his professional interest in sociolinguistics: 'I thought at first of acting the topographer-linguistician (to "do the job properly") but soon decided against.[18]

The same process of becoming a member which gave Lee knowledge of village speech and its constitutive significance for the 'confident selfhood' and 'liveliness of personality' he discovered there, also stopped him from doing research:

> Suppose one were to 'do' such a place scientifically, even no more than in a thorough or scholarly way: put your tape-recorder in front of people: get your note-pad out: deploy your phonetic script, your 'technique' or your 'methodology'. What have you done but alter the relation, create another sort of curiosity, distance people from yourself, from themselves, yourself from yourself? They have become an object of interest to someone else who is

not himself but a person who has something to do ....So
their language is taken from them, away from them it goes
'out there' ....It is the way to kill the thing you love.[19]

In my terminology, Lee is saying that even the most dedicated
attempt to reproduce situated reality within the constitutive
realm of the text can result in nothing more than a curious
object to stare at, as we stare at museum pieces, restored pio-
neer villages and exhibitions of folk-art.

Lee's guilt-ridden outcry - recalling W.H. Auden's stern
commandment, 'Thou shalt not commit a social science' - is, of
course, too strong to be representative but it stems, I believe,
from the same source of tension underlying milder symptoms
familiar to social scientists: the demand that reports make room
for anecdotal detail and qualitative data; that interviews should
always encourage respondents to elaborate responses in their
own words; that researchers should express themselves in their
reports, perhaps through providing research biographies or,
more radically, by expressing moral commitment and personal
feeling.[20]

The search for symptoms of repressive tension between textual
and situated reality construction can then be pursued at the
level of personal misgivings and disciplinary debates over the
practice of social research. It could also be done through examining thematic obsessions in sociological theory: the Marxian
theme of overcoming alienation in the practice of a truly common life; the Durkheimean concern with moral community and
the threat of anomie; various expressions of nostalgia for community structured by Tönnies' distinction between gemeinschaft
and gesellschaft; yearnings for wholeness, integration, belonging; distinctions between secondary and primary ties, formal
and informal relationships; and the phenomenological preoccupation with intersubjective fusion as the deep core of sociality:

When the fusion is very weak and only integrates superficial
layers of consciousness ... sociality is *mass*. When minds
fuse, open out, and interpenetrate on a deeper, more inti-
mate plane, where an essential part of the ... acts of personality is integrated in the 'we', without, however, attaining
the maximum of intensity in this integration, sociality is
community. When, finally, this most intense degree of union
of 'we' is attained ... sociality is communion.[21]

My argument is that all such themes are experientially grounded in the passage from situated to textual reality construction;
a passage occurring as the separative negation of situated
fusion in being brought to writing which then allows for looking
back and looking below to what has been negated. The problem
I wish to address is how that negation is decisively accomplished
so as to leave nothing behind but a factual report.

Factual reporting as rhetorical transformation
Rhetoric includes reflection on the power of writing to draw
readers into composed meaning structures. Consequently, given
the idea of objective social inquiry as a linguistic turning of
situated experience into a reported world which is real and
factual in being read, it is reasonable to suppose that the treatment of reports as rhetorical artefacts would be fruitful.[22] For
our purposes, an analytic scheme of special appeal is one proposed by the literary critic Harold Bloom.[23]

Starting from the problem of a poet striving to fashion something original out of the originary influence of strong predeces-
sors' words, Bloom proposes a creative process (a 'revisionary
dialectic') which has suggestive resemblances to our notion of
factual reportage. In each case there is an emergent differentia-
tion of a seemingly self-sufficient meaning structure from a
prior fulness of meaning. A finished poem from precursive words
an authoritative report from situated experiences.

Creating proceeds through three cumulative cycles of limiting
and representing an original fulness of meaning. The actual work
of limitation and representation is carried out by three pairs of
rhetorical tropes: one pair for each cycle (Irony and Synechdoche; Metonymy and Hyperbole; Metaphor and Metalepsis). At
the level of specific textual content this transformation work
is marked by characteristic images associated with each trope.

As will be shown below, Bloom's schema provides a useful
explication of textual reality reconstruction. It allows us to
grasp it firmly as a semiological organization of meaning built
up as reading proceeds. There is, however, another aspect of
Bloom's enterprise continuous with our own: an intent to promote
in his readers an interpretive defence against stultifying obei-
sance to any words before them. Readers as much as poets face
the problem of how to do anything more with precursive words
than merely repeat them. Bloom's reconstruction of how a poet
'misreads' prior words in order to make room for his own must
be understood as a figurative model of emancipatory reading
(i.e. emancipation from mere literal repetition). The significance
of his equation between 'misreading' and 'dialectical revision'
is that all dialectical revision involves an enlivening recollection
of some originary source of activity which has necessarily been
forgotten in the course of the activity itself. The emancipatory
importance of a trope, for Bloom, as the following passages
make clear, is its status as a mistake of literal meaning which
allows both for creative writing and reflection on the necessity
of mistaking for creativity (including, of course, the creation
of an objectively knowable social reality in writing):

> A trope is a willing error, a turn from literal meaning in
> which a word or phrase is used in an improper sense,
> wandering from its rightful place. A trope is therefore a
> kind of falsification, because every trope (like every
> defense, which is similarly a falsification) is necessarily

an interpretation, and so a mistaking. Put another way,
a trope resembles those errors about life that Nietzsche
says are necessary for life.[24]

If all tropes are defenses against other tropes, then the
use of influence as a composite trope for interpretation
may be that it will defend us against itself. Perhaps, at
this belated time, interpretation has become the reader's
defense. Must we indeed interpret as a way of gaining
power over the text?[25]

Bloom's schema is then doubly promising. It offers an analysis
of the mechanics of textual reality construction which is intended
to break their hold on the reader. To assess how far the promise extends, and what work Bloom leaves us still to do, I will
apply his three cycles of revisionary dialectic to factual reporting and specifically to the 1834 Poor Law Report.

Rhetorical transformation in the 1834 Report
The revisionary dialectic of the report begins with ironic limitation expressed in images of absence and presence (or absence
in presence). As ethnomethodologists have shown, everyday
social life is replete with interpretive procedures, sense-making
practices, members' methods, ensuring the accountable orderliness of that life. Orderliness is already there as rational accounting in practice. It is ironic then that wherever the 1834 Report
looks at the 'practical operation of the Poor Laws' - in giving
out-door relief or in-door relief, to the able-bodied or the
impotent, in rural parishes or urban parishes - it finds absence
of rational accounting and orderliness. Situated practice is
characterized in terms of maladministration, mismanagement,
evils, abuses, neglect of duty, lack of responsibility, indiscriminate (arbitrary) decision-making. The naming of absence
which calls for inquiry can be done more moderately, for
example, by identifying a problem, puzzle, or gap in knowledge,
but all involve an originary act of limitation against situated
reality construction. Policy research begins in a declared
deficiency of order in situated practice while at the same time
positing a discoverable orderliness through observation of what
is there. Value-free observation, faithfully pursued, will find
a virtual presence of social order in recording the details of
a declared absence. Research work cannot proceed, however,
within the ironic shuttle of absence and presence, consequently
situated practice is brought back again in a different form as
a universe of instances, cases or indicators of a presumably
patterned world. Factual reporting now represents situated
reality in terms of part standing for whole or whole for part,
i.e. in the trope called synechdoche. In the methodological
self-consciousness of contemporary social science, part-whole
representation appears as sampling theory and the operationalization of concepts; in the 1834 Poor Law Report it appears more

simply as a concern to show that its partial data are fit to stand
in place of all the facts and that the total pattern will be present
in these particulars. The theme of part-whole substitution is
played out in three forms: as an unquestioned presumption that
patterns were there for the finding; as an admission that the
practicalities of reporting required extraction from the evidence;
and as a denial that such extraction involved partiality. These
topics are raised in the first three pages of the report - the
'Statement of Proceedings' - and in Supplement 3, 'Instructions
to Assistant Commissioners'.

The unquestioned presumption of pattern - of an orderly
whole waiting to be detailed - can be seen in the astounding
confidence with which the commissioners set about amassing
vast quantities of information, in the full knowledge that legislators wanted a report one year hence, yet with no doubts that
this could be done. Not only did they send lengthy questionnaires to all rural and urban parishes (around 15,000 in all,
of which just over ten per cent responded) and solicit written
evidence from large numbers of knowledgeable individuals in
the United Kingdom and various foreign countries, they also
recruited twenty-six assistant commissioners to do field reports
covering eight general areas of inquiry. The original timetable
required all evidence to be in by November 1832, so that a
report could be ready for the printers early in 1833. Given
that there was no technology of data-processing available to the
commissioners, we can only suppose that their confident anticipation of speedy completion was founded upon a belief that the
information, however voluminous (and it eventually extended
into thirteen bulky volumes of appendices) would dispose itself
into discernible patterns. Faith in the inherent orderliness of
the realm of inquiry is asserted directly in the statement of
proceedings (p. 3).

It appears from this narrative that the magnitude of the
evidence has been the great difficulty with which we have
had to struggle. But we believe, on the other hand, that
that very magnitude gives the principal value to our inquiry.
All evidence is necessarily subject to error, from the ignorance, forgetfulness, or misrepresentation of the witnesses,
and necessarily tinged by their opinions and prejudices.
But in proportion as the number of witnesses is increased,
those sources of error have a tendency to compensate one
another and general results are afforded, more to be
depended upon than the testimony of a few witnesses, however unexceptionable.

The same faith, expressed here in the quasi-statistical doctrine
of central tendency as the emergent truth of deviating detail,
reappears in the instructions to the field investigators as a
taken-for-granted assumption that they will recognize what
places are worth reporting when they come across them. Each

assistant commissioner was sent to a broadly bounded geographical area, armed with open-ended questions, and instructed
(p. 248) to

> use his own discretion as to the places which appear to be
> most deserving of investigation, and as to the points of
> inquiry which may be most successfully investigated in
> each parish ... principally he should dwell on those facts
> from which some general inference may be drawn and which
> form the rule rather than the exception.

The prior existence of objective patterning guarantees not
only that each observer will readily distinguish instructive from
uninstructive parishes and rule-governed from exceptional facts,
but that twenty-six untrained, unprofessional observers will
do so in a common way which will allow their particular reports
to be gathered into a single general report. In this context, it
is relevant to add that each investigator was asked to submit
periodic reports as he went along rather than give one at the
end of his journeys. Here the thematization of inquiry as movement between part and whole is played out in the notions of
sub- and preliminary reports. It is most explicitly articulated
where the commissioners justify extraction in advance of the
total body of evidence still to be published and insist that their
extracts are fully representative of all that is to come. They
speak here to the inescapable paradox of all factual inquiry in
aspiring to represent the whole picture impartially on the basis
of incorrigibly partial observation. Lacking the consolations of
sampling theory, the commissioners can only plead practical
necessity and claim innocence from bias (p. 3):

> In the hope of diminishing the difficulty of making use of
> this voluminous evidence, we have embodied a considerable
> portion of it in the following Report; and wherever it has
> been practicable, we have subjoined to our quotations refer-
> ences to the pages in the Appendix from which they were
> extracted. But as the Appendix, owing to the obstacles
> which we have already stated, is still incomplete, and much
> of it unpaged, many of our references are unavoidably left
> blank.

The restorative display of situated reality as having an
immanent order which makes it reportable threatens reporting
with a passivity which would inhibit the project of replacing
situated with textual reality construction. One presence can
only be replaced by another stronger one not by a faithful copy.
Following Bloom's schema the insufficiencies of the first cycle
of limiting and representing call for a second cycle, beginning
with a new form of limitation which can be described as metonymic troping. Bloom refers to metonymy as 'an emptying out of
a prior fullness of language',[26] and, elsewhere, as 'a change of

name, or substituting the external aspect of a thing for the
thing itself, a displacement by continuity that repeats what is
displaced, but always with a lesser tone'.[27] Further assistance
is provided by Bloom's suggestion that a corresponding psychic
defence mechanism is the isolation of past thoughts and actions
through segregating them from one another and taking them
out of context. In factual reporting, metonymic limitation occurs
in the reduction of particular persons, places, events, opinions
and so on to examples of general categories; limiting their
significance to the exemplary function. Particulars are separated
from the context in which they were found and rearranged to
form repetitions of say, a standard practice, a trend or a type
– collections of different instances, signifying the same thing.
Situated particulars are reduced, through analytic resemblance,
to a common meaning. The descriptive section of the report
moves through a variety of topics – relief in kind, relief in
money without labour, wage supplements, the roundsman system,
parish employment, the workhouse, the effects on those involved, magistrates, overseers, the laws of settlement, etc. –
using the same technique of presentation; namely, the inter-
spersing of authorial commentary and witnesses' words. Whereas
in quantitative social research the renaming of 'raw data' as
generalizations is accomplished through translatory devices
such as descriptive statistics and classificatory tables, in this
case it is done through standard phrases placed around clustered
quotations: 'the following extracts show the extent of these
practices', 'from the preceding evidence it will be seen how',
'the following answers are specimens of', 'similar feelings show
themselves in the following answers', 'the following replies are
further testimony to the same effect', 'the reports are full of
the same evidence', 'the following testimony is an instructive
example', 'a similar opinion is expressed by', 'we shall proceed
to illustrate these views by'. In this way, the diverse words
of a vast multitude of magistrates, overseers, assistant overseers, vestry clerks, vicars, labourers, farmers, etc. which
threaten reporting with an incoherent babble of noise are transformed into orderly messages. As the authors of the report
state: 'We felt it to be of utmost importance that we should ourselves be masters of the contents of all this evidence.' (p. 2)
Any descriptive survey, including our present survey of the
1834 Report, relies upon metonymic limitation both in order to
get done and to show that it is a descriptive survey. In ethnomethodological terms it is an indexical property of reporting.
    Since emptying out is a negation of source, reporting cannot
rest there and turns to another restorative trope: to what
Bloom calls the excesses of hyperbole. Abstractions are imbued
with the active powers of living entities; polarized types struggle in superhuman combat; Olympian figures are constructed,
out of all proportion to the individuals they represent. In less
hyperbolic terms, reportage engages in the reification of concepts. Referring to 'out-door relief', for example, the 1834

Report endows 'it' with extraordinary powers - 'it appears to contain in itself the elements of an almost indefinite extension; of an extension, in short, which may ultimately absorb the whole fund out of which it arises'. (p. 25) Subsequently, the report quotes (p. 26) approvingly the remarks of an assistant overseer who sees out-door relief as giving rise to a contagious disease called pauperism:

> the malady of pauperism has not only got amongst respect-able mechanics, but we find even persons who may be con-sidered of the middle classes, such as petty masters, small master bricklayers, and other persons, who have never before been seen making application to parish officers, now applying.

Those infected by the disease become monstrous caricatures of ordinary, decent people (represented particularly in the figure of the independent labourer); quoting approvingly (p. 51) from a collector of poor-rates:

> Paupers are dirty in their persons and slothful in their habits; the children are allowed to go about the streets in a vagrant condition. The industrious labourers get their children out to service early. The pauper and the charity-fed people do not care what becomes of their children.

Hyperbolic restoration need not, of course, be conducted in so strong a tone; it is enough that particular events be represented as animate forces or that typified figures - the able-bodied pauper, the impotent pauper, the independent labourer, the soft magistrate, the inefficient overseer - become the 'real' actors in the dramatic moments of the report, just as age, sex, social class, racial, ethnic and other categories form the dramatis personae of modern sociological studies. This trope does not depend then on an overtly impassioned use of language, neither does it matter whether general concepts are declared to be nominalist conveniences, heuristic devices, ideal-type constructions, collective realities or transcendent totalities; it is sufficient that common nouns be attached to verbs, adverbs and adjectives which at the time of reading give them a life of their own, imbuing them with inherent capacities such as spread-ing, growing, contracting, declining, thinking, feeling, willing or evaluating. No report can do without this.

In terms of manuals on research methods, hyperbole cor-responds to analytic description of the data, a defence against the emptiness of mere fact-finding. Its referential fulness, however, blocks the projected completion of social reporting, which is to stand completely in place of situated practice as its essential truth, as the realization of its virtual rationality. Reporting is completed in explaining the present and pre-empt-ing the future. In the theoretical practice of research, the

latter occurs as predictive application to further testing; in
the 'political' practice of research, which is our concern here,
it occurs as recommendations for reform (i.e. as prescription),
I am suggesting then that explaining corresponds to the final
limiting trope of metaphor, while prescription corresponds to
the trope of metalepsis.

Metaphoric limitation functions in the same way as sublimation;
through displacing an activity which cannot be fully admitted,
properly named, onto substitute objects. That which cannot be
admitted into a report is the strongly constitutive activity of
reporting itself since to do so would disrupt the project of
establishing its reality as reality per se, a project which depends
upon the claim to do nothing but reproduce what is there.
Explanation points to causal factors out there which are sufficient to account for the presence of persons and events in
analytic categories plus changes in distribution between categories. Responsibility for the location of particulars in these
categories and those patterns is thus displaced from the
reporters onto a variety of substitute objects outside the activity
of reporting. As Bloom remarks, metaphor creates 'a perspectivism of inside against outside, another subject-object dualism'.[28]
The structuring of subject-object dualism in factual reporting
is, however, different than in poetry because the inner movement of the writing is not towards individuation - the distinctive-
ness of this poem from earlier ones - but towards the absorption
of authorial voice in the impersonal, passive voice of reality
speaking for itself through the mouths of investigators. The
struggle is to locate constitutive achievement in the object, to
show that it can account for itself.

The 1834 Report names the inner dynamics of the Poor Law
system as vested interests, typical motives and typical weaknesses of character. It is through these pushes, pulls and
pressures that the system is articulated and sustained. As the
system itself is imbued with all the properties required to produce and reproduce what the report has described, the activity
of reality construction is displaced from inside the text to the
'outside' realm it refers to. Metaphorical substitutes for textual
reality construction are to be found here in typical forces working upon malleable, ambiguous or misguided laws to form a
self-sustaining system of action. Given their wholly negative
characterization of the system as involving the demoralization
of labourers, depression of agricultural wages, diversion of
funds from capital investment in farming, an increasing burden
of rates on property owners, the encouragement of vice, etc.,
it is not surprising to find commissioners expending considerable interpretive effort in accounting for its continuation. The
more defective (inefficient, stupid, immoral, etc.) the reality
a report has claimed to observe, the greater the amount of
metaphoric displacement required to preserve the constitutive
innocence of the text. The following passages detail displacement work in the 1834 Report.

Firstly, the report says that the system of relief is fed by claims from the impotent and the able-bodied poor. The former are accounted for in large part by derelictions of duty and want of natural affection (p. 25):

> The duty of supporting parents and children, in old age or infirmity, is so strongly enforced by our natural feelings that it is often well-performed, even among savages ....We believe that England is the only European country in which it is neglected ... if the deficiencies of parental and filial affection are to be supplied by the parish, and the natural motives to the exercise of those virtues are thus to be withdrawn, it may be proper to endeavour to replace them, however imperfectly, by artificial stimulants, and to make fines, distress warrants, or imprisonment act as substitutes for gratitude and love.

The latter, the primary concern of the report and the dominant feature of the system it sees, are explained as follows (p. 149):

> Wherever inquiries have been made as to the previous condition of the able-bodied individuals who live in such large numbers on the town parishes, it has been found that the pauperism of the greater number has originated in indolence, improvidence, or vice, and might have been averted by ordinary care and industry.

A later passage (p. 155) adds the desire to defraud other people of their money to the list, then states the adequacy of this account of origins:

> One of the most encouraging of the results of our inquiry is the degree in which the existing pauperism arises from fraud, indolence, or improvidence. If it had been principally the result of unavoidable distress, we must have inferred the existence of an organic disease, which, without rendering the remedy less necessary, would have fearfully augmented its difficulty. But when we consider how strong are the motives to claim public assistance, and how ready are the means of obtaining it, independently of real necessity, we are surprised not at the number of paupers but at the number of those who have escaped the contagion.

The claims pushed forward by these inner springs of conduct are processed in such a way by overseers, vestrymen and magistrates - acting through a mixture of soft-headed charity, lack of appropriate knowledge, monetary self-interest, fear of reprisals and indifference to public duty - as to not only reinforce that conduct but undermine the motivation for independence in others. Each parish through its governing body -

the vestry - appointed one of its members to serve one year as overseer. The position was unpaid and acceptance mandatory. In law, the overseer was responsible for determining the amount of relief money required, from what persons and in what proportions; also, for distributing relief to claimants on the basis of his judgement of need and merit. Sufficient reasons are provided making it inevitable that any ordinary man entering the position (dedicated men are named for their exceptionality) will distribute relief in such a way as to ignore the distinction between genuine and fraudulent need, and to make the situation of the able-bodied pauper more eligible than that of the honest labourer. There are only three visible checks on their 'profusion or partiality, or fraud'.[29]: the share of the burden they bear as rate-payers, the supervision of the vestry, and the powers of magistrates. Each is shown to be defective, indeed to promote rather than restrain the profligate distribution of relief already encouraged by the desire to avoid trouble and do favours. Magistrates, for example, not only fail to question parish accounts but promote indiscriminate relief through good-hearted or soft-headed intervention on behalf of refused applicants (p. 57):

> If the overseers refuse relief, or grant less than the applicant thinks himself entitled to, they may be summoned before the justices to defend themselves against the charge of inhumanity and oppression; and if they do not comply with the magistrates' order, they are punishable by indictment or fine.

In these ways the report provides all the reasons anyone could want for making sense of the methods for processing claims and distributing relief. All that is now required to close the explanatory circle is an account of how the methods of relief themselves suffice to reproduce paupers. One important reproductive mechanism is the temptation to make false claims afforded by the laxness and corruption of the system (p. 48):

> The principal of the further evils which it [the proposed system] would extirpate is the tendency of that system to constant and indefinite increase, independently of any legitimate causes, a tendency which we have shown to arise from the irresistible temptations to fraud on the part of the claimants.

Another major feed-back linkage arises from the vague terminology informing administrative practice. For example, that 'the poor' are entitled to 'reasonable', 'fair' or 'adequate subsistence'. The commissioners comment (p. 29):

> It is abundantly shown in the course of this inquiry, that where the terms used by the public authorities are vague, they are always filled up by the desires of the claimants,

and the desires always await upon the imagination, which is
the worst regulated and the most vivid in the most ignorant
of people.

Since there are no clear limits on what a poorly defined poor
person has a right to expect, the system generates an infla-
tionary spiral of expectations (p. 29):

The paupers are discontented from their expectations being
raised by the ordinary administration of the system, beyond
any means of satisfying them ....Whatever addition is made
to allowances under these circumstances excites the expectation of still further allowances, increases the conception of
the extent of the right, and ensures proportionate disappoint-
ment and hatred if that expectation is not satisfied.

Finally, and most significantly for the commissioners, the
methods of poor relief turn independent labourers into paupers
(p. 127):

Throughout the evidence it is shown that in proportion as
the condition of any pauper class is elevated above the
conditions of independent labourers, the condition of the
independent class is depressed; their industry is impaired,
their employment becomes unsteady, and its remuneration
in wages is diminished. Such persons, therefore, are under
the strongest inducements to quit the less eligible class of
labourers and enter the more eligible class of paupers.

What is provided then in the explanatory moments of the report
is a system capable of accounting for whatever has been and
might be observed as instances of its own operation. The constitutive activity of reportage has been transferred to an
objective system as its functioning. A reality which accounts
for itself stands in place of active reality construction as a
metaphorical substitute for it. Indeed, there is a double substitution involved here. Reporting, having taken the place of
situated reality construction (its originary place), is now
displaced into the preoccupying object (the objective, self-
sufficient system of action) which it has turned itself into. This
pre-emption of all constitutive activity is so decisive as to
threaten a reduction of reporting itself to inactive passivity
and practical impotence: to the status of something upon which
reality has been impressed. This would be an impossible ending
for a form of writing informed from the beginning by a practical
intent to reform the world. Consequently, the completion of a
report demands a final restorative turn so as to negate passivity.
This is provided in the trope called metalepsis.
  Metalepsis is a compound form of metonymy whereby new
words stand as substitutes for the words of previous tropes.
In Hegelian terms we might say that previous tropes are sub-

lated through renaming. Metalepsis is a comprehensive gathering together of what has gone before. Bloom calls it 'the revi-
sionist trope proper'[30] and provides several marks of its
presence in a text. Most relevant for us is the suggestion that
metalepsis appears as 'a scheme ... that refers the reader back
to any previous figurative scheme ... either a projection and
distancing of the future and so an introjection of the past ...
or else more often a distancing and projection of the past and
an introjection of the future'.[31] The 1834 Report, in its recommendations for a new administrative order which will realize
the true intent of old legislation, incorporates both possibilities.
Certainly its prescriptive passages and reviews of past legislation are full, as Bloom's map requires, of images of early and
late. More specifically, Bloom identifies two forms of metaleptic
transumption: the substitution of 'early words for late words
in a precursor's tropes' and 'substituting late words for early
words in previous tropes'.[32] In applying his definitions to the
text, I have equated 'precursor's tropes' with the words of
previous pauper legislation but it could, of course, include any
prior inquiries or reports (it is conventional in social science
to begin with a review of the literature). 'Previous tropes' I
take to be the five moments of limitations and representation,
the self-constitutive moments of the text as report, which have
been described above. A further interpretive amendment to
Bloom which should be stated in advance is that the terms
'early' and 'late' have different meanings in the two forms of
substitution. Given that late can mean dead as well as recently
arrived, and that early can mean old as well as arriving in
good time for something about to begin, this volatility is hardly
surprising.

Substitutive work on precursors' tropes is evident in renaming past legislation as sound principles to be revived, harmful
errors to be destroyed or good intentions to be realized in a
new administrative practice. Positive idealization of the past is
specified particularly as the sound principles of the 1601 Act
(referred to as the 43 Elizabeth); an Act considered so
important that it is reprinted in the Supplement to the Report.
It is called 'the basis, but certainly not the origin, of our
present system' (p. 8), an ambiguous phrase suggesting that
while its soundness fits it for serving as a foundation (an
introjection of the past) it should not be regarded as the source
from which present evils grew (a distancing of the past). This
is made clear in the opening sentence of the descriptive section
(p. 9):

> It is now our painful duty to report that in the greater part
> of the districts which we have been able to examine, the
> fund which the 43 Elizabeth directed to be employed in set-
> ting to work children and persons capable of labour but
> using no daily trade, and in the necessary relief of the
> impotent, is applied to purposes opposed to the letter, and

still more to the spirit of that law.

Subsequently, the report returns in two ways to the task of reviving the late spirit of 1601; through contrasting it with bad legislation, and advocating its incorporation in a new administrative system. Bad legislation is that which has spoiled the strict clarity of the 43 Elizabeth: relief must be limited to that necessary to sustain life; it must be given only to the destitute (not the poor and certainly not anyone in employment) and, if ablebodied, only in return for supervised work of an onerous kind. The section on magistrates recalls the legislative abandonment of these principles, culminating in the 36 George III (1796) 'the great and fatal deviation from our previous policy' which 'recognized as objects of relief, industrious persons, and enabled the magistrate, at his just and proper discretion, to order it to be given in a way which should not be injurious to their comfort, domestic situation and happiness'. (p. 72) The second way in which the words of 1601 are transumed is through renaming them as general principles for new legislation. For example, the first principle declares that 'all relief whatever to able-bodied persons or to their families, otherwise than in well-regulated workhouses (i.e. places where they may be set to work according to the spirit and intention of the 43 Elizabeth) shall be declared unlawful' (p. 146). The report goes on to argue that since experience shows 'there is scarcely one statute connected with the administration of public relief which has produced the effect designed by the legislature', (p. 156) the spirit of 1601 can be realized only through embodiment in a central board of control armed with suitable powers. At this point it is clear that the substitution of early words (new beginnings) for the late (moribund) words of precursors merges with its apparent opposite, the substitution of late words (recommendations) for the early words (methods, data, analysis) of the report. Justification merges with deduction in a hoped-for future (p. 148):

We shall now show, from portions of the evidence as to the administration of relief upon a correct principle in towns, that by an uniform application of the principle which we recommend, or, in other words, by a recurrence to the original intention of the Poor Laws, other evils produced by the present system of partial relief to the able-bodied will be remedied.

And (p. 204):

It will be observed that the measures which we have suggested are intended to produce rather negative than positive effects; rather to remove the debasing influences to which a large portion of the labouring population is now subject, than to afford new means of prosperity and virtue.

We are perfectly aware that for the general diffusion of
right principles and habits we are to look, not so much to
any economic arrangements and regulations as to the influence of a moral and religious education; and important evidence in the subject will be found throughout our appendix.

The revisionary cycle of limitation and representation is now
complete. The report stands in place of the system; a truly
rational order stands in place of a specious one; textual reality
stands in place of situated reality as its inner truth.

Limits of schematic analysis
Bloom's schema has provided a useful device for drawing out
what was intended in saying that objective reports are procedures of textual reality construction which begin and end in
determinate negations of situated reality and its methods of
construction. Indeed, the demonstration model is so strong
that it might seem tempting to stamp Quod Erat Demonstrandum
on our thesis and proceed by way of further application and
amendment. However, Bloom himself has left two warnings
against such a procedure: one by precept, the other by example.
    His preceptive warning arises from the observation that
readers need to mistake meaning in order to assert their autonomy against the regulative power of a text: 'Tropes then are
necessary errors about language, defending ultimately against
the deathly dangers of literal meaning, and more immediately
against all other tropes that intervene between literal meaning
and the fresh opening to discourse.'[33]
    From this it appears that the reader faces two possibilities of
regulative capture: first, in the literal meaning of content
(referential capture); second, in the interpretive devices that
may have been used to transcend literal meaning (schematic
capture). Referential capture may be avoided by a strong
interpretive schema (say, Freudian, Marxian, Bloomian) but at
the risk of secondary capture in it as the definitive meaning,
which would mean the establishment of the schema as the last
word rather than being a 'fresh opening to discourse.'
    Parts of Bloom's own text exemplify the dangers of schematic
capture. Whereas the discourse dances and excites as it moves
between Kabbalism, psychoanalysis, and rhetoric to compose
the map of misreading, it becomes curiously pedestrian and
mechanical when reiteratively applied to poems by Wordsworth,
Keats, Shelley, etc. The last word is more of the same.
    The conclusion to be drawn is that to take Bloom's or any
strong analytic schema as literally equivalent to analysis would
be a stultifying mistake.[34] I have found it helpful, even indispensable, to impose certain concepts in advance of the materials
so as to obtain a sighting and take a bearing on the phenomenon
to be investigated. Beyond this, however, concepts must be
developed cautiously, out of immersion in textual detail, if a
short-circuiting of inquiry is to be avoided. The question of

what these particular reports are as knowledge-constitutive
reading events cannot be addressed by seeking illustrations
of answers borrowed from a prior schema. Analytic explication
of text work and the reading process must come from specific
engagement in that work and process, not from a repetition of
starting points.

SUMMARY

Starting from the premise that we know, reason, cognize,
recognize within the medium of language, plus the proposition
that language is differentiated into two distinct epistemological
realms (hearing-speaking and reading-writing), I have formulated the difference as a tense boundary relation between situated and textual reality construction. In sociological terms, the
former is the realm of personal interaction, the latter that of
administration and government (i.e. the superordinate organization of society into categories and classes).

Speaking and writing involve two irreducible ways of recognizing significant properties and making them into intelligible,
accountable realities. Tension between them is played out politically as conflicts between organizers and organized, administrators and citizens, officials and people. These are a marked
feature of what Dorothy Smith has called the social organization
of documentary reality, studies of which have brought out the
significance of writing procedures as governing devices. The
political direction of this analysis is given by a concern to
resist the unreflective equation of rationality in writing with
rationality per se: an equation which is a potent source of
unexamined authority in our society. Our concern to make
recollective claims on behalf of situated reality construction
resonates with older struggles on behalf of the individual against
the state, community against bureaucratic association, personal
identity against institutional identity. The intention is to do
political critique.

These considerations provide us with a motivated framework
for inquiry, a need for reflexive theorizing about textual reality
construction. I have argued, however, that the need cannot be
met adequately by focussing upon the concrete organizational
practices through which records, documents, reports and so
on are assembled and used, but only by extending to reading
and writing the same close questioning of methods for accomplish-
ing knowledge and reality effects which ethnomethodology has
addressed to situated speech. From this standpoint the thesis
of tense negation between textual and situated reality construction appears as an analytic proposition describing the organizing principle of factual social reports, rather than an observation
about the basis of bureaucratic administration.

In order to obtain a firmer grasp of our object of analysis,
textual reality construction, a preliminary demonstration model

has been constructed, taking categories from rhetorical analysis and applying them to the 1834 Poor Law Report. The task still remains, however, of recovering the specific production practices of the reports from engagement with their detail. Schematic abstraction is not enough to open up textwork and the reading process to critical reflection. I conceive the task as being that of achieving an emancipatory reading of factual reportage texts.

In the next chapter the task will be further pursued through a critical analysis of how the Poor Law Reports have been read by others. I will be concerned there with methods of reading and not with the merits of individual authors, since my aim is to show how limits on emancipatory adequacy are inherent to prevailing methods of reading regardless of the skill, sensitivity or scholarly competence of anyone using them.

CHAPTER 2

How the Reports have been read: a critique of reading methods

In order to resist schematic abstraction I have grounded the discussion in particular writings about the reports. On the other hand, since particular writings typically display mixed reading methods, I have been forced to detach the latter from their contexts of use so as to conduct an examination of reading rules rather than a review of publications. The relationship between those sets of rules and the particulars in which they appear is, however, to be understood as being like that between generative grammars and realized utterances rather than heuristic abstractions and concrete details. We would not want to engage in a critical analysis of mere boxes.

Our procedure will be to identify and illustrate major methods of reading in the literature, showing for each one: (a) the emancipatory interest contained in its aims and aspirations; and (b) its outer limits as an emancipatory reading. Two observations must be made on the task of specifying the limits of a method. First, in order to show that the limits are essential and inherent rather than contingent or corrigible, they must be demonstrated as constitutive necessities of the method in question. Second, since all reading methods are bounded by presuppositions and commitments, the mere demonstration that limits exist is not enough. It must be shown that the limits are such as to close off reflexive awareness of participation in an active process of knowledge and reality construction. Our interest is in limitations of reflexivity, not limitation per se.

The literature on the Poor Law Reports is almost entirely governed by three reading methods: reading the reports as evidential inquiries; reading the reports as events in historical narratives; reading the reports either as expressive indicators of authorial consciousness or as documentary evidence of an embracing socio-cultural pattern. (Clearly, the third method contains two potentially distinct interpretive sets which, if one was dealing with, say, literary rather than historical documents would have to be separated. I treat them together here because the utmost that both allow for in the way of an emancipatory reading of historical-factual documents is the same, namely a thoroughgoing sociology of knowledge reading.)

None of the three methods is incompatible with the others (though, as we will show, the third may come close to destroying their security). Indeed, the literature - in spite of scholarly disputes and contestations - has the form of a single, albeit trihedral, discourse. I will discuss the methods in the order given above.

READING THE REPORTS AS EVIDENTIAL INQUIRIES

The aim of this method is an assessment of logico-empirical
adequacy. Its primary accounting devices are (a) an evaluative
model of good inquiry specified as research using adequate
procedures of data collection and processing; and (b) a conception of the true facts of the situation as revealed by adequate
research procedures. Exactly what counts as adequate will
depend upon the level of sophistication in research techniques
accessible to the interpreter. All we need suppose, however,
is that some rules of social inquiry as empirical research have
been made authoritative so that critical assessment can take
place as a contrastive movement between actual and adequate
procedures, and between given data and virtual data (the true
facts of the reality investigated).

It would be disingenuous, given the grounding of our study
in critiques of empiricist methodology, to ask whether or not
this reading method can be emancipatory in a positive sense.
We need only remind ourselves of two essential features that
operate as impassable limits to reflexive awareness. First, the
positing of reality as an externally existent domain waiting to
be corrigibly discovered, investigated, and known. Second, the
conception of knowledge as a coming into correspondence with
reality dependent upon a methodical purging of all constitutive
inputs on the side of the knower (moral values, political purposes, aesthetic prejudices, etc.), on the ground that they are
sources of error and distortion. These founding assumptions
are commonly referred to as objectivism and objectivity; the
former securing an ontological, the latter an epistemological
boundary around the empiricist work site. Empiricism cannot
possibly understand its work as a mode of reality and knowledge
construction because the overcoming of mere constructions is
precisely its task. This is how it recognizes the difference
between knowledge and illusion, invention or make-believe.
Habermas neatly summarizes the outcome (using 'philosophy of
science' and 'positivism' to name empiricist self-understanding):
'the philosophy of science renounces inquiry into the knowing
subject...the positivist attitude conceals the problems of world
constitution'.[1]

However, given the declared aspiration of the empiricist reading method to undertake critical assessment it is worth asking
if it can be emancipatory in the negative sense of disturbing a
literal reading of these (and any other) reality reports. At first
sight this seems obviously to be the case. The method applies
the scientific norm of organized scepticism to a report in question, deliberately suspending the claims of its referential content
to be findings about reality so as to examine the possibility that
they could be a function of the procedures used to collect them.
The enactment of sceptical distancing as a breach of literal
reading is exemplified in Mark Blaug's well-known examinations
of the 1834 Report. Developing a full critique in paired articles,

Blaug seeks to destroy as 'myths' these crucial findings of the
report: (a) that the Speenhamland system of wage subsidies and
scaled allowances had caused a progressive demoralization of
workers, depression of wages, depression of rents and increase
in poor-rates since 1795; and (b) that the system was still
widespread at the time of inquiry. He proceeds through a dual
process of critical discrediting. First, by making comparisons
between the empirical claims of the report and the 'facts of the
situation' (shown by proper analysis of official statistics),
Blaug discredits the right of those claims to represent reality;
secondly, through revelations of improper research procedures
and lack of objectivity he discredits the report as inquiry.
Blaug's reading method (the method dictating his text) yields
critical judgements of this kind:

> There is no evidence whatever of that most popular of charges
> levied at the Old Poor Law: the 'snow-ball effect' of outdoor
> relief to the able-bodied [Blaug, 'Journal of Economic History',
> June 1963, p. 167.]

(The evidence of proper analysis shows their evidence to be no
evidence at all.)

> What little evidence they did present consisted of little more
> than picturesque anecdotes of maladministration ... as evi-
> dence of a social malady it has little value. [Blaug, ibid.
> p. 177.]

> the questions were poorly framed and the respondents were
> given licence to answer as they pleased: often the replies
> were ambiguous or irrelevant; sometimes the questions were
> not answered at all. [Blaug, 'Journal of Economic History',
> June 1964, p. 230.]

> The evidence they collected in the town and rural inquiries
> [but did not analyse properly] should have convinced the
> commissioners that they had misinterpreted the consequences
> of the Old Poor Law. But their minds were made up, and
> where they did not ignore the findings, they twisted them
> to suit their preconceived opinions. The Report of 1834 is
> not only a 'wildly unhistorical document', as Tawney once
> said, but also a wildly unstatistical one. [Blaug, ibid.
> p. 243.]

It should be added that while evaluation in terms of proper/
improper research procedure is essential to the empiricist reading method, an accusation of wilful distortion (such as twisting
the data) is only a possible way of naming impropriety, and by
no means necessary. Others writing as agents of the method
have named the faults of the report-as-inquiry through terms
like naivety and primitive technology, shifting the burden of
blame from the producers of the report to the means of production currently available to them. The Checklands, for example,

describe the instructions for data collection issued to the
assistant commissioners as 'a curiously naive invitation to preconception', but resist moralistic judgements (like those of
Blaug) with the reminder that 'There was an almost total lack
of experience and precedent in survey technique. It was impossible to apply scientific principles to the collection of evidence,
for none existed.'[12]

   We turn now to the question of what is the most that a strictly
empiricist reading method could hope to achieve in freeing us
from a literal reading of social inquiry findings. Certainly, as
Blaug and others demonstrate, it can successfully undertake
emancipatory criticism against the literal reading of this or that
particular report, but the essence of the criticism is only that
a particular report is not good enough to be read literally. In
other words, the criticism issues from and is directed towards
the utopian concept of a perfectly literal correspondence between
representation and reality. The utopian nature of the concept
does allow (but only allows) for limited reflexivity in the form of
an indefinite reapplication of criteria defining adequate scientific demonstration. For example, Blaug's own data and procedures
have been criticized by a fellow economic historian, James
Taylor, on such grounds as failure to push back far enough his
time series index of poor relief expenditures, distortion of index
numbers, factual errors, etc. In general, 'he arrives at too
many conclusions from too few data'.[9] Taylor's verdict is that
Blaug's account of the Old Poor Law system may be correct but
only detailed local studies of its operation will really tell. Behind
(and ahead of) the verdict is the ultimate aim of empiricist
reading: the completion of a truthful representation of reality
where text and reality alike are fully redeemable by literal reading. The method can challenge this or that literal reading in
particular but only in the name of a perfect realization of
literal reading itself (which would fulfil the ancient aspiration
to make reality an open book).

READING THE REPORTS AS EVENTS IN HISTORICAL NARRATIVES

The reading method examined here – that of narrative reconstruction – is to be understood as something inherent to and
required by the writing of history. In Habermas's terms:
'Historical descriptions in principle have a narrative form;
they are tied to the frame of reference of narrated stories.'[14]

   Although Habermas presents the rules of that frame from the
viewpoint of historical writing, we intend to consider them
from the other side as an incumbent convention for history
readers. First, however, I willl signpost the relevant literature.

   There are three main stories through which the Poor Law
Reports have been written up (and thus made readable) as
events in history. First, the story of collective efforts in

English society to cope with the problem of poverty. The classic work here is the Webbs' typically massive history of the poor laws; more concise, updated narratives of poor relief policy are provided by Poynter, J.D. Marshall and Michael Rose.[5]

Second, and always including the first as an element in its plot, the story of how English government and public administration underwent changes towards recognizably modern forms. Examples are, again, Sidney and Beatrice Webb, whose history of the poor laws appears as volumes VII to IX in their even more massive history of English local government; Maurice Bruce's history of the welfare state in Britain; and MacDonagh's history of Victorian government.[6]

Finally, the story of how a pre-industrial, often anti-industrial, population was formed into a work-force suited to mechanized factory production. It relates processes of residential, institutional, psychological uprooting and disciplining to a narrative framework of class conflict. Thompson's history of the English working class is a strong example here.[7]

While the narrative literature abounds in interpretive disputation and value clash over the reports, it is itself bound by two constitutive features which provide both for the existence of the literature as a collectivity of texts and for history writing and reading as work in a common field. The first is a working rule that whatever narrative pattern is used, it must be presented as though it had an objective existence in chronological time. This is necessary in order for particular events (say the events of an official inquiry and its consequences) to be held interpretively accountable to a pattern as instances of its unfolding. In other words, a pattern in narrative use is endowed with exteriority and constraint relative to particular details: it has the Durkheimean properties of a social fact. All the narratives cited above (and all others which might be discerned or created within the disciplinary province of history) conform to this rule. A pattern (like a theory in science) may, of course, be challenged. For example Bruce's contention that 'the story of the poor law from the sixteenth century until its final abolition in 1948 is the story of the slow widening of the area of responsibility, from the parish, through the Union (1834) to the Local Authority (1930), and eventually ... to the nation as a whole,'[8] might be challenged by Michael Rose (echoing Richard Titmuss) as a 'historical romance of "Welfare Statism"'.[9] But any such challenge would presuppose an eventual identification of the true story relative to which a charge of romance (or any other term for usurpatory fiction) could be made good.

The second feature is utilization of commonsensically known springs of human action to make the movement of line-by-line narrative reading into a transparently rational movement of events in themselves. Habermas has specified culturally given conceptualizations of normative action, subjective purpose, motivated conduct, communicative meaning, decisional rationality, etc. as generic elements of the narrative frame of reference, adding:

However we reconstruct this intuitively mastered system of basic concepts, the history writer must move in this system when he both describes and explains a context of events narratively. The historian masters these basic concepts by virtue of the competence which he (independently of his professional expertise) has as a subject capable of language and action; he shares this competency with all other adult members of his society.[10]

The postulate of narratory confinement to concepts derived from (and indexical to) societal membership allows Habermas to draw the logical conclusion that history writing cannot do more than reconstruct what has happened in the past according to the sense-making practices and (re)cognitional forms ordering everyday life in the present. However much history writing might enrich and sophisticate 'naive narrative' through, for example, borrowing concepts from the social sciences, it is in the end condemned to composing what Harold Garfinkel likes to call Just So Stories. The following observation by Habermas permits a specific linkage between the emancipatory impotence of history writing in relation to prevailing socio-political practices and its methodological closure on reflexive reading:

> Historical descriptions are action-oriented knowledge; they are on the same plane as the historic consciousness of contemporaries. As between the participant in discourse and one who takes action, there is no difference of level between the history writer and his public.[11]

Interpreting 'the history writer' analytically to mean the rules of a particular writing genre, and 'his public' to mean the reading posture set by those rules, we can say that historical narrative holds the person who reads to a single plane of understanding in which he is co-existent with text and context through shared conventions of common-sense accountability. The plane itself is closed to examination in being used as an explanatory resource. We must be careful, however, not to make too strict a judgement. The mere act of removing words from an original setting – for example, the contents of the Poor Law Reports from the framework of factual inquiry and reportage – so as to incorporate them via quotation, paraphrase and interpretation into a history narrative is in itself a disturbance of a literal reading and to that extent emancipatory. The removal, however, is always a relocation in a conventionally secured zone of interpretation and the most that can be done is to update narratives as conventions change. History is continually rewritten to restore and preserve the constitutive innocence of history writing for the time being.

A cautionary note must also be entered on the issue of practical-political effectivity. In endorsing Habermas's negative judgement, I do not mean to say that history writing is incapable of

promoting the practical values claimed for it: offering lessons
to decision-makers, teaching humility to the powerful, clarify-
ing attitudes by refracting them through time, cultivating group
consciousness, fostering moral sensitivity through narratives
of suffering, etc. It must surely be admitted that history writing, if publicly amplified (as in party programmes, manifestos,
mass media messages) and connected to conduct through organized action, has power to shape events. Established regimes,
new ruling classes and revolutionary groups have been famously
interested in the writing and teaching of history. But that
serviceability of history to diverse shapings of political consciousness which attracts the interest of practical men of power
precisely betrays its lack of power as critical reflection. The
methodological closure of history as a discipline against reflection on the constitutive nature of its reading-writing practices
means that it can only enter social practice non-discursively as
part of a technology of preservative or oppositional power.
Admittedly the latter polarity is often named as a liberation or
freedom movement, but the other side of antagonistic struggle
(coming to the fore when a movement succeeds and becomes a
government) is loyalty to a cause, commitment to a mission,
solidarity with a historic community of heroes, martyrs, victims,
prophets, brothers, sisters, and the like. Whatever liberational
function a given version of history may have, it is entirely political in character and depends not on itself but on the situation
of the group (or public or class) from whose viewpoint that
history is written. History (because it is in principle tied to the
narrative frame of reference) cannot in principle challenge the
hegemony of intuitive social knowledge established by virtue of
group membership. History is always writing from and towards
such membership, caught inexorably within its forms of thought.
Its emancipatory potential is completely realized and released
in service to group conflict.

There is at least one positive lesson to be drawn from these
comments (providing a theme for subsequent elaboration).
Namely, that the problem of emancipation in practice is not at
root a matter of moral will and political determination but of
cognitive capacity to theorize unrecognized methods (significatory structures, accounting devices, the 'grammatical' rules
of cultural membership) determining social reality construction
in a certain way. (Karl Marx understood this in dedicating his
life to the formulation of a critique of the conceptual categories
of political economy, entering secondarily and ambivalently
into the organizational work of revolutionary overthrow.)[12]
The emancipatory demand made of reading and writing as critical
reflection is to effect a breach of constitutive continuity with
everyday, 'natural' practices of rational accounting. However,
the strategic question of how best to meet the demand goes
beyond the present topic and must be postponed.

I will conclude with some comments on the first feature of
narrative reconstruction noted above: reliance upon an

objectified pattern of events to make story-telling into researchable truth-finding. Objectification of narrative pattern is not a
discrete, done and finished thing but the continuous maintenance
of a certain reading posture in and through the organization of
a text. Testification to the objective standing of the story in
use is a functional imperative of all history narratives; an
organizing principle which all topical detailing must serve.
With regard to histories that include the Poor Law Reports this
means that the interpretive movement of reading they require
is always from the reports and towards some extrinsic chain of
events they belong to. My point here is not simply that the
inward movement of constitutive analysis is, so to speak, in
the opposite direction from the outward, onward movement of
reading enjoined by the flow of narrative writing but that it
involves a theoretical breach with such reading, and this can
only be done through concepts beyond the categories to which
narrative is tied. Something like an orthogonal intercept is
pushed down and through them, putting interpretation on a
different plane than what Habermas refers to as an intuitively
mastered system of concepts. If it were to be objected that my
own interpretation of modern administration as a radical deepen-
ing of the subordination of situated to textual reality construction itself posits an objective temporal pattern and is, therefore,
liable to the judgements levelled against history writing, I would
plead guilty to patterning but argue in mitigation: (1) the
formulation of the pattern is such as to turn reflective attention
towards instead of from the constitutive dynamics of the reports;
(2) those dynamics are explicated through categories transcending yet reflexively open to members' methods of knowing social
reality. The emancipatory limit of history resides in its being
unreflexively open to members' methods: this is what constitutive theorizing seeks to remedy, not openness itself. Certainly,
we do not wish to follow the remedial example of scientistic
sociology which mistakenly equates transcendence with super-
ordination, seeking to substitute formal for societal concepts
and methods in the name of a superior rationality. Emancipatory
social theory demands an interception of planes, not a separation
into hierarchical levels of domination. It remains now to be
seen if that demand can be met by the third method through
which the reports have been read.

READING THE REPORTS AS EXPRESSIVE AND/OR DOCU-
MENTARY INDICATORS[13]

Repeating a previous point, two distinguishable methods of
reading are merged here - one pointing to a hermeneutic of
authorial consciousness, the other to a hermeneutic of ideational
coding - on the ground that the farthest both can go towards
an emancipatory reading of social reality reports is a sociology
of knowledge interpretation. Intimations of such a reading are

found in the critical thrust of discussions of the 1834 Report towards unmasking as lies and unmasking as ideology. The former is shown in Blaug's charge, quoted above, that the Commissioners twisted the findings to suit preconceived opinions. Thompson moves to the second kind of unmasking by specifying those opinions to an 'ideological dogma' called 'Malthusian-Benthamism', itself belonging to an Individualistic-Utilitarian-Methodist ethos of English capitalism, and serving to legitimate the forceful formation of a disciplined, docile work-force. Behind the mask is, of course, the economic interest of the entrepreneurial class in labour as a factor of mechanized production. For Thompson, then, the 1834 Report belongs with the temperance movement, the Society for the Suppression of Vice, legal prohibition of working-class entertainments, condemnation of traditional fairs and holidays, clock regulation of work and leisure time, Sunday schools, and moral-legal assaults against 'Cobbler's Monday' (also known as St. Monday),[14] as documentary indicators of a ruling-class ideology. In similar, though non-Marxian manner Finer interprets the report as the triumph of a certain concept of public administration, represented by Edwin Chadwick, against a view of poor relief predominant among the governing classes (a view dictating that the poor had no right to public relief, that the poor laws should be abolished, and that the most effective solution to poverty was the emigration of surplus labourers). That concept is traced back to Chadwick's erstwhile mentor, Bentham, and Bentham depicted as the theorist of a 'radical' sub-set of the industrial middle-class whose practically rooted world-view included a hard-headed contempt for mere tradition and conventional wisdom; a horror of waste; a high valuation of efficiency, cheapness and uniformity in all spheres of management; and a conviction that the public interest (the greatest happiness of the greatest number) could be achieved through rationally ordered dispositions of pains and pleasures.[15] Finer does not pursue a whole-hearted debunking of the report, contenting himself with the verdict that the remedies proposed were 'inadequate to the extent that the diagnosis was lop-sided'.[16] His verdict reveals something of the emancipatory potential in the documentary-expressive method of reading.

The extent to which he is able to read the report as lop-sided is the extent to which he reads it as an ideational code and an expression of authorial consciousness. To this extent he frees himself from reading its content literally as a reality report. What is at issue, however, is whether the tactic of displaying truth claims as a function of social origins and cultural context must itself be grounded in an objectivist ontology. A decision demands that we uncover the necessary limits of the sociology of knowledge as an emancipatory reading method, and this can only be done through some account which explicitly pushes that method to its limits. At this juncture the work of Karl Mannheim assumes crucial significance for us. A preliminary

indication of its fulness relative to what has been achieved in
the poor law report literature is that unmasking as lies is construed by Mannheim as a preparation for the sociology of knowledge and unmasking as ideology still only a halfway house.

Mannheim's emancipatory intent emerges clearly in his reconstruction of the 'constellation' attending the emergence of the
problem (and method) of the sociology of knowledge in our
time.[17] A significant element was the appearance, out of rational-
ist scepticism of an oppositional science called sociology. Its
significance is found not in the ideas which were opposed but
in the method of 'unmasking' that the new science used as an
oppositional strategy:

> This is a turn of mind which does not seek to refute, negate,
> or call in doubt certain ideas, but rather to *disintegrate*
> them, and that in such a way that the whole world outlook of
> a social stratum becomes disintegrated at the same time.[18]

Mannheim elaborates his meaning through a strong distinction
between 'denying the truth' and 'determining the function' of
an idea. The first operation takes place on the same plane as
the disputed idea: the disputant enters a significatory structure around the idea and opposes it through the combinatory
possibilities of its own discursive set (e.g. Blaug disputing
the truth of certain propositions made in the 1834 Report). The
second operation sinks as it were a vertical shaft through the
horizontal plane of the discourse by pointing to its 'extra-
theoretical' grounding in non-discursive practices, interests,
purposes, situations: 'Only then, do I achieve an "unmasking"
which in fact represents no theoretical refutation but the
destruction of the practical effectiveness of these ideas.'[19]

Disintegration of ideas, then, results from bringing to consciousness a hitherto unthought, hence unquestionable, integration with a mundane, worldly context. In our terms, this is
something like a destruction of constitutive innocence. Mannheim
goes on to distinguish between two kinds of unmasking achieved
already in social thought (and which are, for us, possible
methods of emancipatory reading). The older one questions the
moral character of the speaker/writer in order to show an
intent to deceive, and unmask an idea as a lie. It is metaphorically interesting that a lie also means a horizontal position and
a resting place. An idea in that position and place is one that
seeks assessment purely in terms of its logical-empirical validity.
All unmasking procedures disturb such assessment by showing
an idea to have a vertical, extra-theoretical dimension, to be
more than just an idea, and hence liable to other criteria of
judgement. In this first type the vertical dimension consists of
the moral character of an addresser and the criteria are those
of personal honesty.

In the second type, unmasking an idea as ideology, the
dimension is defined by some partial theory of the sociological

determination of thought and held to a philosophy of social
morality and/or the meaning of history. Mannheim names Marxist
class warfare as its sphere of origin, adding that it 'later
became the prototype of a new way of transcending theoretical
immanence in general'[20] – a new way of angling in and out of
the flat plane of purely discursive assertion and refutation.
Using Wittgenstein's terminology one might say that whereas
the first type proceeds by showing that an apparent move
in a discursive language-game of representing reality is
actually a move in an ethical game of sincerity and deception,
the second does so by showing that what appears to be a single-
game discursive move is really a complex move in at least two
games at once, where the rules of a hidden social game are
dominant.[21]

    The crux of Mannheim's argument is that unmasking as
ideology does not provide complete transcendence of 'theoretical
immanence' because it aims only at the social relativization of
certain ideas (those of one's opponents) and not at ideas (all
thought and knowledge) in general. The analytic challenge –
and reflexively disturbing problem – of the sociology of knowledge is to make relativization total:

> We cannot refrain from concluding that our own ideas, too,
> are functions of a social position ....What we have to grasp
> is that both our 'ideas' and our 'existence' are components
> of a comprehensive evolutionary process in which we are
> engaged. This overall process, then, is posited as our
> ultimate 'absolute' (albeit a changing and evolving one).[22]

Mannheim provides here a direct statement of knowledge production as participation in an active social process: abstractly
meeting one of our requirements of emancipatory adequacy in
an interpretive method. More closely, the aspiration of emancipatory reading to dispel the discursive hold of a text (specifically, a text written in the form of a social reality report) is
recognizable in Mannheim's aim to transcend the 'theoretical
immanence' of social thought by showing that it does not confront a standing reality outside of itself but simultaneously
articulates, changes, and is changed by an embracing process
in which we as communicants (speakers-hearers, readers-
writers) are engaged. The question is, however, whether the
application of the sociology of knowledge as a reading method
can realize its emancipatory intent. In speaking of application,
I mean that Mannheim's method, like any interpretive sign-
system, subjects anything entering it to determinate transform
devices making it intelligible in certain ways. The task is to
specify the basic rules of the system to see what it would make
of something like a Poor Law Report. My argument will be that
they are such as to thwart the intent announced as its mission
(at least, in terms of the problem of reading – I will not comment
here on the political aspect of Mannheim's programme).

The integrity of Mannheim's method - its boundary against what is negatively other than itself - is established with reference to three possibilities of epistemological capture. First, there is the innocent absolutism of thought operating thoughtlessly as something natural and taken-for-granted. Mannheim says at the beginning of his major book, 'Ideology and Utopia', that 'strictly speaking it is incorrect to say that the single individual thinks', rather he is socialized into 'preformed patterns of thought' whose hold can only be shaken if membership is made deeply problematic.[23] Subsequently, in the title essay of the book, Mannheim compares this emancipatory movement to the experience of a man living contentedly within the provincial sphere of a narrow, unquestioned perspective ('the scope of a small town or limited social circle') until some 'crisis of disillusionment' forces reflection upon his way of life so that he sees it as only partial and particular within a broader totality:

> Once the individual has grasped the method of orienting himself in the world, he is inevitably driven beyond the narrow horizon of his own town and learns to understand himself as part of a national, and later of a world, situation. In the same manner he will be able to understand the position of his own generation, his own immediate situation within the epoch in which he lives, and in turn this period as part of the total historical process.[24]

The emancipatory virtue of relativization in critically dissolving innocent absolutism (which, for us, is literal membership of a social reality report) is by no means assured, however, by the comforting metaphor of concentrically expanding horizons. Critical consciousness may be caught in two further possibilities of epistemological capture which now arise: the despairing circle of aimless relativism; and a reimposed absolutism - the dogmatic resolution of wandering. The crisis of our time is an excess of disillusionment, a multiplicity of ways of thinking experienced as 'intellectual unrest' and lack of a common ground. It is simultaneously an opportunity and a danger:

> We must realize once and for all that the meanings which make up our world are simply an historically determined and continuously developing structure in which man develops, and are in no sense absolute....But, [if this is not done] the vision may disappear the opportunity may be lost, and the world will once again present a static, uniform, and inflexible countenance.[25]

Mannheim's totalization of ideological analysis does not aim at complete unmasking but, rather, to prevent the mask which has slipped from the face of social life in our time from being

replaced. The apparently non-evaluative concept of ideology
which is at the centre of the sociology of knowledge needs, as
its programmatic warrant, the evaluative purpose of negating
relativism (which we must remember is also its methodological
source) in order not to be confused with it. Directly following
the above passage there is an impassioned outcry against those
who would exploit 'our contemporary intellectual plight' by
laying false claims to certainty:

> attempting to pass off to the world and recommending to
> others some nostrum of the absolute ... (to satisfy) ... the
> need for intellectual and moral certainty felt by broad sec-
> tions of the population who are unable to look life in the
> face.

Mannheim then confesses the need informing his own enterprise
as a belated recognition of something not visible at its outset:

> Thus it appears that beginning with the non-evaluative
> conception of ideology, which we used to grasp the flux of
> continuously changing realities, we have been unwittingly
> led to an evaluative-epistemological, and finally an onto-
> logical-metaphysical approach ....Here, as in so many other
> cases, only at the end of our activity do we at last become
> aware of those motives which at the beginning drove us to
> set every established value in motion, considering it as part
> of a general historical movement.[26]

The meaning of this confession, as stating a constitutive feature of the sociology of knowledge as an emancipatory interpretive method, is more fully revealed in a footnote to an earlier
essay. Here the ambivalent tension between relativization as a
theoretical resource and relativity as an imminent threat is
additionally revealed by a symptomatic profusion of bracketing
marks (invitations not to take words literally):

> What we mean by 'self-relativization' of thought is by no
> means epistemological 'relativism' but merely the opposite of
> 'autonomy'. One may very well assert that thought is 'rela-
> tive to being', 'dependent on being', 'non-autonomous',
> 'part of a whole reaching beyond it', without professing
> 'relativism' concerning the truth value of its findings. At
> this point it is so, so to speak, still open whether the
> 'existential relativization' of thought is to be combined with
> epistemological relativism or not. In any case, however, we
> would like to go on record, at this point, that we cannot
> share the at present widespread fear of relativism. 'Rela-
> tivism' has become a catchword which, it is believed, will
> instantly annihilate any adversary against whom it is used.
> But as to us, we definitely prefer a 'relativism' which accent-
> uates the difficulty of its task by calling attention to all

those moments which tend to make the propositions discoverable at any given time, partial and situationally conditioned
- we prefer such a 'relativism' to an 'absolutism' which loudly
proclaims, as a matter of principle, the absoluteness of its
own position or of 'truth in itself', but is in fact no less
partial than any of its adversaries - and, still worse, is
utterly incapable of tackling with its epistemological apparatus the problems of the temporal and situational determination of any concrete process of thought, completely over-
looking the way in which this situational conditioning enters
into the structure and the evolution of knowledge.[27]

Of course, frankly stated and stylistically cultivated confes-
sions of uncertainty do not themselves provide an epistemological
apparatus either. Nor is it enough to boldly proclaim that
instability in the concept of ideology 'is part of the technique
of research'.[28] The sociology of knowledge has to be applied
as a working method which will use the technique of social
relativization, while containing its dangers, in the course of
detailed encounter with particular materials. The evaluative
declarations of 'dynamic relationism' are insufficient to maintain
the integrity of the system in actually doing interpretation.
Something more is needed in moving beyond the programmatic
level. This is provided by a return to objectivism: positing an
external reality resistant to thought about it. The specifically
analytic promise of dynamic relationism is announced in the
opening section of 'Ideology and Utopia': 'A new type of
objectivity in the social sciences is attainable not through the
exclusion of evaluations but through the critical awareness and
control of them.[29]
In interpretive research practice, control of evaluations
becomes a methodological problem of securing intersubjective
validation of accounts: a peculiarly sensitive problem for a
method which relativizes all knowledge, including its own. Mannheim resolves it by introducing two objectivist closures on this
'flexible and dialectical' turn of thought around itself (which
might otherwise become the giddy spin of mere relativism): the
ontological positing of a single reality which is partially glimpsed
from historically conditioned standpoints - a perspectivism distinguished from relativism by an ontology of 'the same'; and
the hypostatization of styles and patterns of thought as investigative objects to which ideas can be referred as an intermediate
form of relativization (styles and patterns are in turn relativized
to social factors transcending thought - factors ultimately
grounded in the single reality which partial thought glimpses).
The first closure appears in Mannheim's discussion of the
sociology of knowledge, where he endorses Max Scheler's insistence that even though a cultural object (say Hellenism) can only
be cognized through multiple interpretations from various angles
that object still has a standing identity in itself, a 'real being',
which serves to rule out 'arbitrary characterizations':

To mention an example by means of which we can illustrate
the meaning of perspectivism most clearly: human consciousness can grasp a landscape *as landscape* only from various
perspectives; and yet the landscape does not dissolve itself
into its various pictorial representations. Each of the possible pictures has a 'real' counterpart and the correctness
of each perspective can be controlled from the other perspectives ....The historicist standpoint, which starts with
relativism, eventually achieves an absoluteness of view,
because in its final form it posits history itself as the Absolute.[30]

The inescapable need of the method to posit a single reality
as the ultimate control on arbitrary multiplicity (i.e. the
reflexive disintegration of the method itself) surfaces again
in Mannheim's evaluation of ideological and utopian thought as
temporally warped perspectives (the former through lagging
behind, the latter through leaping ahead of what is demanded
in the present):

The attempt to escape ideological and utopian distortion is,
in the last analysis, a quest for reality ....We begin to
suspect that each group seems to move in a separate and
distinct world of ideas and that these different systems of
thought, which are often in conflict with one another, may
in the last analysis be reduced to different modes of experiencing the 'same' reality.[31]

For our purpose, the significance of this reduction does not
reside in a last analysis but in what it authorizes for any particular analyses that might be undertaken: in the fact that it
reserves a place, within the absolute totality called history but
outside thought, from which social factors can operate as objective forces shaping, conditioning and influencing thought.
   The second closure, which completes what is necessary to the
sociology of knowledge as a new type of objectivity, is most
clearly displayed in Mannheim's essay on conservative thought.[32]
It begins with an acknowledgement that at the heart of the
method is 'the concept of a style of thought', taken over from
art history. From this starting point, the analysis proceeds as
a gathering process whereby particular ideas are brought in as
demonstrative details of the conservative style of thought and
its negatives. The interpretive movement enjoined by the method
is from instances to hypostatized patterns and back again. The
latter include the 'isms' (liberalism, capitalism, rationalism,
scientific positivism) which called forth nineteenth century
German conservatism as their antithetic response, and the
mediating 'isms' (romanticism, historicism, traditionalism)
through which that style of thought took shape. Their standing
as existential entities is explicitly stated at the beginning of
the second section:

Acting along conservative lines ... means that the individual
is consciously or unconsciously guided by a way of thinking
and acting which has its own history behind it, before it
comes into contact with the individual. This contact with the
individual may under certain circumstances change to some
extent the form and development of this way of thinking and
acting, but even when the individual is no longer there to
participate in it, it will still have its own history and development apart from him. Political conservatism is therefore an
objective mental structure, as opposed to the 'subjectivity'
of the isolated individual.[33]

We can now specify the basic structure and dynamics of the
sociology of knowledge, conceived as a reading method. A
particular document, such as the 1834 Report, will be received
into its system of interpretation through placement in a significatory space corresponding to the concept of 'the isolated
individual'. It does not matter whether the document is
addressed as a concern to understand its particular authors or its
particular content, the important point is that its isolated particularity must be overcome by showing membership of broader
mental structures which are themselves historically generated
and socially conditioned (like the provincial man who needs to
be driven from the narrow horizon of his own town in order
to transform isolation into understanding). Isolated particularity,
objective mental structure and socio-historical context provide
three significatory locations between which something like a poor
law report can be shuttled to weave an interpretation. The
interpretive dynamic is always away from isolated particularity
(because the emancipatory imperative of the method is always
away from innocent absolutism, dogmatically imposed absolutism
and theoretical immanence), and between the other two as
objective, concentrically organized spheres of reality (they must
be objectively secure in order to close off relativism as an
inner danger to interpretive validation; there must be an outer
circle of 'absolute' reality so that a stand can be taken against
relativism as nihilistic despair). One result is to dictate a reading method which is systematically incapable of treating the
objectivity of the structures it relies on in interpretation as
something produced in practice. Mannheim comes distantly close
to acknowledging this incapacity in a footnote to the confession
of 'metaphyical-ontological value judgements' quoted previously:

This unavoidable implicit ontology which is at the basis of
our actions, even when we do not want to believe it, is not
something which is arrived at by romantic yearning and
which we impose upon reality at will. It marks the horizon
within which lies our world of reality and which cannot be
disposed of by simply labelling it ideology. At this point we
see a glimmer of a 'solution' to our problem ....The exposure
of ideological and utopian elements in thought is effective

in destroying only those ideas with which we ourselves are
not too intimately identified.[34]

Of course, Mannheim intends to talk of moral, ethical and
existential limits to the disintegrative thrust of his method, not
of investigative limits imposed by the rules of the method itself
on what can be made topics of inquiry. But it is not, I think,
arbitrary to understand him in the second way, given his commitment to fashioning an openly reflexive, dialectical form of
knowledge about knowledge. I am not holding Mannheim's method
to some impossible requirement of questioning everything at
once, including all its grounds for questioning, all its constitutive rules and fixities. The decisive basis for objection here
lies in what it cannot question properly, namely objectivity,
which is an essential property of that which it wants to understand, i.e. knowledge. As a consequence, the fate of the sociology of knowledge was to be its unresisting reduction from an
emancipatory response to the crisis of thought in our time to
an obscure, provincial sub-area within scientistic sociology,
its practitioners studying knowledge within a division of labour
erected upon an objectified reality whose sameness guarantees
the coherence of their specialized work into a comprehensive
scientific programme. (It is ironic, yet revealing, that Mannheim
should have once used precisely these metaphors of division of
labour and scientific comprehension to describe the imperial
prospects of the sociology of knowledge itself.)[35] However, we
must try to be more precise about the meaning of objectification
as constitutive rule and investigative limit when the interpretive
dynamics of the method are applied as procedures of textual
analysis.

The meaning emerges in Mannheim's methodological writings
as a critical distinction between grasping ideas from within and
grasping them from without, plus an interpreter's rule to
transcend the former through the latter. Mannheim insists that
the difference 'is not merely one of point of view but is the
result of a fundamentally different attitude toward the same
intellectual phenomenon'[36] (toward, say, the ideas of the 1834
Report on poverty and its relief). Grasping from within 'means
that the subject, in a particular way, is absorbed by the intellectual phenomenon, that he "lives" in it ....Their grasp "from
within", therefore, may also be defined as the unconditional
fulfillment of the "positing" that is prescribed in the intellectual
phenomenon.'[37] It means being grasped by the innocent demand
of utterances that they be treated as nothing but ideas: Mannheim refers to this elsewhere as capture in the immanence of
thought. Limited degrees of freedom are offered by 'intrinsic
interpretations' (limited because they do not depart from the
ideational plane but merely articulate its attitude of grasping
from within). These include: interpretation of authorial intention; history of ideas; examination of presuppositions, interior
logic, latent meanings; juxtaposition with another system of

thought; and documentary interpretation. The last of these, involving reconstruction of the total 'global outlook of an epoch' - a 'Weltanschauung' manifested in the plastic arts, music, morals, etiquette, interaction rituals, literature, as well as ideas of an era - is given a special significance because it provides a transition from intrinsic to extrinsic interpretation. The proper task of the latter is to expand the interpretive frame of reference so that it is now an existential (social) rather than merely cultural totality:

> We have to do here with an act of breaking through the immanence of thought - with an attempt to comprehend thought as a partial phenomenon within the broader field of existence, and to determine it, as it were, starting from existential data. The 'existential thinker', however, asserts precisely that his ultimate position lies outside the sphere of thought - that for him, thought neither constitutes objects nor grasps ultimately real matters of fact but merely expresses extra-theoretically constituted and warranted beliefs.[38]

The new objectivity, like the old, succumbs to the paradoxical yearning of all thought understanding itself as contemplative reflection to be at one with a reality transcending thought, to achieve a self-effacing harmony with reality called truth. The conceptualization of that transcendent reality as dynamic and historical, rather than eternal and universal, certainly has a claim to be called newly different: not least because it cultivates the latent paradoxes of objectivist epistemology and raises them to the level of overt discursive conflict (witness Mannheim's ambivalent struggle with the topic/opportunity/resource/danger of relativism). For our purpose, however, the interest of this is not as a dramatic spectacle of self-destruction but in the fact that even a reflexively intended objectivity cannot formulate the interpretive task of breaking away from the ideational spell of textual content except as an outward movement from inner to outer, from text to context, which is to say by evacuating the text. The sociology *of* knowledge declares in its title a strong line between social existence and thought. The line is constitutively essential because passage across it, to and fro, is its research practice: the way in which it makes itself a rationally accountable inquiry. As a reading rule the line authorizes and requires a division between intrinsic and extrinsic standpoints of interpretation. In conjunction with the objectivist equation of the latter with the standpoint of social reality, and its positing as the only place from which an emancipatory grasp of ideational content is possible, this amounts to a ruling out of the kind of solution we have proposed to Mannheim's problem of 'breaking through the immanence of thought'. For us, with social reality reports in mind, the immanence of thought means the power of a text to withhold attention from its own constitutive methods so that it appears to have been shaped by the

reality it refers to. Mannheim's strategy, like our own, is to
break the literal frame of reading by locating the methods on a
plane orthogonal to the surface of the text. He does so, however, by stepping out of the text into an ontologically secured
reality consisting of objective mental structures and their cor-
relates:

> Intellectual and cognitive standpoints ... do not float in
> thin air or develop and ramify purely from within, but
> must be put in correlation with certain tendencies embodied
> by social strata ....We can show that a certain style of
> thought, an intellectual standpoint, is encompassed within
> a system of attitudes which in turn can be seen to be related
> to a certain economic and power system ....Thus the con-
> struction of a sociology of knowledge can be undertaken
> only by taking a circuitous route through the concept of
> the total system of a world outlook.[39]

The programmatic concept of an all-encompassing totality (the
sphere in which the 'existential thinker' circuitously moves) cannot be sustained in analytic practice: it is consequently reduced
to a series of objectified variables - 'intellectual standpoints',
'social strata', 'economic system', 'power system', and so on.
In contrast, our method is to resist the directive pointing of a
text away from itself by, as it were, moving in the opposite
direction: attending to textual methods of reality and knowledge
construction as processes located in the overlooked space between
the printed page and the reading eye. It is in this reading
space that we might hope to develop an emancipatory reading
'from within' which escapes the ideational plane. Mannheim
cannot formulate such an alternative in terms of his antithesis between inner and outer. Moreover, his commitment to
objectivity means that he can only understand constitutive
theorizing as the invalid assertion that 'thought constitutes
objects'. We also reject that formula as inadequate but replace
it with the working hypothesis that reality and knowledge effects
are constituted by specifiable practices of reading-writing. In
this respect we find ourselves close to Walter Benjamin's rejection of the 'unfruitful antithesis' between form and content as
a method for analysing the societal dimension of literature and
to his claim that 'the concept of technique' - the mode and
relations of literary production a text embodies - offers a
superior, because dialectical, starting point for literary criticism
with a political intent.[40] That starting point, represented in our
question of the textwork through which knowledge effects are
produced, is inherently dialectical because it makes problematic
the place, presence and function of the person who reads.
   Mannheim does at one point come close to placing the problem
of constitutive mechanisms on his research agenda. This is in a
discussion of the 'objective meaning' of cultural objects and
social actions as something distinct from their expressive and

documentary meanings. Objective meaning is 'rooted in the structural laws of the object itself';[41] for example, the melodic and harmonic organization of a piece of music, or the spatial composition of a painting.

Clearly, Mannheim's illustrations from the fine arts contain the possibility of analogical extension to the text as something having its own structural laws and dynamics. This would require, however, a strongly constitutive conception of writing in relation to reality, whereas Mannheim's objectivist commitment to reality constrains him to see writing either as an intermediary vehicle expressing, documenting something beyond itself, or as something immediately presenting an objective meaning. In the case of art, immediate presence can be understood as sensory experience but this is not so with writing and Mannheim can only conceptualize it as an immanent meaning somehow present in the words themselves. Its recovery, in research practice, is reduced to the instruction that objective interpretation 'starting from the author's own premises, tries to draw correct conclusions from them. (Example: "To understand Kant better than he understood himself")'.[42] Objective interpretation ends up, in the final analysis, as a subsidiary undertaking on the ideational plane, belonging with other established hermeneutic practices to the intrinsic side of the inner-outer classification and, therefore, to that capture in the immanence of thought which the sociology of knowledge must transcend through social relativization. The potential closeness of Mannheim's concept of the objective meaning of cultural objects to our own concept of the constitutive power of a text is decisively negated by the necessities of his method.

In conclusion, my verdict on this, the most promising of existing reading methods, is that the rules governing its practice ultimately exclude the emancipatory interest announced in its programme. A significant result of the contradiction is that Mannheim, in 'Ideology and Utopia', turns increasingly to an instrumental mastery and technical control framework of self-understanding for his enterprise (i.e. to what Habermas has identified as the knowledge-constitutive interest of natural science, strongly contrasted with the interest of critical science in emancipatory self-reflection).[43] Mannheim comes to declare the social value of his method in almost scientistic terms:

> Increased knowledge does not eliminate decisions but only forces them farther and farther back. But what we gain through this retreat from decisions is an expansion of our horizon and a greater intellectual mastery of our world ... advances in sociological research into ideology ... will enable us, as we have already indicated, to calculate more precisely collective interests and their corresponding modes of thought and to predict approximately the ideological reactions of the different social strata ....Those who fear that an increased knowledge of the determining factors which

enter into the formation of their decisions will threaten their 'freedom' may rest in peace. Actually it is the one who is ignorant of the significant determining factors and who acts under the immediate pressure of determinants unknown to him who is least free ....Whenever we become aware of a determinant which has dominated us, we remove it from the realm of unconscious motivation into that of the controllable, calculable, and objectified.... Motives which previously dominated us become subject to our domination.[44]

The critical limits of the sociology of knowledge are revealed here in the fact that it can be enrolled in precisely the same project of rational domination and control served by social reality reports, as a means of making the projected control more complete and extensive. The 'new objectivity' realizes its value in social planning; it articulates a 'prosaic attitude ... in large measure to be welcomed as the only instrument for the mastery of the present situation, as the transformation of utopianism into science'.[45] This is the logic of the method, and Mannheim's belated praise of utopian thought as a salvation from the Weberean nightmare of a completely rationalized, matter-of-fact, social order is helpless to resist it. It is our position that only a critical method grounded in a conception of language as the constitutive medium of social reality and knowledge could hope to do so.

CHAPTER 3

Reading and reality effects

In choosing to begin with an account of reality effects, placing these before knowledge effects, we retain Kant's insight that the judgemental work of knowledge proceeds upon the prior base of something given as real. Statements can only be construed in terms of probability, possibility, causal connection, validity and so on by accepting them as reality references. Whereas, however, Kant's problematic - the knowability of experience - at least made it plausible to posit an a priori sensuous intuition as that which provides a continuous flow of reality for cognition, such a mechanism could not hope to explain the production of reality effects in encountering signs on paper. Moreover, the fact that texts vary in the strength and duration of such effects; that, for example, truth-claim texts are readily distinguished from realistic novels and science-fiction, suggests that we should be looking at textual self-display methods for an answer rather than at 'the reader's' constitutive faculties. The concrete individual who reads should not be confused with 'the reader' as a posture required by a text as a condition of membership to it. Such an equation - or reduction - can, of course, occur in practice; it describes, in fact, the ordinary experience of literal reading against which interpretation struggles. Interpretation itself, however, is inconceivable without an individual capable not only of entering but of transcending the role-requirements dictated by a text. Reading, like any other social process, is a dialectical movement between self-captivation and self-retrieval. To understand reality effects on paper, we must concentrate on captivation as a textual achievement (certainly not as a failing or weakness on the part of the individual who reads), but this is done only as a first step. The identification of textual methods is conceived as the beginning of interpretive retrieval and not as an attempt to efface the individual, which would be an abandonment of emancipatory interest. In dialectical terms, the individual exists as an affirmation of identity in the face of dispersal, including dispersal into role-requirements, so that actual experience of dispersal - for example, as capture in the constitutive realm of a text - is indispensable to a real, as opposed to a rhetorical affirmation of identity. The emancipatory interest is realized in preserving this kind of tension, not in annulling it by false alternatives. We assert the concept of the reader as a textually demanded posture, in deliberate opposition to that of the reader as the substantial person scanning the page, precisely because the

conventional strength of the latter threatens to dissolve this
dialectical dualism of dispersal and identity, captivation and
retrieval. Its predispositions are an obstacle to constructionist
analysis and must be bracketed in order to move ahead.

READER AS PERSON AND READER AS POSTURE

There are two dominant conceptions of reading in our culture:
reading as an instrumental skill, and reading as the establishment of a personal relationship with the author. Although sometimes found in polemic opposition to one another, they both
express a one-sided view of reading as an individual achievement, as that which the reader does, and are elaborations of
the reductionist idea that the reader is nothing but the person
who reads. To put the objection differently, they both posit
the concrete individual as the appropriate unit of analysis for
an account of reading and thereby open themselves to all the
objections that have been levelled in social analysis generally
against the doctrine of methodological individualism.[1] These will
not be pursued, however, since the purpose here is not to
renew old debates but to clarify our own position through contrastive distancing. For this it is sufficient to describe what
is being resisted. The following are offered as samples of both
standard conceptions of reading and allow us to see what they
have in common.
     A dramatic increase in the numbers of people going through
schools, colleges and universities in modern societies plus an
equally dramatic increase in the amount and variety of printed
materials they are expected to absorb have given new significance
to reading as an instrumental skill. The exigencies of fast processing in diversified curricula cannot be met by elementary
reading ability and have stimulated the appearance of quasi-
technical manuals to enhance personal proficiency. Such manuals
reflect and reinforce the idea of the reader as someone who
does something to a text. A prominent example is Adler and
Van Doren's reading aid.[2] Their manual begins by equating
good reading with active reading, the activity being that of first
raising oneself to the author's level, then examining him and,
finally, transcending the particular book at hand by locating
it in a literature, debate, tradition or corpus. The reader's
progress occurs as a cumulative elevation through four levels -
elementary grasp, inspectional skimming, analytic explication
and synoptical overview - each one finely divided into stages
negotiable through basic rules and practical hints. The essentially passive role of the text is clearly marked in this description of active reading: 'a mind, with nothing to operate on but
the symbols of the readable matter, and with no help from outside, elevates itself by the power of its own operations'.[3]
     In practice, this image of perfect self-sufficiency is not sus-
tained; the work of elevation requires continual reference to

an independent other - the author - who must be listened to, respected, interrogated, argued with and placed in a collective context of discourse. The author's presence functions as a guarantee that the text encodes a determinate message which can be recovered and passed on with objective certainty. Anxious resistances within literary criticism to the doctrines of semantic autonomy and authorial irrelevance display this objectifying function of the personalized author with particular clarity. Hirsch, for example, speaking from a concern to establish criteria for judging the relative validity of different interpretations of the same text (including all kinds of texts, not merely literary works), argues that if interpretation loses the anchorage of author's intent, the vacuum may be filled by the interpreter's own needs, fantasies and predilections: 'when critics deliberately banished the original author, they themselves usurped his place'.[4]

If the meaning of a text is not the author's no determinate meaning can be posited and interpretation relapses into solipsism. Hirsch summarizes his position as follows:

> meaning is an affair of consciousness and not of physical signs or things. Consciousness is, in turn, an affair of persons, and in textual interpretation the persons involved are an author and a reader. The meanings that are actualized by the reader are either shared with the author or belong to the reader alone ....What has been denied here is that linguistic signs can somehow speak their own meaning.[5]

The fact that Hirsch can retain that position, even though the concept of 'intrinsic genre' used to establish it shows precisely how linguistic signs can speak their own meaning (we will return to it subsequently), gives added force to the contention that the personalized concept of reading is a normative affirmation of cultural values which hinders textual analysis. In short, it is an ideological concept.

The values affirmed by Hirsch with respect to competing interpretations, and by Adler and Van Doren with respect to reading books, reflect an orientation, let us call it instrumental activism, informed by the will to gain mastery over things through the application of correct rules. Sociologists drawing upon Max Weber's analyses of the Puritan ethic and the rationalization of conduct, have long recognized it as a defining feature of Western industrial societies. In return for submitting to the authority of rules as method or technique, individuals receive the promises of rational ends-means control and objective certainty. Rules of correct reading and valid interpretation belong with rules for making friends, influencing people, rearing children, achieving sexual joy, and making a happy marriage as extensions of instrumental activism from material to social processes. There is, however, another value

complex in our culture which sustains a personalized conception
of reader and author. It includes duties like self-cultivation,
self-fulfilment and self-enrichment, and may be called humanistic activism. A strong example is an early 'how-to-read' book
by J.B. Kerfoot.[6]

Kerfoot, no less than Adler and Van Doren, regards good
reading as an active process, that is, as something more than
the receptive capacity to decode written signs. In his case,
however, the activity is not externally directed towards an
objectively given meaning but is an inwardly directed movement
of self discovery and enhancement. Kerfoot's good reader does
not move in order to take possession of the text but for the
sake of movement as an expression of personal being and,
therefore, a resource for self-reflection. Like a conscientious
artist, the reader links life to performance in a spiralling
circuit of improvement:

> For reading consists of our making – with the aid of the pat-
> terns and hints supplied by the author, but out of *our*
> mental stock, which we have produced by living – something
> that never existed before; something that only exists at all
> is so far as we make it.[7]

A text provides the equivalent of script, props, costumes,
etc. from which the reader constructs a performance. Kerfoot
describes serious reading as seeking oneself through projection
and play; it differs both from escapist reading to forget oneself and utilitarian reading for information. Given the strongly
subjectivist bent of Kerfoot's early chapters, there seems no
compelling reason for him to introduce the author at all except
as a convenient way of referring to a text. Cultural habit proves
too strong, however, so that in the final section we find Kerfoot
deep into an objectivist conception of the author's meaning which
dictates an account of 'right' reading directly opposed to that
of playfully creative reading quoted above. The aspiration now
is to formulate 'the thing that the author is trying to show us';
the reader is required to suspend all preconceptions in an
'open-minded seeking-out of the author's attitude of observation'; the ultimate criterion of right reading is 'proper collaboration with the author'.[8] In other words we are back squarely to
Hirsch's enterprise of discovering the determinate meaning of
a text. The fact that Kerfoot can effortlessly embrace seemingly
opposite notions of reading (sometimes in the same sentence) is
readily explained by the proposition that both are legitimated
by the same ideological concept of reader as person.

The main points of our discussion can be summarized as follows:

1 Accounts of reading confined to a substantialist concept of
reader as person oscillate between two possibilities: either a
radical subjectivism in which the text becomes whatever the
present reader makes of it, or an objectification of the text

as the author's intentions, meanings, problems, solutions, and
so on.
2 The correlate of an objectified text is a definition of right
reading as the personal reader's quest for correspondence with
authorial intent. This is the hermeneutic equivalent to scientific
truth-seeking.[9] Correspondence may be sought in an attitude of
respect, puzzlement or criticism but the basic activity is still
viewed on the conversational model of one person entering the
meaning space of another: a model which is incapable of seeing
a decisive difference between speaking and writing, or talk
and text.

My concern here is not with what the metaphor of reader as
person allows for (which, in all honesty, is a great deal) but
what it excludes. In particular that it excludes serious consideration of the reader as a response called for by a text, and
having no existence independent of it. If the reading act is
conceived interpersonally as collaboration with the author or as
interrogation of the author then the constitutive activity of the
text is simply not seen. It functions as an unexplicated resource
for collaborating, interrogating, and so on: a device for seeing
which cannot itself be seen except by a shift of vantage point.
The concept of an active text is posited as a means for accomp-
lishing such a shift since the spell of a dominating concept
cannot be broken except by imagining how things could be
otherwise. It must be admitted, however, that even this shift,
carried out in deliberate opposition to the personalized concept
of reader as active subject, is itself open to the accusation of
having invented a new subject – the active text – and thus
exchanging one fiction for another. In Nietzsche's terms we
are still caught in 'the seduction of language' whereby we cannot perceive a process or action without attributing it to an
active entity, and are, therefore, liable to his judgement that
'there is no "being" behind doing, effecting, becoming; "the
doer" is merely a fiction added to the deed – the deed is
everything ....Scientists do no better when they say "force
moves", "force causes", and the like ... our entire science still
lies under the misleading influence of language and has not
disposed of that little changeling, the "subject".[10]

Certainly, we have not disposed of it – but then, neither did
Nietzsche until his relapse into madness and silence. It must
be stressed again that the purpose of separating the individual
subject who reads from the reader required by a text is to
affirm the significance of the former, not to dispense with him.

The general idea I wish to establish is that there is a virtual
reader in a text prior to anyone becoming that reader. The
virtual reader can also be described as a response anticipated
by a text, a redemptive posture present in the writing, or as
a place waiting to be filled. Since preliminary exposition is a
matter of using figurative language to imagine what something
is like, it is an advantage to multiply metaphors.

Critical reference was made previously to Dorothy Smith's

account of the manufacture of reality in documentary form on
the grounds of taking the economic production metaphor too
literally. Applied to the reading process, however, it provides
useful imagery for our purpose. A printed text, in so far as it
is written for multiple replication and public sale (unlike, say,
a private letter written once for someone in particular), has
some of the attributes of a commodity and can be thought of in
terms of mass production. That is to say, production oriented
to an anonymous set of wants, needs and interests where the
product is structured by an anticipated type of consumer. A
mass-produced automobile, for example, has a typical driver-
buyer built into it prior to anyone actually becoming that driver.
To consume a commodity is to become an instance of a pre-given
form of usage. At the heart of every production process is an
empty core around which the product forms. The core anticipates
a consummatory act through which the potentiality of the product will be realized. It is empty because the actual consumer
is not yet present; there is only a place waiting to be occupied
by a fitting anyone. 'The reader' is imaginable as such an empty
core or place at the heart of writing as a productive process.
The methods of a text (its generic conventions, stylistic devices
and so on) can then be thought of as ways of drawing the
person who reads into that place. These may or may not be
deliberate, may or may not be noticed, and may or may not be
successful. People commonly say of a book they have failed to
read, 'I just could not get into it.' At this point, however, we
are in danger of being distracted by spatial images away from
the main point, which is to establish the temporal and constitutive priority of 'the reader' over the person who reads. Again
we turn to literary criticism for assistance.

The evolution of the novel in modern times is marked by the
appearance of complex texts which, in defying orthodox methods
of appraisal have forced a re-examination of the reading process.
One such work, the subject of a recent critique of the vocabulary of literary criticism by Peter Rabinowitz, is Nabokov's
'Pale Fire'.[11] The novel centres around a poem by a deceased
professor-poet, John Shade, and an introduction, commentary
and index by his former neighbour and colleague, Charles
Kinbote. Kinbote's elaborate exegesis relates the content of the
poem to events in a country called Zembla which climax in the
escape of its ruler, King Charles, at the outbreak of the Zemblan
Revolution. Kinbote claims to be King Charles and is regarded
as insane by his colleagues. Not surprisingly, the novel has
engendered considerable disagreement among critics as to its
meaning. Some have claimed that Kinbote is 'really' another
member of Shade's university called Botkin; others that Shade
is Kinbote's invention; still others that Kinbote invented Shade.
One critic, John Stark, argues impatiently that only Nabokov
and the text are real but then proceeds to criticize Shade for the
narrow realism of his poem and praise Kinbote's 'purely imaginary' commentary!

After reviewing this confusion, Rabinowitz proposes that to address the question, What is really happening in 'Pale Fire'? demands a vocabulary for coherent talk about truth in fiction. He finds a useful lead in Gibson's distinction between the real reader (the one who scans the text) and the 'mock reader' whose place the real reader fills in order to recover the text's meaning, but criticizes Gibson's model (as well as the related work of Walter Ong) on two grounds. First, it does not take seriously the difference between fictional and non-fictional modes of address; second, it obscures a necessary distinction between the overt narrator and the implied author as sources of address in fictional texts. In order to secure the distinction - which turns out to be crucial for separating fictional from factual modes of address - Rabinowitz suggests that reading a novel involves participation in four possible types of audience: actual, authorial, narrative and ideal narrative. Now it is clear from a footnoted reference that Rabinowitz wishes to think of an audience as a role which a text forces on the person who reads and not as a substantive social category or group. Unfortunately his intention is thwarted at the outset by the inclusion of the 'actual audience ... the flesh-and-blood people who read the book'[12] as part of the typology. This is the kind of audience which is counted and classified by readership surveys; analysed by sociologists; and investigated by experimental psychology. It is not generated by a text in the course of reading but by activities, procedures, purposes beyond the text. To hold on to the idea of a text-generated audience we must conceive of an audience as a way of being drawn into writing; a posture induced by being addressed in a certain way. The interpretation of audience as posture allows us to make better sense of the other three types and to avoid Rabinowitz's relapses into concrete, substantialist formulations.

The 'authorial audience' is defined by Rabinowitz as a hypothetical one the author has in mind when composing the work - a set of assumptions about linguistic competence, familiarity with conventional writing codes, worldly knowledge, moral sensibility, empathic capability, and so on. Certainly, such a set is encountered by the person who reads as conditions for entering, following and comprehending a text but it is unnecessary and misleading to locate it in the mind of the author. The set is in the text itself. The author's mind is a secondary, derivative concept which distracts attention from what actually goes on in reading. Part of what goes on is the emergent shaping of an initially diffuse desire to understand by the semantic and structural contours of the text in the course of going through it. As long as this interested negotiation of the text proceeds smoothly, the person who reads is within the authorial posture but not aware of it. Only when the desire to understand is thwarted - and by something more than snags removable by dictionary work - is the authorial posture attended to as a problem articulated by such questions as What does he mean?

What is the author getting at? What is intended here? Notions
like the author's mind and collaboration with the author can
now be seen as hermeneutic tactics to restore an inhibited desire
to follow the meaning of a text. Restoration itself, however,
does not occur through a mystical reunion with a departed
spirit accomplished through a hermeneutic seance, it occurs as
a reorganization of the field of action.

If Rabinowitz's 'authorial audience' is construed as a posture
called for by any text whatsoever to satisfy a desire to understand it, then his other types may be seen as specialized requirements in following particular kinds of texts, especially complex
novels.

A generic trait of the novel as a recognizable form of text is
a narrative of events. The narrator in a novel is typically an
imitation of a non-fictional type of reporter - an historian,
a biographer, a journalist, a diarist, etc. - through whose
eyes we see characters, scenes, situations and the unfolding
of events. The narrative audience is the posture required to
enter the narrator's world as a real place. Rabinowitz suggests
that as long as that world conforms to common-sense understandings no problem of acquiescence arises. Where, however,
the narrator's world is odd, unfamiliar or fantastic - as in
science-fiction, 'Alice in Wonderland', or Kafka's 'Metamorphosis'
- then the reader is made conscious of the element of pretence
involved in retaining membership of the narrative audience
and experiences a separation or distance between narrator and
author. With this in mind, Rabinowitz comments:

> One way to determine the characteristics of the narrative
> audience is to ask.... 'What sort of person would I have to
> pretend to be - what would I have to know and believe - if
> I wanted to take this work of fiction as real?'[13]

By retreating into a substantialist, psychologistic notion of
the reader, Rabinowitz subsequently obscures his own highly
significant insight, to be elaborated subsequently, that the
production of reality effects in writing depends upon textual
devices for collapsing the authorial into the narrative audience.

Having argued that the maintenance of authorial posture can
be complicated by content which deviates from everyday experience (i.e. seems to be governed by different rules of space,
time, causality, social interaction, motivation and so on),
Rabinowitz shows that it can also be complicated by making the
narrator more than a medium of observation. This occurs, for
example, where the narrator reveals himself to be a dreamer,
liar or ingratiator trying to enlist the sympathy and good will
of the person who reads. More indirectly it occurs whenever a
narrator brings himself into the narration. The audience thus
addressed is called the ideal narrative audience and involves
the person who reads in making judgements of the honesty,
sincerity or authenticity of the narrative. Such judgements are

required in order to retain membership of the authorial audience, the posture governing the total process of reading.

Armed with these concepts, Rabinowitz returns to the question of what is really happening in 'Pale Fire'. His discussion has, for us, two virtues: a negative one in demonstrating the abortive effects of using a personalized concept of reader to analyse the reading process, and a positive one in allowing the notions of literal and emancipatory reading to be formulated more precisely. Taking the negative first, Rabinowitz responds to his own primary question by posing a set of supplementaries which must be answered beforehand. I have italicized the personalizing elements in them. For example, Does the narrative audience *believe* that Shade and Kinbote actually exist or does *it believe* that one has invented the other? Does the narrative audience *agree with* the ideal narrative audience that Zembla really exists? Is Shade's poem a *good one for* the narrative audience as well as the ideal narrative audience? My objection is that the questions can be conceived as answerable only by positing concrete audience consisting of people who could be questioned. But this would turn all the audiences into *actual* audiences available for investigation, thus destroying the value and rationale of the analytic scheme. Rabinowitz aborts his own inquiry and ends with nothing but complaints about the impossibility of deciding what the book is saying. Surely, however, it is the capability of Nabokov's text to generate an indeterminate structure of reading postures, between which the person who reads must move, which tells us what the book is about. It is about the ability of a text to hold itself open against attempts at definitive exegesis. What is really happening in 'Pale Fire' is a textually enforced movement between multiple reading postures which reflexively unsettles the person who reads. *This movement precisely defines what is meant by emancipatory reading*. We can distinguish strongly now between complex texts of this kind which enforce emancipatory reading, and simple texts which induce settlement into a single posture and against which emancipatory reading must be a hard-won struggle. Factual reports, such as the Poor Law Reports, induce settlement into the single posture of the narrative audience, that is to say literal reading. 'Pale Fire' is a text which requires no special effort at meta-reading to achieve emancipation in it because the text itself makes capture in a single posture untenable. It is already what emancipatory meta-reading seeks to make of all simple texts, and what we seek to make of the Poor Law Reports.

Before moving on it should be pointed out that although the idea of reader as posture has been explicated through using literary criticism, it could also be developed through combining George Herbert Mead's model of the act with the proposition that reading is an act to which that model is applicable. Although Mead bases his model on sensory experience and the act of perception it is readily extendable to linguistic experi-

ences and the reading process. Its advantage for us is that
it helps to place the teleological notion of a virtual reader on
a sounder theoretical basis than the metaphor of commodity
production could provide for. To ensure continuity we will
relate Mead's account of the act to Rabinowitz's discussion of
a complex text and, in general, take everything he says as
if it were a description of reading and the hermeneutic process
of meta-reading.

An act is a unitary experience analysable as an organization
of stages in which the final stage of consummation is already
present at the beginning as an anticipatory attitude. The first
state is marked by sensory stimulation plus a reaction towards
that stimulation:

> This reaction, in so far as the perception does not go out
> into instantaneous overt activity, appears in consciousness
> only as an attitude, but as such it is the first stage in the
> complete response or group of responses which the stimula-
> tion in question calls out.[14]

Let us say then that the text stimulates an as-yet-unspecified
anticipatory attitude of complete readership. The next stage,
perception, involves selective attention to the properties of the
source of stimulation so that it is constituted as a definite object
for the actor. At this stage the object has been separated out
as something in particular, it has been identified and characterized (e.g. this is a comic novel, a biography, an official
report, written by - concerning -), but because it has not
been incorporated into the actor's behaviour through 'contact
experience' is still what Mead calls a distant object. (It should
be added that touching is not the same as contact experience.
To hold an apple, or a text, is not yet to enter the contact
experience anticipated in that holding.)

The promises and invitations of distanced properties are
realized through two successive stages of 'manipulation' (in
which these properties are replaced by contact characteristics
arising through practical engagement with the object of
perception), and 'consummation', where the act is completed.
The teleological nature of the act receives strong emphasis
at this point:

> We approach the distant stimulus with the manipulatory
> processes already excited. We are ready to grasp the ham-
> mer before we reach it, and the attitude of manipulatory
> response directs the approach ....It is the later process
> already aroused in the central nervous system, controlling
> the earlier, which constitutes the teleological nature of the
> act ....Such an aroused future act always has a hypothe-
> tical character. It is not until this initiated response is car-
> ried out that its reality is assured ....In this sense the
> future is already in the act.[15]

With the qualification that anticipatory response is grounded immediately in a shared network of linguistic meaning (what Mead elsewhere calls significant symbols) rather than the central nervous system, we may take this as a reasonable point of departure for describing the reading process. It remains to be shown, however, that Mead's model can provide an account of complex or difficult texts and of consciously interpretive reading (i.e. hermeneutic striving for meaning).

Mead argues that as long as the conduct called out by an object (say a text) moves towards the consummation anticipated originally, then the object is simply there and taken for granted. Where the unfolding of the act is disturbed by the failure of the object (as perceived) to respond appropriately, then reflection occurs to reconstruct the object:

> From the standpoint of future conduct explanation is such a reconstruction of the object, toward which conduct has failed to elicit the proper response, that this defeat may be avoided in the future. Explanation is substituting another object, with which we will be en rapport, for that which confessed its unreality in the experimental test of conduct.[16]

Rabinowitz, for example, reflects upon 'Pale Fire' as a problematic object arising from inhibitions of response in the intended act of a completed reading of it and seeks to reconstruct it through the notion of four audiences. He confuses that task, however, with the separate one of reconstructing referential objects - Shade's poem, Kinbote's commentary, the state of Zembla - 'within' the text. He treats 'Pale Fire' both as an object to be reconstructed and as a container of objects. By focussing ultimately on the latter, he treats the novel as though it were a factual report, shows it to be incomprehensible in that form, and thus ends with a justification for giving up rather than restoring the reading act towards it. More interesting than the failure of Rabinowitz's restoration project, however, is the ability of that text to disturb reading responses in the first place for anyone who engages with it. Mead suggests that disturbance of conduct arises through the simultaneous arousal of mutually inhibiting responses, a suggestion echoed in Rabinowitz's analysis of ambivalent distance between reading audiences. But how could the person who reads encounter a problem of completion - a problem grounded precisely in the possession of linguistic competence rather than its lack - unless the text itself generated mutually inhibiting reading responses? And how could a text do this, how would a complex text be possible, except through containing multiple reading postures which the person who reads is constrained to enter? What Mead, in the following passage, says of interaction with physical things applies with equal force to reading texts:

The necessary condition of this physical but cooperative 'other' getting into experience, so that the inside of things, their efficacy and force, is an actual part of the world, is that the individual in a premonitory fashion should take the attitude of acting as the physical thing will act, in getting the proper adjustment for his own ultimate response.[17]

A necessary condition for realizing the meaning of a text is that the person who reads should engage in a co-operative sharing of attitudes with it such that premonitions of what is going to happen are confirmed in the event. In a simple text this emergent fulfilment of anticipatory promises is organized within a single frame of reference. The idea of reader as posture corresponds to an organizing frame rather than the specific responses co-ordinated within it. In order now to confirm the ability of Mead's model to allow for complex texts and hermeneutic meta-reading, we must turn from his discussion of the act in general to the social act in particular.

A social act (which we take reading a text to be) involves the acting individual (for example, the person who reads) in taking the role of one or more others within a communal perspective or what Mead more often refers to as the generalized other. The following passage can be taken as an analogical description of the hermeneutic quest for meaning:

Thus in group activities the individual finds himself, by his gestures, not only mediating the actions of the group but also inspiring in himself the beginnings of their parts in this common activity ....When the activity is an organized one in which the different roles because of their organization all call for an identical response, as in an economic or political process, the individual assumes what may be called the role of the generalized other, and the attitude is a universal or rational attitude. The rational attitude which characterizes the human being is, then, the relationship of the whole process in which the individual is engaged to himself as reflected in his assumption of the organized roles of the others in stimulating himself to his response.[18]

Our interest, however, is not in resolving the role-taking problems of disorganized texts but in restoring tension to texts so well organized that the person who reads becomes nothing but a standardized role-player in an unproblematic, hence unexamined, community. In using the term community I do not wish to be heard as making a metaphorical reference to the characters who populate a text or to the interrelationships between them which make up its narrative content. Rather, I am making a direct reference to the constitutive rules and methods which allow an assembly of words on paper to be experienced as a knowable social reality. If a community is a bounded set of rules for endlessly generating visibles and tangibles as instances of itself through the mediation of members, then the rules of any game as well as generic forms of artful composition – the sonata, the portrait, the lyric poem, the realistic novel or the factual report – can be seen as communal in nature. This point has been stressed by Hirsch in attempting to account for the possibility of shared meanings between author and reader or reader and text.[19] The topic of sharing, of having an experience in common, is articulated through the concept of genre, subdivided into heuristic, conventional, intrinsic and extrinsic types.

To interpret any text one must approach it with provisional expectations of what sort of thing might properly be found there – pre-understandings of permissibility. A reader (decoder) has a generic conception of the text which initiates the hermeneutic circle of part-whole interpretation. Hirsch shows, for example, how the meaning of a poem is transformed by reading it as an old folksong rather than a nineteenth century love poem. Whereas, however, the reader relies upon provisional assessments, liable to correction in the course of reading, the author relies upon a determinate constitutive genre to encode his meaning. Hirsch calls this the intrinsic genre to stress its stability and invariance relative to the heuristic assessments of the decoder. The author, having willed the operation of an intrinsic genre 'is constrained by its properties'.[20] Valid interpretation, the aim of good reading, is then defined as tuning into the intrinsic genre of a text. The imposition of any other determinate frame (for example, a psycho-analytic reading of a poem) is the establishment of a false or extrinsic genre. Clearly, generic conventions are involved both in encoding and decoding but only as common resources. The intrinsic genre of, say, Byron's 'Don Juan' is not sufficiently identified by calling it an epic poem, even though Byron relied upon the conventions of that form to realize his project, i.e. the intrinsic genre he intended.

The similarities between Hirsch's account of reading a text and Mead's teleological model of the act are too obvious to require comment. It is worth remarking, however, that Hirsch's hermeneutic aspiration to achieve harmony with the intrinsic genre of a text has implications for reading identical with those derivable from Mead's account of collective participation as entering the universal and rational attitude of the 'generalized other'. Both enjoin a pious orientation to the proprieties of a text. In the case of reports on social reality this would amount to a prescription to be a literal reader, that is, the ideal member posited by the constitutive rules of such a text. Clearly then our quest for emancipatory meta-readings must from this perspective be seen as impious even though, from the viewpoint of our political interest it can also be seen as a pious regard for origins and the proprieties of social life and language.

TEXTUAL DEVICES AND REALITY EFFECTS

In this, the last of my preparatory discussions, I explore two propositions. First, that methods for producing reality effects on paper include, indispensably, devices for securing the constitutive innocence of the text. Second, that a strong distinction is called for between the playful securing of such effects as art and their serious accomplishment as factual reporting. I will refer to the former as conventional and the latter as transcendental reality effects.

The theme of constitutive innocence can be detected in the following quotation from Rabinowitz's discussion of truth in fiction:

> At the extreme end of realism, narrative and authorial audiences are so close as to be almost indistinguishable .... When the distinction between the two disappears entirely, we have autobiography or history.[21]

David Goldknopf begins his analysis of realism in the novel with an almost identical statement. Having asserted that early eighteenth century England witnessed the introduction of fictional narratives whose novelty consisted in representing mundane experience readily referable to those of 'ordinary readers', Goldknopf adds:

> Realism was further cultivated by literary devices and prose styles which strengthened the illusion of reportage. In short, the authors tried hard to create the impression that the narratives weren't fictional at all.[22]

The task faced by early novelists was made more difficult by the fact that the prevailing proprieties of narrative compelled them to tell stories in the first person singular. As Goldknopf points out, the appearance of an I-narrator on the page is immediately distractive in that it raises identification questions. Is this a he or she, a young person, an old person, a normal person, a sick person, or what? In short, the emptiness of the blank, universal 'I' constitutes a problem – a source of interpretive insecurity – in realizing the project of an empirical narration because the success of such a project depends upon the confinement of hermeneutic circling to the horizontal plane of the narrative, to the mutual fulfilment of plot (or story) and detail. The unsecured I-narrator cannot be taken for granted and keeps open the imminent possibility that the details are to be read as indexical expressions of his or her character or psyche rather than taken literally. In such a state of ambivalence either the story or the narrator may be the focus of part-whole interpretation: empirical narrative requires decisive resolution in favour of the former. Goldknopf discusses the novels of Daniel Defoe as interesting case-studies in the

accomplishment of fictive realism within the problematic convention of I-narration. Defoe often used a device whereby the
author represents himself in a preface as editor of certain
memoirs which have happened to come his way (for example,
'Memoirs of a Cavalier', 'Moll Flanders', 'Colonel Jack'). The
notion of fortuitous encounter provides for the objective status
of the memoirs as something already existent in the world waiting to be found (i.e. as facts) and simultaneously absolves the
author of any constitutive activity beyond the innocent one of
editing: 'Defoe has faked an editorial function to conceal an
authorial one.'[23]

The objectivity of the memoirs – the reality of the communicative channel – is further established by editorial explanations
of gaps and incompletions. For example, missing pages, illegible
passages, censorship of offensive material. In 'Robinson Crusoe',
the incompleteness of the I-narrator's journal is attributed to
the exhaustion of his ink supply. In such ways the text is
visibly marked with the traces of real world events which bear
witness to its historicity. From the viewpoint of resolving the
problem of interpretive ambivalence, the beauty of Defoe's
device is that revelations of subjective identity, of selective
perception, become further confirmations of the authenticity
of the memoirs as records of experience (this is the sort of
writing one would expect from a person like that) while, at the
same time, the secured reality of the memoirs allows for the
discounting of distortions and personal colourations as distortions and colourations of things that really happened. Allowing
for bias provides for reading the I-narrator as an eye-witness,
for seeing through him as it were. We will return to the themes
of editing and corrigible bias in analysing the reports.

A significant extension of our vocabulary for analysing
constitutive innocence and reality effects can be derived from
a recent attempt by Robert Scholes to say how 'literariness'
occurs as a recognizable property of texts.[24] His guiding
principle is that literariness is an experience of duplicity in
some aspect of a communicative act. (Clearly, this can apply to
any form of communication but we will confine ourselves to
reading-writing.) Scholes uses Jakobson's six-feature model of
the communicative act to specify possibilities of duplicity (i.e.
loss of innocence). Three obvious features are an addresser
conveying a message to an addressee. Beyond these, however,
are three less obvious features essential for communication to
take place. There must be a referential context (let us say a
context of sense) which is or can be put into words; a contact
medium; and a code available to communicants as recoverable
operating rules in situated usage. An operative code may be as
complex as primitive myth, as subtle as an artistic genre, as
overt as a written grammar or as mundane as the competences
which sustain conversational glossing practices (i.e. the
ethnomethods of everyday talker-hearers). Scholes's argument
is that 'we sense literariness in an utterance when any one of

the six features of communication loses its simplicity and
becomes multiple or duplicitous'.[25] From this, as a provisional
statement liable to amendment, we may say that the work of a
reality report is to preserve simplicity in regard to all six
features of communication. Two questions now arise: What might
simplicity and duplicity look like in texts concerned with a
realistic representation of social life? and, How can the schema
be used to differentiate between realistic fiction and factual
reporting? Before answering, it should be said that the
appropriation of Jakobson's model for our own needs requires
caution since, first, it was formulated out of the speech act,
and, secondly, is from the viewpoint of a substantially present
addresser. As the burden of the whole preceding discussion
has been to establish speech and text as distinct constitutive
realms and, within the latter, to bracket the notion of a substantial author in order to focus on the text as a postural placing of the person who reads, we would not now wish to make
light of that burden merely for the sake of possessing an
analytic scheme. With this in mind we turn to the first question.

At the risk of exaggeration, empirical sociology can be seen
as a prolonged effort to secure textual simplicity in all six
features of the communicative act – a single addresser, single
addressee, single message, single code, single contact, single
context – in the face of inherent ambivalences of the enterprise.
Methodological criticisms are undertaken as duplicity displays
in the higher interest of truth to reality. Such displays show
us what loss of simplicity looks like in factual reportage and
what kinds of tasks the textual production of reality effects
endlessly undertakes.

Addresser duplicity occurs as the sense that the conveyor
of an utterance is not really its maker (for example, that the
narrator is a real author's dummy). Familiar display procedures
in sociological criticism include (a) assertions that the nominal
reporter is a witting or unwitting spokesman for dominant-
class interests, and, (b) reminders that behind the scientistic
attribution of findings to the communal operation of a method
lurks the personal I of the investigator (the absented author).
Responses to (a) include renewals of methodological rigour;
responses to (b) include confessional increments to reports in
the form of prefatory statements of value commitment, anecdotal
footnotes, and research autobiographies. These are inoculatory
injections of mild duplicity given in the interest of preserving
simplicity for the whole act.

Since 'addresser' and 'addressee' in a text are, for me, correlative aspects of the reading posture, duplicity in one must
necessarily be implicated in the other. That they are distinct
aspects, however, may be seen in the fact that whereas writing
has been thematized as a problem within empirical sociology,
reading has not. Border control procedures are so strong that
complex texts (in the sense of equivalents to 'Pale Fire') are
not allowed in as sociology. They are distanced as social

philosophy, pre-sociology and the like, from which the sociology
has to be abstracted. As, for example, the theory of class conflict and the concept of alienation have been abstracted from
Marx's texts as the readable sociology in them. A sense of
addressee or reader duplicity is recorded merely as the verdict
that whatever this is it is not (or not quite, not yet) factual
social inquiry. Amplifications of such a verdict include typical
charges of confusion between description and prescription;
confusions avoided in proper reports by the simple device of
compartmentalizing the postures of reading fact and reading
practical recommendations. One of the elementary ways in
which a social reality report is made recognizable as just that
is through typographical separation into sections so that at
any given point a single reading posture is unambiguously
given.

Duplicity of message has come to view in empirical sociology
as denunciations of wilfully strange or obscure language. A
good example is found in John Rex's argument that if sociology
is to accomplish its historical mission of demystifying the social
world - making it intelligible for everyman - then it must start
by putting its own linguistic house in order. Talcott Parsons -
once C. Wright Mills's favourite target of satirical jibe - is again
held up to ridicule but Rex has a new name to place in the
rogues' gallery of obscurantists: that of Harold Garfinkel.
Since Rex's strictures strike against the analytic foundations
of the present enterprise, I will take time out to respond to
them. The accusation is stated as follows:

Ethnomethodology has suffered peculiarly from the unique
language of its founder, which has unfortunately been copied
by his disciples. Thus, for example, on the first page of
Garfinkel's chapter What is ethnomethodology? ('Studies in
Ethnomethodology', 1967) we find the following:
'The central recommendation of these studies is that the
activities whereby members produce and manage settings
are *identical* with members' procedures for making those
settings accountable. The reflexive and incarnate character
of accounting practices and accounts makes up the crux of
that recommendation. When I speak of accountable my
interests are directed to such matters as the following. I
mean observable-and-reportable, i.e. available to members
as situated practices of looking and telling. I mean too that
such practices consist of an endless, ongoing, contingent
accomplishment; that they are carried on under the auspices
of, and are made to happen as events in, the same ordinary
affairs that in organizing they describe' ...[26]

Rex then comments:

Strange language indeed ... the mischief of it lies in its
turning away from any study of social structures, which

are the starting point from which making things accountable must begin.[27]

Now Garfinkel would undoubtedly find the last comment wonderfully ironic since his strong accusation against all ortho-dox sociology (and this would include Rex's eclectic compound of Weberean methodology with humanistic and empirical Marxism) is that it is unable to study social structures – to take struc-turing as a topic of inquiry – because it shares the common-sense view that social structures are, in the final analysis (after mundane duplicities have been stripped away) external things out there open to look-and-tell reporting. Its task then – its superiority to ordinary consciousness of the way things are – can only be to observe and report these structures more accurately, objectively and comprehensively. Garfinkel's insight, however, is that any account which takes existing social structures as its 'starting point' is from the beginning caught up in the situated practices through which members continuously generate and sustain the structured accountability of whatever they are doing. A basic condition for the successful operation of such practices is that they are typically unremarked and unremarkable (i.e. familiar, trivial, banal). Their sheer simplicity, in the sense of not being duplicitous, removes them from practitioners' inquiry and thus sustains the experience of social structures as objectively given for factual reporting. Orthodox sociology can hope to do more of the same in its practices – to generate more and different properties of social structures than ordinary language can manage, to compare, contrast, quantify, classify and interrelate such properties in endless detail for the sake of 'theoretical' and/or political practice – but only at the price of maintaining the unremark-ability of the constitutive work which provides factual structures for further looking and telling. Rex's obvious starting point (which is also the starting point for the Poor Law inquiries and all factual reportage on social reality) is at the same time an inherent limitation on what can be inquired into. If Rex had been less eager to satirize Garfinkel he might profitably have used him to raise a significant question against his own enter-prise of demystification. Namely, if unremarkable language is the medium through which objective social structuring is accomplished, and if unremarkability (let us say constitutive innocence) is a condition of that accomplishment, then how can that unremarkable language be used, as Rex demands, to open social structuring to understanding? How can it break the spell of deep, i.e. constitutive, innocence? Would not Rex's project require a language 'strange' enough to wrench inquiry out of the normal perspective? This, it seems to me, is the measure of Garfinkel's greatness as a social theorist. In any case, we are now in a better position to see that simplicity (or trans-parency) of message is a constitutive feature of social reality reporting, and that calls for plain, workmanlike prose have a deeper significance than a fastidious concern for good writing style.

What has been said about the constitutive significance of transparent prose applies also to the avoidance of code duplicity; indeed the topics are closely entwined. In literature, duplicity of code is most clearly marked where a text juxtaposes past and present styles or conventions or genres. An extreme example is the hospital episode in James Joyce's 'Ulysses' which unfolds as a chronologically ordered pastiche of styles extending from early Anglo-Saxon narrative myth, the medieval roman, the Authorized Version Bible, the early eighteenth century essay, the styles of Lamb, de Quincey, Newman, Pater, Ruskin, up to modern slang and the American hot-gospel sermon. The factual report is a conservative genre which is intolerant of such protean shifts of code and relies upon strong delimitations of form and style to ensure a pious reading.[28] Attending to reality is a serious business requiring security from distraction. In order to be readable as nothing but a report, a text must strictly observe the proprieties of this form of reading-writing. Rex's strictures against Garfinkel are in this sense accusations of impiety.

Turning now to duplicity of contact, Scholes remarks: 'If spoken words are presented to us in writing ... either the writer or the reader must supply the features of oral communication lost in this translation.'[29]

If it was the case that writer or reader must supply the lost features of oral communication in order to preserve contact simplicity, then social reporting, which relies so heavily on talk (e.g. interviews) for its information, would display a chronic preoccupation with the matter. The fact that it does not, that, on the contrary, verbatim quotation from informants is used as an unproblematic resource for securing the authenticity of a report, shows that no restoration of lost features is called for as a condition of doing a report. Where attempts to restore lost features are attempted by the writer – as in the insertion of symbols to indicate upward and downward intonation, pauses, stretching of words, accentuation, broken words, etc. – the result is precisely to display contact duplicity, not to resolve it. The full reproduction of speech in writing cannot help but appear as a blatant artifice, as a stranger from an alien realm. Written speech requires the exclusion of the constitutive features of oral communication in order to be read unproblematically (that is to say simply) as real speech. In social reality reports 'real speech' is readily accomplished through the conventional device of annotated quotation, a device sustained by the deeper convention that alphabetic script is merely a convenient means for representing and reproducing the spoken word. In terms of the interests sustaining my analysis, the contact dimension is of low importance within the technical question of how texts achieve reality and knowledge effects but of primary importance in specifying the political significance of the achievement. The

intent of my argument concerning the relationship of dialectical
negation between textual and situated reality construction is
to make contact duplicity a moral problem for social reporting,
conceived as a political activity. When humanistic sociologists
and concerned intellectuals rail against scientist jargon and
undue abstraction, demanding that the subjects of inquiry be
allowed in reports to speak for themselves in their own voices,
they are symptomizing the problem without quite realizing what
it is. This is evident in their construal of the problem as entirely
soluble within the conventions of textual reality production
itself. The inadequacy of their demands to satisfy the concern
which calls them out is clearly revealed in the case of the 1834
Poor Law Report. It would be difficult to find a social report
more replete with the 'voices' of subjects. As Mark Blaug has
written: 'Anyone who has read the Report of 1834 can testify
to the overwhelming cumulative effect of the endless recital of
ills from the mouths of squires, magistrates, overseers, and
clergymen'[30] - and yet, as will be shown, it would be equally
difficult to find a report which so clearly demonstrates the
negation of situated reality construction as a constitutive feature
of textual reality construction. The recitals to which Blaug
refers do not come from the mouths of squires, magistrates,
overseers or anyone else, they are embedded as quotations in
an annotated text. This is, for me, a difference that makes
(or is made by) a crucial difference.
    The discussion so far has identified five aspects of written
communication to which problems of duplicity and textual devices
for securing simplicity can be specified. These are, however,
secondary to the terminus ad quem, the essential technical task
of a social reality report, which is to maintain a reading of its
referential context as phenomenal and concrete even though it
is on the page necessarily semiotic and abstract. The overall
triumph of constitutive innocence in a reality report is to make
an absent phenomenal context present on paper for reading.
(The paired terms semiotic/phenomenal, abstract/concrete,
absent/present are all taken from Scholes's discussion of context
duplicity.) Glossings of duplicity in regard to addresser,
addressee, message, code and contact provide as it were a
frame through which substantive content is windowed as a
phenomenal, concrete presence. With this in mind we are now
able to make a decisive distinction between fictional and factual
realism. Whereas the latter has a serious (i.e. self-constitutive)
commitment to projecting content as a reality encounterable
beyond the page, as something which can be brought into what
Mead calls the manipulative zone of the actor, the former does
not. To put it another way, fictional texts engage in the production of conventional reality effects while factual reports produce
transcendental reality effects. Texts recognizable as literary
or fictional make-believe are those which playfully rather than
seriously gloss their duplicities. Like arch coquettes they deny
their artificiality only in order to draw attention to their art.

The ultimate triumph of fictional simulation is not merely to draw the addressee into itself, to produce a reality effect but to do so in a way which draws attention to this effect as a constitutive achievement to be admired. Fiction has to provide signs of its duplicity in order to provide for recognition of its artful achievement. The stylized conventions of the novel, like those of the theatre, are not handicaps to be overcome but resources which are relied upon to make their accomplishment visible. The effects are, however, accomplished within the confines of a cultural form or a genre and typically end when the book closes or the curtain falls. Transcendental reality effects are so-called because they extend beyond such boundary conventions. The referential content of a factual report has to be experienced as something re-searchable or re-formable, that is, as encounterable beyond the text. The covers of, say, the Poor Law Reports are not like novel covers or theatre curtains but like open horizons extending backwards in time as real history and forwards in time as possible lines of action; horizons which confirm and invite traversal. Admittedly it is possible to find confusions between conventional and transcendental reality effects; for example, in 'Don Quixote', and among devotees of Sherlock Holmes who take pilgrimages to Baker Street and use actual nineteenth century weather reports to determine the precise dates of 'his' investigations. On the other hand, Don Quixote is displayably mad because he read romantic inventions as encounterables, and the Baker Street pilgrims are only recalled to smile at their mild craziness. The fact that their transgressions can be seen as such testifies to the effective reality of the boundary they ignore. Failure to observe such limits of normal form immediately mark one as abnormal, as one not knowing the difference between reality and illusion. No such possibility arises in factual reportage since it authorizes infinite extendability beyond the reading performance. It operates under the sober categories of truth, error and falsehood rather than the playful ones of reality and illusion.

Having developed a vocabulary sufficient to begin the interrogation of the Reports, we can now move on to ask how they secure themselves from the imminent duplicities of writing about social reality and by what methods they produce transcendental reality effects. Such methods will be referred to as 'reality indexicals' and are to be thought of as constitutive properties of the reportage form of writing, not just as identification tags. The point requires emphasis because we are not merely interested in what makes reports recognizable as such for classification purposes - as, for example, one might be interested in the stylistic properties which allowed Rosenblum's uninstructed students to reliably sort photographs into newspaper, advertising and fine arts categories[31] - rather we are interested in reality indexicals as generic properties which can be linked to the tasks of keeping the frame innocent and bringing the content to reading as encounterables in real-world time and place. It is not being argued that reality indexicals relate solely to the production of reality effects and not at all to knowledge effects; in the situated process of reading these are merged together as a unitary experience and it is only because they are separable for reflective analysis, whether provoked by a flawed text or the desire to disturb an achieved innocence, that we treat them separately here.

CHAPTER 4

Reality effects in the Poor Law Reports

My procedure is to work through the texts, noting what aspects
come to attention through the notions of constitutive innocence
and reality indexicals and seeing whether they can be worked
up to the level of constitutive features essential to social
reality reporting per se.

THE AUTHORITY TO INQUIRE

The 1834 Report opens with an address to the monarch, conventional in Royal Commissions:

> We, the Commissioners appointed by Your Majesty to make
> a diligent and full inquiry into the practical operation of
> the Laws for the Relief of the Poor in England and Wales,
> and into the manner in which those laws are administered,
> and to report our opinion whether any and what alterations,
> amendments, or improvements may be beneficially made in
> the said laws, or in the manner of administering them, and
> how the same may be best carried into effect, humbly certify
> to Your Majesty, in manner following, our proceedings in
> the execution of Your Majesty's Commission, and the opinions
> which they have led us to form.

Behind the specifics of the address - its stylistic mannerisms
and surface content - there are two features of crucial significance for achieving constitutive innocence: firstly, that the
source of inquiry is located beyond the inquiry itself, and,
secondly, that the inquiry proceedings were such as to allow
reality to exercise a formative influence on the minds of those
carrying them out. Generalizing the first observation, it is
proposed that every reality report, to be read as such, requires
an inquirendo - an authority to inquiry - emanating from beyond
itself so that it is construed as something which has been externally called for and not, say, as something creatively invented
or wilfully fabricated. The conventional inquirendo of research
in the social sciences is the unfinished business - the gaps,
puzzles, contradictions, inadequacies - of some relevant community of inquirers. References to existing research, others
in the field and the state of the topic might be seen as functional
equivalents to acknowledging appointment by Royal Warrant or
legislative decree. Recalling that the Latin root of royal is

egere, to rule, we might say that inquiry is constituted as
a response to an imperative call, a command, located outside
the particular individuals who execute it.

This formulation is plausible as far as it goes but there is a
basic difference between the *inquirendo* of Royal Warrant and
that of unfinished business in a community of inquirers which
reveals it as inadequate. The difference is that in the latter
case the call comes directly from the same place that inquiry is
to be directed towards rather than from a diffuse authority to
inquire. We might surmise that science is the disciplinary equivalent to 'Your Majesty' in the narrow sense of providing a
taken-for-granted sign of legitimacy which is at the same time
an imperative calling, but such speculation turns attention
away from the texts in question and, specifically, from the
question of whether there are in the reports equivalents of
the *inquirendo* of unfinished business in disciplinary research.
The question is particularly pointed when aimed at the 1834
Report because, as the Checklands remind us, it was 'inhibited
by the primitive state of social inquiry'[11] at the time; there was
'an almost total lack of experience and precedent in survey
technique. It was impossible to apply scientific principles to
the collection of evidence, for none existed. Indeed the question
- how does a society take an objective view of itself in social
terms? - had hardly yet been posed.'[12] The 1834 Report could not
then be located in a cumulative research agenda, selectively
recollected as current gaps, puzzles, etc., but it does contain
a weak approximation to that practice in the form of a historical
review of previous legislation which provides the report with a
self-transcending frame of relevance.

This first comes to view as a preliminary section titled 'Progress of the law' which, having identified the 43 Elizabeth (1601)
and its intentions as the principled core for establishing a
good poor law system, traces prior legislation to make those
intentions clearer. Thus we are told that early pauper legislation, dating back to the fourteenth century, was an attempt to
control the movements of people viewed as prospective threats
to public order. In 1388 labourers were prohibited from leaving
their locality without an authorizing letter from the justices of
the peace; 'impotent' persons were required either to stay put
or, if the local people refused alms, to go back to their birthplaces. The 1495 Act required beggars unable to work to go to
the 'hundred' where they resided, or were best known, or were
born, and not to beg outside the boundaries. In 1531 justices
of the peace were directed to assign the 'impotent poor' to begging areas, while any able-bodied person caught begging was
to be whipped and returned either to his birthplace or the place
where he last lived for three years consecutively, there to offer
his labour to anyone wanting it. The Act of 1536 legislated
charity for the impotent and work for 'sturdy beggars'; the
former through requiring each parish to establish a 'common box'
through which almsgiving must be conducted, the latter through

a graded series of punishments for vagrant idleness – first
whipping, then cropping of the right ear, and, finally, execu-
tion for repeated offences. In 1547 milder punishments were
substituted. Able-bodied beggars were to be branded with a
'V' for (vagabond) and given as slaves for two years to anyone
wanting them. If no one did then they were to be kept as labouring slaves in their birthplaces. A runaway vagabond was to
be branded with an 'S' and enslaved for life. The Act also
reinforced almsgiving by ordering curates to continually exhort
parishioners to 'help their brethren in Christ, born in the
same parish, and needing their help'. The Act of 1551 further
institutionalized charity by requiring each parish to keep lists
of householders and of the impotent poor ('the poor in very
deed') and to appoint each year two alms collectors. Householders
refusing their 'gentle requests' were to be exhorted further by
the minister and, failing this, by the local bishop. In 1563
sanctions against the uncharitable were significantly strength-
ened to include and compulsory taxation orders by a justice and
imprisonment for failing to obey such an order. 1572 saw a
return to the severities of 1536 with regard to sturdy beggars
while further strengthening charitable help by concentrating
powers of tax imposition, collection and distribution in the
justices of the peace and their areas of authority rather than
in the parishes. The Acts of 1597 and 1601, however, returned
to the principle of parish responsibility and established the
official ideology of poor relief for the next two hundred years
or more.

The Commissioners do not bother to detail the provisions of
these Acts because they are said to be familiar already; they
do, however, refer the reader to 'the Supplement' where the
whole of the 43 Elizabeth 1601 is reproduced, and draw special
attention in the first paragraph of the report proper, immediately
following the historical review, to its basic premise, namely
that the only justifiable uses of funds are the strictly necessary
relief of the impotent, and relief to able-bodied destitutes
lacking any means of subsistence, but then only in return for
work. A major theme of the report concerns the subsequent
dilution and abandonment of the sensible restrictions of 1601
through a combination of legislative laxity and local maladministration. References to previous laws are interwoven into the
descriptive and prescriptive sections of the text as regular,
recurrent accounting practices. Past legislation is recalled as
the mediation of a concern for social order, articulated through
demographic settlement, with the options of deterrent punishment, charity and setting to work. Their conjunction forms the
social meaning of poverty. (It is the persistence of the semantic
space circumscribed by these attitudes which guarantees that
the poor will always be with us.) The relevance of legislative
recall to establishing the permeability of a text by the flow of
real world events is, I think, obvious but its comparability to
disciplinary recollection as a summons to inquiry is less clear.

Moreover, the previous characterization of it as only a weak approximation needs to be explicated.

Comparability resides in the fact that both are recollections of social laws whose inadequacies call for inquiry. The crucial difference, however, is between social laws construed as man-made legislation and social laws construed as causal forcings beyond will, wish and intention. In the former case inquiry is called for by defects in human artefacts, something like inspectional repair work occasioned by a defective machine; in the latter it is called for by defective knowledge of the basic conditions governing all social existence and placing limits on the efficacy of human will. The inquirendo of the former is the corrigibility of man-made inventions in the light of practical experience, that of the latter is the discoverability of a natural order through scientific method. The former call demands inquiry into practical experience, the latter demands inquiry into that which transcends and imperatively conditions such activity. Because the inquirendo is issued from a place beyond constitutive activity, it conveys a stronger sense of externality, a more decisive reality effect. Constitutive innocence is more deeply secured in this way.

The 1909 Reports also rely upon legislative recollection as an inquiry warrant. Both Majority and Minority Reports, for example, make constant reference to the 1834 Poor Law Act. They do, however, possess an additional resource resembling disciplinary recollection in the accumulation of previous inquiries on their topics. The Majority Report opens by depicting a domain of inquiry so vast as to have been only partially touched by the 'nearly one hundred Reports of inquiries into subjects connected to the Poor Law since 1834', adding that 'none of them included in their preview pauperism as a whole'. The present inquiry thus projects completion of a body of knowledge representing an external object called pauperism. As in disciplinary inquiry the accumulation of investigation around an object is in itself an indexical confirmation of the standing reality of that object. Beyond this resemblance, however, we can detect another generically distinctive feature of policy inquiry. Whereas completion of inquiry is for disciplinary research an ultimate value (truth) which is pursued as a vocation,[3] it is for policy research a practical matter of meeting a dead-line set by the urgencies of decision-making. Action reports always talk of completion as a fight against time, which is to say the time tabled by a decision schedule extrinsic to inquiry.

The 'Statement of Proceedings' in the 1834 Report tells how a concerted attempt has been made to have it ready for the 1833 Parliamentary Session, only to be thwarted by 'the vast bulk of the manuscripts' and the engagement of the Parliamentary printers in other matters. Even now, they say, the Report is flawed by missing and 'occasional false references' to the evidence due to working from unpaged and unindexed proof sheets. To have waited longer, however, would have meant postponing remedial measures until the 1835 Session and 'such a delay appeared to us a greater evil than the imperfections and inaccuracies to which the course which we have adopted must expose us' (The 1834 Report, p. 3). Similarly, the 1909 Report points to its procedural imperfections as symptoms of the pressure of time. Having begun by inviting written submissions from every administrative body and organization concerned with the relief of poor persons, plus eminent officials, experts and 'persons of experience', the Commissioners confess on p. 3 that the project of checking and completing all this evidence through oral examination had to be abandoned:

> As the inquiry proceeded, it soon became apparent that it would be impossible, within the limited time at our disposal, to obtain by oral examination of witnesses, a body of evidence which could be taken as even approximately indicative of the views of the country as a whole .... The exigencies of the situation compelled us, therefore, to select as oral witnesses the authors of statements which contained either special features of interest or ambiguities which it was desired to clear up.

The authors of the Minority Report are even more explicit on the topic of urgency (1909 Report, p. 999):

> throughout the three years of our investigation we have been living under a continuous pressure for a remodelling of the Poor Laws ....We do not regret this peremptory and insistent demand for reform. The present situation is, in our opinion, as grave as that of 1834, though in its own way.

THE NEED FOR OBJECTIVE CRISIS

The relevance of urgency displays to the accomplishment of reality effects on paper is readily demonstrated. Not only do they reference the externality of the call for inquiry but the defects and omissions associated with them also index the permeability of the text by real world events. There is a precise parallel here with Defoe's device of attributing the incompletion of Robinson Crusoe's journal to the exhaustion of his ink supply. What is still lacking, however, in comparison with the inquirendo of disciplinary research is a definitive location of the origin of the call to inquire. This requirement of reality reporting is no better met by decisional urgency than by Royal Warrant. How then is it met in these texts? In brief, by the formulation of objective crisis as that which simultaneously demands and directs inquiry. It is not enough for a report to state that a problem exists - that much is presupposed in setting up a commission in the first place; the problem must be produced as

a crisis visible for reading, in directive detail, on the page.
Displaying the crisis is, in my terms, an essential constitutive
feature of reality reporting conducted under the warrant of
policy research. Without it the redemptive process of literal
reading is disturbed since the non-secural of an objective
origin as the researchable destination of inquiry leaves room
for the possibility of subjective origin as creative intent, i.e.
a loss of constitutive innocence occasioned by salience of authorship.

A previously cited article by Mark Blaug broaches our topic
by showing that the questionnaire data collected by the 1832
Commission does not substantiate the crisis claims made in the
report.[4] For example, only 7 per cent of parishes outside the
four rural counties associated most closely with the Speenhamland system reported wage subsidization and even within that
area only 11 per cent did so. Similar small percentages are
shown for other pauperizing practices such as 'the Roundsman
system' and the 'Labour-rate system' which are prominent
targets of the report. There is no difficulty in amplifying and
extending Blaug's procedure for bracketing crisis claims. To
satisfy myself on this point, having, as it were, already been
taken in by the text, I analysed some of the quantitative and
qualitative data contained in the responses to the rural and town
questionnaires (the rural data are in 'Reports from Commissioners', Session 1834, vol. 30; the town data are in vol. 33).
On the question of a financial burden, one item shows per
capita poor law costs for the years 1803, 1813, 1821 and 1831,
calculated by parishes. A quick scan of the raw data (no tabu-
lations are given) suggested a typical pattern of a rise in 1813
and again in 1821, followed by a decline between 1821 and 1831
to levels at or below those of 1803. A check on the last time
period showed that of 368 town parishes for which data was
available, 40 had remained the same (within plus or minus 5
pence), 103 had gone up (of which 34 were within the City of
London) and 225 had gone down. Of 1533 rural parishes, 96
were the same, 358 up, and 779 down. Certainly it would be
difficult to formulate a financial crisis from the figures at hand.
The qualitative data is similarly ambivalent as to the presence
of a crisis demanding reform. For example, Q. 45 of the Rural
Queries asked for opinions on the effects of forbidding magistrates to authorize relief to any person refusing to enter the
work-house or the poor-house (in effect banning out-door
relief, which the Report identified as the critical evil of the
existing situation). Most respondents (a mixture of overseers,
assistant overseers, clergymen and magistrates) were either
non-committal or did not respond, which in itself could have
been interpreted as a sign that out-door relief was not a matter
of widespread concern; and of those expressing a definite opinion 145 were favourable to the suggested reform and 128 against.
The general point derivable from the qualitative data (there are
several other questions of the same kind) is that most poor law

practitioners saw nothing particularly wrong with the existing
situation, and that while a minority expressed alarm, an approximately equal minority argued the virtues of the status quo.

It is possible then, through revisiting the data of 1834, to
show that no crisis is self-evidently present either in the
statistical data or in the perceptions of poor law practitioners.
A comparable critique could be directed against the 1909
Majority Report. Having introduced at the beginning a chapter
whose object is 'to show statistically the dimensions of the
problems with which we are called upon to deal' (p. 15), the
Commissioners struggle hard to ensure that the reader is seeing
the problems in the figures. Their survey begins with the size
dimension: the magnitude of the pauper host. Standard administrative procedures required that a day count of paupers be
conducted twice a year; those of 1 July 1907 and 1 January
1908 are used as a first estimate in bringing home the size of
the problem. For this purpose, the numbers of insane and
casual (vagrant) paupers are set aside, implying that it is the
number of sane, regular paupers which is of real concern. They
cannot readily be distinguished from normal members of society,
consequently their presence in the count is not immediately
accountable and signifies a problem. Thus on 1 July 1907, there
were 745,794 problematically present paupers on the books.
The raw number is then reworked in various ways to ensure that
it is read as symptomatically alarming (1909 Report, p. 15):

One out of every 47 persons was a pauper on July 1, 1907....
The numbers represent ... 21.3 per 1000 of the estimated
population ....The number of paupers on any given day is
approximately equal to the population of the largest provincial city in England and Wales, viz. Liverpool.

Further safeguarding of the numbers problem is immediately
provided by the claim that persons who are periodic but not
continuous regulars might be missed by a day count. This is
substantiated by comparing a specially commissioned year
count for 1906-7 (excluding lunatics and vagrants and counting
each person only once regardless of how many times he went
on poor relief) with the average of the two official day counts
for that period. The former figure is calculated as 2.15 times
larger than the latter, a total of 1,709,436 individuals almost
equal now to the combined populations of the three largest
provincial cities in England.

Further instances could be generated. For example, the
statistical survey of 1909, having brought size to view as a
cause for concern, sets off on a search for worsening trends
since 1872 (when comprehensive day counts covering the whole
country began). Having established that the rate per 1000 had
in fact declined appreciably from 1872 to 1896 and remained
stationary thereafter, the Commissioners quickly block any
temptation to read the figures as good news by citing negative

features that the figures obscure: for example, that the rate of
reduction has slowed down and now levelled off; that the
absolute number on relief has increased since the 1880s; that
nearly all this absolute increase has been amongst adult males;
that while out-door relief has declined, in-door relief has
increased, and so on. Yet it is still difficult to see the seriousness in the figures and there is no doubt that a sophisticated
re-examination of the data would, like Blaug's analysis of the
1834 Report, be capable of rendering them doubtful as grounds
for crisis claims. The question must now be raised, however,
as to whether any such critique of the data can decisively
disturb the crisis claims of a reality report. Assuming that
empirical critique can only undermine empirical grounds for
assertions, its capacity to do so depends upon whether such
claims are, in the final analysis, empirically grounded. Certainly
the Poor Law Reports with their constant appeals to statistical,·
oral and written evidence would appear to meet this requirement.
Closer reading, however, shows that this is not the case. All
three texts at some point formulate the crisis as something
existing independently of what these witnesses can say or
those figures show. For example, the 1834 Report, having
advanced some expenditure figures to show the progressiveness
of the financial burden, adds (p. 32):

the statement of the mere amount directly expended,
whether estimated in money or in kind, affords a very
inadequate measure of the loss sustained by those who
supply it. A great part of the expense is incurred, not
by direct payment out of the rates, but by the purchase
of unprofitable labour.

It is admitted that such expenses are incalculable and that
employers may even appear to be profiting from cheap pauper
labour; nonetheless, it is asserted, this is a false appearance
for reasons to be given subsequently. The fact that reasons
(the corruption of the work-force) are subsequently docu-
mented does not invalidate the observation that at this place
in the text a crisis claim is asserted independently of what the
particular evidence at hand can show. My argument is not
that practical reality reporters set out to establish crises as
autonomous entities beyond empirical evidence but that whenever and wherever evidence is wanting or seems contradictory,
crisis is asserted anyway.
Reference was made previously to the conspicuous lack of
alarm revealed in the views of those directly involved in administering the poor laws. In a section called 'Objections to amendment', the Commissioners note a lack of alarm, indeed a general
approval of the status quo, among precisely those groups upon
which the burdens and evils of the system most heavily weighed
- the employers of labour and the owners of rateable property.
The question insinuating itself here is basically the same as

that which occurs to a naive bourgeois in reading a Marxist
critique of the evils of modern capitalism. If things are so bad,
why do the afflicted and oppressed seem so contented? The
answer also is basically the same, viz. false consciousness.
Having reviewed contentment with the system, the Commissioners
state on p. 36 of the 1834 Report:

> It appears, therefore, necessary to state at some length
> the effects of the existing system both to show how short-
> sighted are the views of those who think that they continue
> to profit by it, and to show, before we suggest any remedy,
> *the absolute necessity that some remedy should be applied.*
> [Italics added]

Shortness of sight is not to be attributed to the myopia of
viewers, however, but to the nature of the effects themselves,
which being long-term, aggregative and unintended, are under-
standably beyond any view but that of systematic inquiry. Thus,
each farmer might see immediate benefit in hiring subsidized
pauper labour, or even in forcing his existing workers onto the
parish in order to shuffle off part of his wage bill onto a poor
fund which many beside himself contribute to. What he cannot
immediately see is the resulting transformation of diligence into
idleness, honesty into fraudulence and skill into incompetence,
or the way in which immediately profitable individual decisions
aggregate into long-term losses to all through, for example,
the growing reluctance of investors to commit their capital to an
industry (farming) whose most important instrument of production (skilled labour) is undergoing deterioration. The slow
formation of particulars into patterns is too gradual for the
normal vision of participants to record at the time, as noted in
the 1834 Report (p. 41):

> It must be carefully remembered, however, that these evils
> are gradually evolved. Ultimately, without doubt, the farmer
> finds that pauper labour is dear, whatever be its price; but
> that is not until allowance has destroyed the industry and
> morals of the labourers who were bred under a happier
> system, and has educated a new generation in idleness,
> ignorance and dishonesty.

Comparable passages could be cited from the 1909 Reports,
especially where they bring to view the newly discovered problems of chronic underemployment and distress born of cyclical
fluctuations in the economy; these belong more centrally to
the production of knowledge effects, however, so we will content
ourselves with this passage from p. 1214 of the Minority Report,
reading it as a typical expression of the crisis work which
practical inquiries must constantly undertake in order to
reflexively display their own identity:

The first step is to make the whole community realize that
the evil exists. At present, it is not too much to say that
the average citizen of the middle or upper class takes for
granted the recurrent destitution among wage-earning
families due to Unemployment, as part of the natural order
of things, and as no more to be combated than the east
wind. In the same way the eighteenth century citizen
acquiesced in the horrors of the contemporary prison administration, and in the slave trade; just as, for the first
decades of the nineteenth century, our grandfathers accepted
as inevitable the slavery of the little children of the wage-
earners in mines and factories, and the incessant devastation
of the slums by 'fever'. Fifty years hence we shall be looking back with amazement at the ignorant and helpless
acquiescence of the ruling class of the United Kingdom, at
the opening of the twentieth century, in the constant
debasement of character and physique, not to mention the
constant draining away of the nation's wealth, that idleness combined with starvation plainly causes.

The disengagement of crisis from the risks of empirical demonstration is not an evasion specific to certain reports unsure of
their ground, but an inescapable element of all reports within
the practical action genre. This is implied in the proposition
that representation of an objective crisis is a constitutive feature
of action-oriented inquiry. To say that it is a constitutive
feature is to say that it is something essential to such inquiry,
something which it cannot do without. Crisis cannot be equated
with the subjective experiences of those involved nor with what
the data can show because what is essential cannot be left to
the vagaries of empirical happenstance. This is why, in the
face of imminent empirical discrediting, and as an unshakeable
safeguard against it, practical reports locate crisis below the
surface of what actors might say and beyond the reach of
what particular evidence can now reveal. Attempts like that of
Blaug to empirically discredit crisis claims are, therefore,
ultimately helpless to do so. They can only scratch the surface.
Do we wish to say then that crisis claims are arbitrary impositions, ungrounded affirmations impelled by functional necessity?
By no means. There is, as will be shown in the analysis of
knowledge effects, an irremediable and therefore unfailing
source of crisis sustaining all reality reporting whatsoever.
It is not, however, political, economic or moral in nature,
but epistemological. Social reality reporting is always an attempt
to make situated constructions of reality knowable in writing,
i.e. within the constitutive rules of textual reality construction.
Since one of those rules is the transcendence of situated
accounting practices (objective knowledge is trans-situational),
the textual way of knowing must always encounter situated
reality construction as a want of rational accountability and its
operations as an existence of crisis (a crisis of knowability).

Further discussion of this matter is postponed, however, until the review of textual devices for achieving reality effects has been completed.

REFERENCING OBJECTIVE ENCOUNTER

We have explicated the constitutive significance of one observation arising from the 1834 Report's address to the monarch – that the source of inquiry is located externally to the inquiry itself – but, it may be recalled, there was a second observation to the effect that the inquiry proceedings were such as to allow reality to exercise a formative influence upon the minds of those carrying them out. Again we ask whether something of constitutive significance can be made of the observation by amplifying and reflecting upon it.

Inquiry is called for by something located beyond itself and the text which reports it; the call is answered by going out to somewhere beyond, and bringing in evidence of what is there. This is described clearly in the self-understandings of the 1834 and 1909 Reports as statements of proceedings. In the former inquiry, the first step was to send out questionnaires to all the parishes of England and Wales so that evidence of poor law operations could be brought back in as practitioners' inscriptions on their blank spaces. The second step was to appoint Assistant Commissioners to supplement and check the evidence through personal investigation on the spot. In order to frame instructions for them, 'two of the Commissioners made excursions into the country, to ascertain by actual experience the sort of duties which the Assistant Commissioners would have to perform'. (The Report of 1834, p. 1.) The instructions themselves required each Assistant Commissioner to go to an assigned area and there 'use his own discretion as to the places which appear to be most deserving of investigation, and as to the points of inquiry which may be most successfully investigated in each parish'. (The Report of 1834, Supplement No. 3. 'Instructions to Assistant Commissioners', p. 248.) The investigator is further instructed to inspect documents, cross-examine witnesses, conduct interviews and engage in participant observation; a daily record must be kept of such activities and a progress report submitted at least once a week in addition to the compilation of a final report. It is interesting to note that the Commissioners, faced with a situation in which no disciplinary format of social inquiry was available, relied upon the same device as early writers of realistic fiction, like Defoe, in that they traded upon the traveller's authority of 'I was there' and secured that authority by embedding eye-witness accounts in an editorial narrative. The organization of such accounts in the report is, however, more complex, effortful and imposing than that of fictive realism. In part it is more imposing (produces a stronger reality effect) because it is authorized by a collective

editorial 'we' and so avoids the distractive insecurity of I-
narration remarked upon previously in discussing Goldknopf:
'I-narration forces us to acknowledge what third-person narration would merely encourage us to surmise: the role of the
interpretive consciousness in the drama before us'.[5]

The constitutive significance of depersonalized narration is
that the person who reads is more firmly drawn into the posture
of following the action. Addressed by a collective voice announcing itself as the executive agent of an investigative method,
the reader's attention is unlikely to oscillate between the identity
of the narrator and its relevance to what is being referred to.
This unitary, referential mode of attention provides an unremarkable frame within which an attitude of looking into scenes
pointed to by the text is continuously sustained. The frame
itself is reflexively sustained in the course of the text through
what we are calling reality indexicals. Depersonalized narration
(signifying observational externality) is such a device; effortful editing will now be displayed as another one.

As mimes well know, effort signifies resistance, and resistance
testifies to an engagement with reality. Effortful editing of
evidence testifies to engagement with a reality so bountiful of
data as to resist summary, and so extensive as to resist comprehension. The following passages from the Poor Law Reports
describe effortful editing in the face of evidential mass:

> The reports of the Assistant Commissioners, though less
> voluminous than the Returns, form altogether a large mass;
> and a large body of testimony consists of the communications
> made to us from every part of England, and from some parts
> of America, and of the continent of Europe. [1834, p. 2.]

> In the hope of diminishing the difficulty of making use of
> this voluminous Evidence, we have embodied a considerable
> portion of it in the following Report. [1834, p. 3.]

> We have selected from the vast body of evidence contained
> in the Appendix respecting the prevalence and effects of
> magisterial interference, the following passages, not as
> peculiarly striking, but because they illustrate most of the
> remarks which we have made [1834, p. 77.]

> We have held 200 meetings, of which 159 have been spent on
> hearing evidence. We have examined 452 witnesses, and the
> questions answered orally exceed 100,000 in number; We
> have, in addition, received statements of evidence, or replies
> to questions as above described, from about 900 persons
> who have not been examined orally [1909, Majority Report,
> p. 4.]

Even this tremendous labour is inadequate however:

> The scope of our reference and the difficulty of deciding
> where to begin and where to stop our inquiries, are clearly
> illustrated in this chapter [an historical review of distress
> due to unemployment]. It was impossible for us to ignore
> causes other than administration which occasioned fluctua-
> tions in pauperism and in the number of applications for
> relief. But a full investigation into such causes would
> have entailed an inquiry into the whole of our social and
> industrial structure, and such a scrutiny was clearly
> impossible, if only from the length of time it would involve.
> [1909, Majority Report, p. 304.]

> We feel very strongly that the subject is too vast to be at
> all adequately dealt with in a six month's period. No biblio-
> graphy of the subject was readily available, and through-
> out the whole of our inquiry new facts and new documents
> have been continually coming to light. The research is very
> incomplete. [1909, Minority Report, p. xxvi.]

It is possible to see in these self-understandings of the
reports the outlines of a rhetoric of reality effects containing
at least three features:
1 A vocabulary of travel, discovery, finding – of coming across
situations and being struck by events. An imagery of encounter
and impingement, suitable to the hardness of facts, which can
be read as a linguistic equivalent to Dr. Johnson's famous kick-
ing of a stone so that his foot rebounded from it to refute
Bishop Berkeley's claim that objects have no independent existence beyond the act of perceiving them.
2 The referencing of evidential mass as the correlate (albeit
only a partial one) of a plenitudinous reality. Rhetorically speaking, it might be said that an evidential mass so vast that it cannot be fully represented in readable form but only alluded to
through footnotes and extracts, has the weight to carry an
audience with it. Or, that the proprieties of reality reporting
require the gravitas of weighty evidence as an indexical expression of seriousness (a crisis is, after all, a matter of some
gravity and should not be lightly treated). Something presented
as factual reportage which was not down-to-earth would be
experienced as a duplicitous code.
3 The referencing of incompleteness as the unavoidable fate of
any particular (i.e. finite) inquiry. The last two quotations
given above identify incompleteness as a practical time-space-
travel problem and, in doing so, project the possibility of
completeness-of full inquiry – as something realizable given more
travel resources. Incompleteness then is construed as an exploration problem soluble by having more inquirers and more time.
This only makes sense, however, if the object of inquiry (e.g.
'our social and industrial structure') is thought of as a spatially

real object since the time necessary for complete inquiry is the time it would take to move across, through and around it. Moreover, the object must be such as to exist independently of the process of inquiry itself; its characteristics must be such that investigative passage is irrelevant to them. How otherwise could the object endure and persist as that which makes knowledge claims about it corrigible and inquiry into it completable? Clearly, the referencing of incompleteness is an affirmation of what philosophers call ontological objectivism and the correspondence theory of truth.

THE EXPERIENTIAL STRUCTURE OF REALITY

The rhetorical topoi of reportage are demonstrably important as devices for drawing the person who reads into the redemptive posture of literal readership. More remains to be said, however, because we have referred only to the imagery of encounter and not yet uncovered the secret of its effectiveness as rhetoric. The deeper problem is brought to view by Schutz and Luckmann's discussion of the everyday world of the natural attitude as 'the paramount province of reality', relative to which all other 'finite provinces of meaning', including the symbolically constructed provinces of science, art, politics and religion, are more or less unreal. To quote Thomas Hardy (Old furniture):

As in a mirror a candle-flame
Shows images of itself, each frailer
As it recedes.

At the far end of unreality, where the 'tension of consciousness' is most relaxed, are the 'fantasy worlds' of daydreams, fairy tales and poetry. Entry into any of them means that 'I am exempted from the urgency of the pragmatic motive under which I stand in the everyday life world'.[6] As much could be said, however, of reading a reality report. It is as true of reading as of a fantasy world that while I remain there I cannot do anything which 'gears into the external world and alters it'.[7] Yet, in spite of this disengagement of gears, a reality report does somehow manage to generate an actual experience of resistant encounter in the course of reading: an experience which grounds the persuasiveness of the rhetoric of reality effects and cannot, therefore, be attributed to it as a result. But how does such an experience get into the reading process? What resistantly encounters what in a text? If a uniquely high tension of consciousness, pragmatic urgency, and corporeal gearing into the external world are constitutive features of situated reality construction which are non-operative in reading, then how are strong textual reality effects achieved? What functional equivalents can we postulate? The questions crowd in like importunate beggars. To gain thinking room it is helpful to recall Heidegger and Durkheim on the topic of facticity. Both look back to our Copernican hero, Kant; the former by way of exegetical clarification, the latter by way of sociological revisionism. Between them they convey a valuable insight into the textual structuring of resistant encounter.

We take up Heidegger's exegesis at the point where he seeks to clarify Kant's argument concerning the twofold determination necessary for something to be an object for knowledge, by examining the word gegenstandt;

> What we are supposed to be able to know must encounter us from somewhere, come to meet us. Thus the *'gegen'* (against) in *Gegenstandt* ....What encounters us must be determined as standing, something which has a stand and is, therefore, constant.[8]

This constancy is not given by mere sensory perception. We do not have a repeated number of sensory encounters and then infer the existence of an object corresponding to them, rather objective cognition is a certain way of experiencing the world:

> What encounters us in sensation and perception and is intuitively given ... only comes to the position of a state of affairs standing in itself when the given has already been represented universally and thought in such concepts as cause and effect, i.e. under the principle of causality in general. The permanent elements of knowing, intuition, and concept, must be unified in a determinate way. The intuitively given must be brought under the universality of definite concepts. The concept must get over the intuition and must determine in a conceptual manner what is given in the intuition.[9]

In the stance of objective cognition, a sensory encounter is experienced as an instance of constant standing against consciousness. Constant standing against is then a general mode of experience – a capability of consciousness – which exists in advance of, and as a condition for, any empirical encounter:

> Experience does not arise 'empirically' out of perception but becomes possible only through metaphysics: through a new conceptual representing peculiarly in advance of the given in the concepts of cause and effect. By this means a ground for the given is established: principles. An object in the strict sense of Kant is thus first of all the represented, wherein the given is determined in a necessary and universal way.[10]

Something confronts us through sensory intuition (through the faculty of sensibility) but it is brought to stand as an object only through the conceptualization of the intuition via the categories of understanding. Since the categories are under the standing of any empirical objects whatsoever and are prior to, as grounding for, actual conceptual judgements, Kant calls them pure a priori categories of understanding.

The Heidegger-Kant formulation of objective encounter is valuable for two reasons. First, it displays the dynamics of reality effects as involving a subordination of immediate experience to conceptual representation. The notion of conceptual subordination is sufficient to provide both for resistant encounter and constancy of standing within the realm of the text. Second, Kant's stern refusal of the adequacy of any empirical psychologistic theory of perception to account for the experiencing of objects carries over to us as a principled refusal of the adequacy of any empirical psychologistic theory of reading to account for textual reality effects. (In principle, empirical theories of effects begin and end with effects as facts and cannot, therefore, make facticity itself a problem. Also, in principle, a psychologistic account of reading must reduce the text either to a stimulus source or an epiphenomenon of processes going on in the person who reads and cannot, therefore, study it as text.)

The formulation does, however, have drawbacks. First, it leaps directly from empirical to transcendental analysis whereas I wish to stick close to the observables of textual methods. To anyone objecting that the analysis must then be empirical I would answer that to attend to the observables within a constitutive framework of theorizing is so different from attending within a representational framework that it is misleading to call both forms of inquiry empirical as though there were no essential difference. Since thought abhors a semantic vacuum I will, for the time being, imitate Habermas and say that quasi-transcendental analysis is being attempted, though what that means only the work can tell. The second drawback is that Kant retains the vocabulary of subject-object dualism even though transforming its significance. The problem here is not so much that he must then posit such awkward concepts as the transcendental ego and the transcendental object of apperception, as that the constitution of reality and knowledge effects is attributed entirely to the subject. Whatever the merits of this approach at Kant's metaphysical level of inquiry, it cannot be applied at the level I wish to work at without switching the focus of attention from text to reader and threatening a relapse into a psychologistic account of reading.

To help overcome these problems of psychologistic relapse and subjective orientation inherent in the Heidegger-Kant formulation, it is useful to appeal to Emile Durkheim's sociological reformulation of Kant. Durkheim's theory of knowledge has its own shortcomings for our purpose but it does possess the significant advantage of locating the possibility of gegenstandt (the experience of objective reality) in a non-metaphysical structure, that of social experience. More specifically, Durkheim

changes the terms of the account from a subject-object to an
individual-collective dialectic.

The notion of standing against initially comes to view in
Durkheim's attempts to formulate the characteristics of the social
fact (this being part of a broader attempt to say what rules
sociological method):

> Certain of these social manners of acting and thinking
> acquire, by reason of their repetition, a certain rigidity
> which on its own account crystallizes them, so to speak,
> and isolates them from the particular events which reflect
> them. They thus acquire a body, a tangible form, and con-
> stitute a reality in their own right, quite distinct from the
> individual facts which reproduce it. Collective habits are
> inherent not only in the successive acts which they deter-
> mine but, by a privilege of which we find no example in the
> biological realm, they are given permanent expression in
> a formula which is repeated from mouth to mouth, trans-
> mitted by education, and fixed even in writing ....None
> of these can be found entirely reproduced in the applica-
> tions made of them by individuals, since they can exist
> even without being actually applied ....
> A social fact is to be recognized by the power of exter-
> nal coercion which it exercises or is capable of exercising
> over individuals ....
> A social fact is every way of acting, fixed or not, capable
> of exercising on the individual an external constraint; or
> again, every way of acting which is general throughout a
> given society, while at the same time existing in its own
> right independent of its individual manifestations.[11]

In his preface to the second edition of the 'Rules of Sociological Method', Durkheim sought to clarify misunderstandings
about the criterion of constraint on individual consciousness,
explaining that the constraint is due 'to the prestige with which
certain representations are invested'. Personal habits have
something of the same quality but

> they rule us from within, for they are in every case an
> integral part of ourself. On the contrary, social beliefs and
> practices act on us from without; thus the influence exerted
> by them differs fundamentally from the effect of habit ...
> the individual finds them completely formed, and he cannot
> evade or change them ... the word 'institution' well expres-
> ses this special mode of reality, provided that the ordinary
> significance of it be slightly extended. One can designate
> ... as 'institutions' all the beliefs and all the modes of
> conduct instituted by the collectivity.[12]

Durkheim's concrete way of speaking about individuals and
collectives would, if taken literally, lead us far away from the

analysis of reality effects in reading-writing, so I propose to interpret his statements as metaphorical descriptions of the nature of textual reality effects. Wherever Durkheim speaks of 'the individual', I will take him to mean particulars or details; wherever he speaks of 'collective habits', 'collective ways of acting' and 'institutions', I will take him to mean types, categories or concepts (recalling Heidegger's statement that the intuitively given must be brought under the universality of definite concepts). From this it follows that the structure of facticity is that of a coercive subordination of particulars to generals, of details to categories. In order not to appear violently disrespectful of Durkheim, I would point out that this metaphorical interpretation allows us to make sense of his otherwise strange claim, in 'Suicide', that a statistical average or a statistical rate is a social fact. He cannot mean that an average or a rate is a collective habit, a social belief, a way of acting, an institution which can exercise a 'power of external coercion' over living individuals; and his subsequent gloss to the effect that an average 'expresses a certain state of the group mind[13] only adds mysticism to difficulty. What he does mean is that an average, like a general concept or category, is a collection device:

> Since each of these figures contains all the individual cases indiscriminately, the individual circumstances which may have had a share in the production of the phenomena are neutralized and, *consequently do not contribute to its determination* [my italics].[14]

The structuring of facticity displayed here is precisely the same as that found in his talk (taken metaphorically) of individuals and institutions: namely that particulars are collected within generals, that the generals exist independently of (are not determined by) what they collect, that the collection is not attributable to the work of collectors but is a neutral function of the collectability of the items and the fact that they can only reveal their essential identity within a collection. What Durkheim cannot yet see in the 'Rules of Sociological Method' is that the collective realm is not 'a category of facts with very distinctive characteristics[15] but describes the constitutive ground of facticity itself. He came to recognize this, however, in his later writings where the analysis of primitive religion develops into a neo-Kantian theory of knowledge. In 'The Elementary Forms of the Religious Life', Durkheim revisits the Kantian categories of time and space through which phenomena are intuited, as well as the 'pure' categories of understanding through which phenomena are brought to thought, and proclaims them all to be 'essentially collective representations'. The categories are imposed on thinking with a priori necessity, which means without the accompaniment of need of proof: 'It (an a priori category) contains within it something

which constrains the intelligence and which leads to its acceptance without preliminary examination.[116]

Echoes of the Kantian theme of constancy and 'standing
against' sound clearly in the following passages:

> Impersonality and stability are the two characteristics of
> truth ....It is under the form of collective thought that
> impersonal thought is for the first time revealed to humanity
> ....A collective representation presents guarantees of
> objectivity by the fact that it is collective ....Impersonal
> reason is only another name given to collective thought ...
> there is something impersonal in us because there is some-
> thing social in all of us, and since social life embraces at
> once both representations and practices, this impersonality
> naturally extends to ideas as well as to acts.[17]

Durkheim's leaning towards a view of reality as socially constructed appears also in his polemic against the pragmatist
philosophy of William James. This is made clear in Steven Lukes's
account of the debate (which apart from being admirably lucid
also points out the continuity of Durkheim's theory of knowledge
with Wittgenstein's analysis of concepts as moves in language-
games rooted in forms of social life).[18] James's equation of truth
with practical success in restoring obstructed courses of action
was deeply abhorrent to Durkheim's rationalistic faith in
necessity, and provoked him to ask what it is that gives certain
representations that obligatory, 'necessitating power' which is
the hallmark of truth. Durkheim's answer, as we have seen,
is to appeal to their origin in collective life. It is this origin,
Durkheim stresses, which explains

> that impression of resistance and that sentiment of something
> transcending the individual which we experience in the
> presence of the truth and which are the very condition of
> objectivity ... it is thought which creates reality, and the
> pre-eminent role of collective representations is to 'make'
> that superior reality which is society itself.[19]

At this point Durkheim seems close to endorsing a radically
constructionist position which would have made his positivist
programme of investigation untenable; he withdraws from the
brink, however, by asserting that representations cannot
become collective (i.e. shared) unless they engender actions
in adjustive correspondence with reality itself - a reality beyond
thoughts, words and concepts. Why does Durkheim need to
make such an assertion (in blatant contradiction to his sociological theory of facticity)? In order to protect the special
status of scientific against non-scientific representations;
especially those called mythology and ideology. In a strange
betrayal of sociological realism, Durkheim relegates 'mytho-
logical' representations to a second-class epistemological status

on the ground that they do not correspond to the reality of things but only to the realities of social life. Mythologies are true to social experience but not true about nature and hence are inferior:

> For a long time yet, there will exist in all societies two tendencies: a tendency towards objective and scientific truth, and a tendency towards truth perceived from within, towards mythological truth. This is ... one of the greatest obstacles to the progress of sociology.[20]

My argument is that Durkheim's positivistic determination to secure the collective as an independent realm of facts accessible to natural science investigation prevents him from following through his own insight that social reality effects exist in the formal structure of collective-individual constraint. The effects cannot be adequately conceptualized as the obedience of individual minds to the authoritative prestige of collective origins but must be thought of as properties present in the collective structuring of particulars. A text produces reality effects not simply because its concepts have their origin in a particular community but because it has a collective organization. A reality-producing text has the form of a social structure in which details and particulars ('individuals') are constrained by generals ('collective representations'). In this light it can be seen that the constitutive significance of the rhetoric of travel, discovery, evidential mass and incompleteness is to provide reflexive confirmation of collective structuring and constraint. Constraint is, for example, textually experienced in the reduction of evidential mass to compacted representations visible on the page: the initial representation of content in descriptive chapter headings; its ongoing representation as marginal sub-headings; the periodic condensation of what has gone before as itemized summaries of findings or recommendations; the final representation of content as an index. That these familiarities of format are something more than reading conveniences is readily illustrated by imagining the doubt that would be occasioned by a novel which contained them all (or a report which contained none). Contents pages, sub-headings, summary packages and indexes do not, of course, exhaust contextual devices for mastering particularity. Others include the annotated orchestration of different voices to say the same thing, the average figure, the tendency time chart, the classificatory table, the representative type, the essential compound (e.g. the essence of pauperism), and the reified group (all of which either have been or will be illustrated in other contexts).

The Poor Law Reports are by no means lacking in Durkheimean awareness; they show it particularly in the notion that uniformity of opinion in the face of diversity of source is an obvious sign of facticity (truth is individual opinion constrained by a common reality).

The Report of 1834, after stating the principle that there is epistemological safety in numbers because as the number of witnesses is increased, sources of error cancel one another out, goes on to stress on p. 3 the sheer diversity of its sources as a reason why any agreement of opinion must be counted as a fact:

The evidence ... comes from every county and almost every town, and from a very large proportion of even the villages in England. It is derived from many thousand witnesses of every rank and of every profession and employment, members of the two Houses of Parliament, clergymen, country gentlemen, magistrates, farmers, manufacturers, shopkeepers, artisans, and peasants, differing in every conceivable degree in education, habits, and interests, and agreeing only in their practical experience as to the matters in question, in their general description both of the mode in which the laws for the relief of the poor are administered, and of the consequences which have already resulted from that administration, and in their anticipation of certain further consequences from its continuance.

Similarly, the 1909 Majority Report after detailing the volume of its evidence, adds on p. 5:

In our opinion, therefore, the value both of our oral and written evidence consists rather in its cumulative effect than in the idiosyncrasies of individual assertion, and when these are eliminated we believe that there will be found a mass of sober and well considered opinion suggestive and on the whole consistent.

The Minority Report understands facticity and truth in the same way. Being dissatisfied with the Majority procedures, its authors appointed three sets of Special Investigators to study the causes of pauperism (rather than how it was being treated) - p. 1151:

The outcome of these investigations was all the more impressive in that it was not what we anticipated. We do not exaggerate when we say that all these enquiries - numbering, with their assistants, more than a dozen, starting on different lines of investigation, and pursuing their researches independently all over the Kingdom - came, without concert, to the same conclusion, namely, that of all the causes or conditions predisposing to pauperism the most potent, the most certain and the most extensive in its operation was this method of employment in odd jobs.

It is a constitutive feature of factual reportage - whether disciplinary or practical - that its finite orderliness is understood as an overcoming of potentially infinite variation. Inquiry is experienced in reading as the revelation of coherence in the midst of scatter. The tension necessary to the experience lies in the juxtaposition of an incipient collection procedure which maximizes potential variation by opening itself freely to the world (at least that part which has called for inquiry), and an emergent consensus showing that possible variation is actually (not artificially) constrained. Reality inquiry must discover orderliness, not impose it. Anything which would limit the initial possibility of variation - for example, confinement of witnesses to those having the same standpoint, spurious evidence dictated by subjective interests rather than by observation, inadequate range of collection - would undermine the authority of an emergent consensus as severely, say, as ballot-rigging would invalidate an election result. As an extreme possibility, if the constitutive tension between potential scatter and actual consensus was completely dissolved, the consensus would lose its authoritative grounding in reality and signify something else such as a value projection or an authorial fabrication. (This is, of course, the intention of ideological debunking, instances of which were considered previously in the review of existing readings of the reports.)

The point I wish to consolidate is that the holding power of investigatory consensus (i.e. its power to hold one to the posture of literal reading) depends upon the consensus being encountered as an inherent order of things rather than a constitutive accomplishment. The poor law inquiries, like any others, are perfectly capable of noting causes for suspicion regarding particular aspects of a consensus but always within the assumption that these can be dealt with by making allowances, doing a little discounting or some other corrective work. The following passage from one of the specially commissioned inquiries of 1909 is especially explicit in the matter:

Opinion is unanimous among all well-judging persons that a successful application for relief, especially in a lax union, encourages neighbours to apply and engenders fraud. Relieving officers can always supply examples of this type readily. Some allowance must, perhaps, be made for their stories. Their work is such as to breed suspicion of their fellow men, and the more efficient the officer, the more he comes to pride himself on his acuteness in ferreting out impostures. But when we have discounted any little proneness to recall the fraudulent and to forget the virtuous it remains true that some women will always be ashamed to come on the parish, others never, and that there is a wavering intermediate class which is swayed towards or away from the parish according as they are influenced by the first class or the second.[21]

What remains when discounting of bias has been done, situational distortions allowed for and individual idiosyncrasies averaged out is what stands against empirical particulars as the guarantee of their corrigibility, namely the general truths of reality. The enactment of a tense interplay between the two, moving towards the sovereign rule of the latter, is a textual method for producing a reality effect. We are reminded here of Charles Peirce's doctrine of the reality of 'generals' - stating that 'there are Real things, whose characters are entirely independent of our opinions about them[22] - and the related propositions of scholastic realism: (a) that the Real is what exists independently of any particular person's thinking about it, and as (b) existence implies continuity over time, which in turn implies generality, then (c) the Real is generality independent of particular thinking but (d) generality can only exist in thought, therefore (e) the Real is thought independent of anyone's particular thinking and the teleological end towards which inferential reasoning by an infinite community of inquirers moves. Whatever doubts the doctrine may arouse as an ontological statement, it captures perfectly one of the constitutive features of textual reality construction. All reality reporting is done as though under its commandment.

FAMILIARITY, COMMON SENSE AND UNREMARKABILITY

To conclude this part of the analysis, I will discuss two other salient characteristics of the reports which hold promise as pointers to textual methods of producing reality effects:
1 Usage of a ready-made vocabulary of poverty discourse: a set of collective nouns, qualifiers, definitions, diagnostic recipes and remedies already embedded in legislative and administrative practice.
2 Reliance upon 'we all know' theorizing to explain and predict behaviour as the typical actions of typical actors.
Analytic promise is held in the prima facie relevance of the first characteristic to the open horizon requirement (an institutionalized vocabulary establishes the openness of a text both to historical flow and practices external to reporting), and of the second to maintaining the constitutive innocence of code and message through common-sense unremarkability. I will briefly document the characteristics in order to explore their analytic promise.

The public vocabulary of poverty
The Report of 1834 was regarded at the time, and has been judged by historians, as a new departure in the administration of relief to the poor. Even a brief consideration of antecedent public debate is sufficient to show, however, that whatever the nature of its novelty may have been, it was certainly not in the categories, concepts, diagnoses and remedies that it deployed.

In this respect it is instructive to recall that the 1832 Royal Commission was not created to remedy a want of knowledge but to resolve a political dead-lock arising from the competing recommendations of two earlier reports: the House of Commons Select Committee Report of 1817 and the House of Lords Select Committee Report of 1818. The Lords Committee was appointed by the government to seek more practical and moderate solutions than the hard-line Malthusian proposals of the Commons Report. Of greater significance for us, however, is the impossibility of moving from the 1834 text to either of those reports without a strong sense of familiarity and déjà vu.

The Commons Report, for example, talks approvingly of the old principles, enshrined in the 43 Elizabeth 1601, of relieving the 'impotent poor' and suppressing 'vagrancy and idleness'. Subsequent departures from them such as giving relief to the 'able-bodied' have undermined socially crucial motivations like self-help, saving for old age and sickness, and limiting family size to suit one's income. The result is that 'whilst the existing poor laws, and the system under which they are administered remain unchanged, there does not exist any power of arresting the progress of this increase in numbers and costs' (p. 292). The dominating themes are the ultimate ruination of rate-payers, dereliction of farms and houses, and the contagious spread of pauper vices until the whole working class is demoralized. Recommendations include the restriction of out-door relief to those both impotent and destitute; able-bodied vagrants and beggars to be placed in workhouses; pauper children to be placed in parochial work schools; and restrictions on the powers of magistrates to intervene in poor relief distribution. The Lords Report similarly deplores departures from 'the true spirit' of the 43 Elizabeth Act (even though they have often arisen from 'the humane exercise of its supposed powers') but supposes that the chief defect - indiscriminate distribution of out-door relief - can be remedied by simplifying the laws, requiring systematic accounting procedures in the assessment, collection and distribution of poor rates and stopping the use of rates to pay wages. The Committee called in thirty-one experienced witnesses for examination and presents a verbatim transcription of the question-answer sessions which reads like a dress rehearsal for the 1834 Report. Testimony is given against the roundsman system of hiring pauper labour, against the capricious laxity of magistrates and in favour of permanent salaried assistant overseers. Familiar dramatis personae flit across the transcripts: the dishonest tradesman-overseer supplying the workhouse from his own business; the fraudulent pauper working the system; the drunken pauper spending his relief money on drink; the lazy pauper preferring the relative comforts of the improperly named workhouse to independent labour.

Of course the Commons and Lords reports do not include the entire range of diagnoses and remedies from which those of 1834 were selected; to show that would require a far wider casting of the documentary net such as Sir George Nicholls's massive review of legislation, books and pamphlets on the poor, extending back to 924 A.D.[23] (Sir George figures prominently in the 1834 Report as overseer of the model parish of Southwell.) From his review it becomes apparent that the commissioners of 1832-4 (and the same would apply to those of 1905-9) fashioned their report from a public stock of knowledge functioning for them as a kind of semantic construction kit. For example, the remedial virtues of the 'well-regulated workhouse' are expounded in the 1697 Act to establish a workhouse in Bristol and the 1703 Act to establish one in Worcester, while the 1711 Norwich Workhouse Act speaks of strenuous workhouse discipline as a cure for 'idleness, laziness and debauchery amongst the meaner sort'; similarly, the 1834 proposal to incorporate small parishes into a single Union to ensure more efficient management is prefigured in the rationale of the 1697 Bristol Workhouse Act.

My point here is not that the commissioners were somehow remiss as inquirers or that they were guilty of merely rehashing old ideas but that a social report in order to produce reality and knowledge effects must be articulated through an existing stock of knowledge containing codes operative beyond the reading process which the person who reads can use without question. Literal reading of a text requires membership of the (ethno)methodological communities whose codes it uses. With regard to specialized communities (for example, those to which early nineteenth century parish poor law officials and Parliamentary legislators belonged) the requirement may be met through the tuition of the text itself – indeed this may be made an explicit purpose, as in anthropological attempts to socialize the reader into an alien culture – but the possibility of such tuition, whether overt or not, depends ultimately upon actual membership of a taken-for-granted code of common understandings. A text must play upon pre-existing plausibility structures in order to achieve referential realism and this is done through evoking the familiar grammar and vocabulary, the significatory rules and semantemes, making up a field of discourse.

Further examination of the Reports shows them to be playing upon two prior plausibility structures in particular:
1 The attribution of actions to rational means-ends calculation.
2 The circumstantial projection of normal courses of action.
The 1834 Report provides sufficient illustration of both points.

The attribution of actions to rational calculation   Max Weber based his ideal type of method for making actions intelligible on the assumption that the most universally understandable, intersubjectively clear form of action is that which can be construed as purposive rationality. Classical economics has made use of the same plausibility structure in building its supply-demand models, and the 1834 Report does so in predictively explaining

poor law practices as strategic games in which rational players
seek optimal pay-offs within a system of rules. Three of these
are the settlement game, the bastardy law game and the labour-
rate game. I will describe the last only.

The game developed from an attempt in some rural areas to
find a better solution to the problem of surplus agricultural
labourers than using poor-rate funds to employ them in make-
work tasks such as breaking stones and digging ditches. The
solution in this case involved (a) designating some portion of
the total rate as a labour-rate, the amount to be assessed according to some quantifiable property criterion such as rental value
or acreage; (b) requiring that amount to be discharged by hiring labourers, failing which the money was to be paid directly
to the overseer. Only labourers legally settled in the parish
could be counted towards discharging the rate. There are two
points of strategic relevance here: first, the larger the labour-
rate in a parish the smaller the residual poor-rate; secondly,
rate-payers varied in their need and ability to hire labourers.
For someone with high labour needs the optimum strategy would
be to maximize the labour-rate component – discharging his
assessment through paying for labour he would need anyway –
and to seek an assessment criterion shifting as much of the
burden as possible onto those with low or no labour needs.
Further refinements of the game are observable in losers'
complaints:

> I am a gunsmith, but do all the work myself; I have not
> any garden or any means of employing a labourer ... my-
> self and many of my neighbours, having no use for a hus-
> bandry man, ought not to pay labour we do not want
> [p. 111].

> I am compelled to contribute to the poor-rate, in alleviation
> of the opulent farmer. The churchwarden as well as the
> overseers of the parish are composed of opulent farmers
> and millers; therefore it is to their interest to uphold and
> support a labour-rate because they alone are benefited to
> the great injury of very many tradesmen, shopkeepers and
> others, who have no opportunity of employing surplus
> labour, and which labour they, the farmers, cannot dispense
> with [p. 112].

Grass land usually had low labour requirements but high rental
value relative to arable land (p. 114):

> I consider the arable farmer ought to take double the men
> as grass farmers do, to make it on a fair scale ... I hope
> there will be a fair difference made between arable land and
> grass land, and I hope all renting farmers will be allowed
> to count their sons as labourers on their father's farms with-
> out being beholden to the overseer to allow just whom he

thinks proper ... if sons are not allowed, it must soon ruin men like myselves with families.

And from a farmer with a large acreage of poor quality sheep-walk land (p. 115):

The occupiers of the good land are more numerous than those of the poor land ... we are out-voted in the select vestry, who agreed that the labour-rate should be levied not by value, but by acreage.

In general, the farmers of arable land - using their voting strength in vestry meetings plus threatened withdrawals of custom from recalcitrant tradespeople - were able to win the labour-rate game. Having made certain behaviours motivation-ally transparent as formally rational actions, the text then weaves them into its overall accounting scheme of moral disinte-gration (invoking collective representations to show their 'real' meaning) - p. 126:

When the direct employers of labour have for some time been sanctioned by the legislature in extorting from others the payment of a part of the wages of their labourers, when the best class of labourers, those who are not settled in the place of their employment, have disappeared, when what now remains of repugnance to relief or of degradation in accept-ing it has been destroyed by its being merged in wages, when all the labourers have been converted into a semi-servile population without fear but without hope, where can we look for the materials of improvement?

A sceptical reader might doubt the hyperbolic tone of this collection passage and call it exaggerated but such criticism would already postulate a reality of which this is an exaggera-tion and confirm the deep constitutive innocence of the text.

The circumstantial projection of typical courses of action There is a well-known distinction in social analysis, attributed usually to Alfred Schutz, between 'in order to' and 'because' accounts of social behaviour. Rational calculation belongs to the former, stressing the teleological drawing out of behaviour by a con-scious goal, while circumstantial projection combines elements of 'in order to' calculation with anterior propulsions of situa-tion and character. The basic plausibility principle here is familiar in journalistic accounts of domestic and world affairs and from mass media depictions of detection work and courtroom scenes, namely, that a concurrence of motive, means and opportunity is sufficient to establish the probable occurrence of a course of action - which is to say, its actuality. As was noted earlier, in applying Bloom's map of misreading, the 1834 Report makes effective use of this device in typifying the behaviour of overseers, magistrates and vestry members. The following quotation from p. 58 on the defects of overseers provides sufficient illustration:

> Further evidence can scarcely be wanted, but if it is required it will be found in abundance in our Appendix. But if there were no such evidence, if the results of the experiment [i.e. the inquiry] were not known, what could have been expected from functionaries almost always reluctant, unless indeed when their object is fraud, who neither come to their office with knowledge nor retain it long enough to acquire knowledge, who have little time and still less motive for attention to its duties, on whom every temptation to misconduct has been accumulated, who have to give or to refuse public money to their own workmen, dependants, customers, debtors, relations, friends, and neighbours, who are exposed to every form of solicitation and threat, who are rewarded for profusion by ease and popularity, and punished for economy by labour, odium, and danger to their properties and even their persons.

There is an open admission here that confirming detail is secondary, even redundant, to the acceptance of a circumstantial projection. We all know, given these circumstances and normal motives, how most people in the long run will behave. The projection stands on its own as a self-evident account of how things in general must be, capable of finding any confirming detail that it requires. And if details arise that do not fit they can always be accommodated as special cases and exceptions to the rule. With Durkheim in mind, I would interpret the passage to mean that details have a reality effect conferred upon them through conforming to the a priori collective representations of common sense. Circumstantial projections convey reality because they stand against and collectively incorporate particulars, not because they are derived from particulars and represent facts.

PRIOR PLAUSIBILITY STRUCTURES AND REALITY EFFECTS

The significance of prior plausibility structures for reality effects is more or less directly stated in a variety of constructionist discourses on social methodology, notably those of phenomenology on knowing the everyday world through the natural attitude, ethnomethodology on facts as social accomplishments, and historiology on how the no longer existent can be knowledge objects. I will cite these briefly (incorporating some ideas introduced previously) in order to extend the dimensions of the topic.

Schutz and Luckmann assert that in the social structuring of everyday experience the particularities of selfhood are trans-

cended through the idealized assumptions of interchangeable
standpoints and congruent relevance systems:

> The fundamental axioms of the social, natural attitude are,
> first, the existence of intelligent (endowed with conscious-
> ness) fellow-men and, second, the experienceability (in
> principle similar to mine) by my fellow-men of the objects
> in the life-world ....If I were there, where he is now, then
> I would experience things in the same perspective, distance,
> and reach as he does.[24]

These idealizations together form the 'thesis of the reciprocity
of perspectives', of which they say:

> This thesis is for its part the foundation for the social
> formation and linguistic fixation of Objects of thought
> which replace, or better, which substitute for the Objects
> of thought present in my presocial world.[25]

I am not interested in this as a possible statement about
cognitive development (the notion of thought objects in a pre-
social world is in any case incomprehensible to me) but as a
description of one of the resources through which it is possible
for textual reality to repressively displace situated reality as
its authentic truth. Similarly, I would treat their further discussion of departures from the face-to-face situation of temporal
and spatial immediacy (the 'thou-orientation' and the 'we-relation') as a description of what is involved in this displacement
(i.e. what the situated realm looks like from within the textual
realm of reality). Beyond the immediacy of the 'we-relation'
others are experienced in the 'they-orientation' as functional
types engaged in typical processes of action:

> Through their detachment from the subjective processes in
> inner duration, these processes ('typical experiences of
> someone') come to contain the idealizations of 'and so forth'
> and 'again and again', that is, assumptions of typical
> anonymous repeatability ....They [typical actors] are
> relevant for me only as they conform to these typifications
> [of attributes, functions, behaviour].[26]

This can be taken as a statement of how reality reports play
upon pre-existing plausibility structures just as the following
can be understood as a description of how others are experienced
in the reading process:

> The more anonymous the type (by means of which a con-
> temporary is experienced), the more strongly objectivated
> is the meaning-context that is foisted upon him ....This
> factual existence of the contemporary is not immediately
> experienced, but only suspected, assumed, or, rather,

posited as taken for granted. In my actual experience the contemporary only has the status of a point of intersection of typical properties.[27]

In their analysis of objective 'meaning-context', Schutz and Luckmann allot a special place to linguistic sign-systems in a way which again anticipates our own discussion, except that their imagery is that of a graded concentric distancing from a central core of immediate reality rather than one of separate and dialectically tensed realms of reality construction. At the immediate centre - the corporeal here and operative now - of experienced reality, linguistic signs are indexical to what is going on in the 'zone of operation', but

After language is acquired as a coherent semantic-syntactic structure, it becomes to a great extent independent to the concrete we-relation and of the immediacy of experience ....Language can then provide knowledge about realities which not only transcend the current experience of the individual but are practically, if not in principle inaccessible to him.[28]

The topic of radically separate realms of reality construction could have been implied in the ambivalent reference to the practical and perhaps principled inaccessibility of the realities of detached language to the current experience of the individual, but that potentiality is subsequently abandoned by the depiction of writing as a mere system of marks objectivating spoken language on a more stable basis, and by asserting the readiness with which 'translation' can be achieved back and forth along the posited dimension of subjective-situated to objective-anonymous sign-systems:

Subjective knowledge can be translated into the 'idealizing' and 'anonymous' interpretive matrices of a system of signs, and it can again be transformed into subjective knowledge by means of an appropriately meaningful retranslation.[29]

Against this glossing of the difference between reading-writing and speaking-hearing as an innocuous separation recoverable by 'translation' and 'retranslation', I am asserting a deep incompatibility which is resolved in social practice as the exercise of political power. To speak of translation is at best a euphemism.

Regarding the specific 'technical' question of the constitutive significance of common-sense reasoning in social reality reporting, I would say (recalling the earlier application of Bloom's 'map of misreading' to our texts) that whereas (a) the person who reads is brought and kept to the page (by devices already described) in a posture of encounter with social reality, it is the case (b) that writing exists as a substitutive effacement of that which it stands for (i.e. situated reality construction) leaving an emptiness (c) which is filled in by the person who reads through recognizing pre-existing plausibility structures in the 'grammar' of the text.[30] It is this recognition of the already known - which is a recognition of how to know rather than any substantive detail - which makes social reality present in reading. The untroubled negotiation of this filling-in process, untroubled that is by loss of constitutive innocence in the course of the act, is what I call literal reading. A comparable point has been made by Murray Murphey in showing how historians depend upon the narrative form of explanation as a functional alternative to scientific explanation grounded on explicit covering laws (i.e. probabilistic or universalistic pro- positions at the top of a deductive hierarchy):

> In scientific explanations, the laws and antecedent condi- tions are made explicit; hence no matter how bizarre the events to be explained may be, the explanation (if success- ful) renders that event intelligible by showing exactly what caused it. In narrative writing, on the other hand, the laws are usually not made explicit. The convincingness of the narrative, therefore, depends upon the presentation of the events of the story in such a way that their sequential occurrence seems to follow causally in terms of laws which are part of the common-sense knowledge of the reader. These laws ... tend to be vague but they are sufficiently clear to permit the reader to recognize at least gross viola- tions. The writer is, therefore, bound by the laws familiar to his readers, and cannot deviate radically from that stock of interpretive knowledge without violating the readers' sense of reality.[31]

I do not quite see it in this way. It is not so much a question of the reader being able to match his common-sense knowledge (grossly or otherwise) with that of 'the writer' as being able to read his common-sense knowledge into the structure of the writing. A text may, after all, refer to strange and distant cultures without loss of reality effect and, conversely, may lose it completely while dwelling upon what is familiar and close. In literature, for example, James Joyce's inclusion of mundane events, Dublin scenes and common place speech in 'Ulysses' do not secure a sense of reality while, on the other hand, the novels of Balzac, Tolstoy, Dostoevsky and others have proved capable of preserving reality effects over time and across translations into foreign languages. Their indifference to cul- tural differences (which are differences of common-sense knowledge) might be taken as evidence of the constitutive power of innocent narration as a communicative form and help to explain its singular utility for historians in their endless quest to stabilize the meaning of past records for present readers. This is a speculative digression, however. The point I really wish to draw from Murphey's formulation is the significance of methodological continuity between reading and extra-reading accounting practices for producing reality effects.

The general topic of continuity as an accounting resource has been brought to view by ethnomethodological observations of how facts for the record are produced through and as organizational work. This sphere of inquiry, being concerned with situated compilations and uses of reality records, lies as it were on the far side of the text as displayed by an interest in reading but its insights are clearly relevant to the issue under discussion. Two references to the literature will be sufficient for our purpose.

Don Zimmerman's study of how workers in a public welfare agency processed claimants' stories into matters of fact sufficient to authorize decisions on assistance includes a section on how they preserved the 'plain fact' character of documents - birth certificates, bank statements, medical records, income tax returns, deeds of ownership, etc. - as part of their work. This was done by seeing them as normal products of ordinary activities involving a record-keeping enterprise:

> Apart from the person undertaking some ordinary activity, there are others involved whose task it is to monitor, facilitate, and record the course and outcome of that activity. In turn, the transaction between such persons is made accountable in terms of the *motivationally transparent* character of their respective roles. That is, the person whose affairs a document reports is a person who, via the account, is seen to be pursuing some commonplace project (for example, buying property) for understandable reasons appropriate to that project, and others are viewed as going about *their* commonplace projects, (for example, selling property, recording titles, assessing taxes, etc.) for reasons appropriate to their occupational obligations ....In short, the authority of various documents is made accountable in terms of the routine, organized ways in which these unremarkable projects are geared to one another under the auspices of typified, generally known interests or motives, and with adumbrated reference to the more or less standardized procedures that presumably control the gearing.[32]

Similarly, the Poor Law Reports make the behaviours and outcomes they document unproblematic matters of plain fact by displaying them as motivationally transparent products of rational calculation and circumstantial pushes and pulls.

The accomplishment of factual reportage in organizational practice is also the theme of Garfinkel's examination of the work of the Los Angeles Suicide Prevention Center in authoritatively determining whether questionable deaths referred to it by the Coroner's Office were in fact suicides or something else. What a Suicide Center inquiry begins and ends with is a death and its remains - 'the body and its trappings, medicine bottles, notes, bits and pieces of clothing ... rumors, passing remarks, and stories - materials in the "repertoires" of whosoever might be consulted via the common work of conversations'.[33] Between the beginning and the end is a rehearsal of the standard ways of living and dying in our society (i.e. the society of interested parties to the death) to see if one provides a more plausible reading of the remains than the others:

> These whatsoever bits and pieces ... are used to formulate a recognizably coherent, standard, typical, cogent, planful, i.e. a professionally defensible, and thereby, for members, a *recognizably* rational account of how the society worked to produce those remains.[34]

So one might say of the Poor Law inquirers that they began and ended with remains - figures on poor-rates and paupers, anecdotes, records of vestry meetings, conversations with overseers and magistrates, written replies to the rural and town 'queries' etc. - and read into these the ways the society could be working to produce them (the society and not the inquiry itself). What is crucial, however, to literal reading is that these ways are already familiar to the person who reads as ways of being in society. Only then will he merge smoothly into the reading posture hollowed out in the structure of the text and be a fitting reader.

SUMMARY AND CONCLUSION

Let us try and draw together what has been said about the function of prior (extra-textual) plausibility structures in the textual production of reality effects and relate this back to our attempted distinction between transcendental and conventional effects (the latter being confined to the limits and allowances of a genre). The question of function must be specified to the requirements of encounterability beyond the page and constitutive innocence. Focussing on the former requirement it can be argued that the presence of such structures in a text makes the outside world present in reading; when the person who reads encounters the 'methodological' practices of his collectivity in the reasoning of a report, he encounters social reality in the Durkheimean sense. It is not the familiarity of substantive content which is crucial here but the familiarity of ethnomethods or what Garfinkel calls accounting practices. A report which is readable via everyday or institutional competence is a social account which is readable for real. At the same time constitutive innocence is secured because the permeation of text by context allows them to be read as one and precludes any strong sense of the text as an authorial artefact. Authorship is obliterated in the collaborative familiarity of 'we all know' theorizing, or, to put it more circumspectly, is reduced to secondary activities of collecting, classifying, editing, annotating, summarizing at the fringes of a text whose centre is filled by an objectively resistant reality beyond these words. But who else is there to do the filling-in at the moment of reading except the person who reads? And how else other than in a frame of constitutive innocence which includes the person who reads?

On the distinction between transcendental and conventional reality effects, it might be objected by a devil's advocate that what we have identified as constitutive features of factual social reportage - crisis display as an external inquirendo, the referencing of evidential mass, the rhetoric of travel and discovery, confessing the necessary incompleteness of the inquiry, the subordination of particulars to generals, the revelation of consensus, an institutionalized vocabulary, and common-sense theorizing - form a conventional writing genre which is no different in principle than genres like the detective story, the narrative novel or the horror-tale; consequently all reality effects are conventional and the distinction posits a false opposition. In a sense this is true and indeed I rely upon that to provide for the possibility of emancipatory reading as freedom from the negative power of unacknowledged conventionality. So I must say 'transcendental' effects to register their underlying dependence on conventional methods of production and as a reminder that those methods include the systematic blanking of that dependence. Whereas works of literature and art rely upon explicit recognition of their generic codes in order to be appreciated as creative enactments of their possibilities, reality reports, governed by the imperative of constitutive innocence, cannot present themselves thus as symbolic artefacts. Moreover, the nature of the conventions involved is quite different even when the genre of factual reportage has been made explicit. Reports are answerable in the final analysis to conventions of knowing, not conventions of creating; they are to be examined in epistemological terms as representatives of social reality, not aesthetically as exemplars of an art or craft. To get behind their conventional denial of convention, however, it is necessary to pose the essential epistemological question, How do you know? in an adequate way. It is conventionally understood as a request (or challenge) for more proof within shared rules of observation and demonstrativity. I wish to put it to the Poor Law Reports, however, as a request for a description of these rules - as How is knowing being done? - and this is a request which cannot be met by showing still more products of the rules.

Before taking up the examination of knowledge effects it would be appropriate, having said so much about the significance of continuity between text and context, to repeat and stress that for me the fascination of reality reports lies in the ways they are discontinuous with contexts and the conviction that these ways are forced upon them by the exigencies of producing

knowledge effects in reading-writing. What makes the 1834
Report of remarkable historical-political significance is its
decisive discrediting of the adequacy of local interactional practices to undertake poor relief; the report expresses a radical
discontinuity with situated reality construction marking the
beginnings of modern social administration in Great Britain. An
ambivalent endorsement of what was being passed by (though
left underneath rather than behind) can be found in the 1818
House of Lords Committee Report:

> From lapse of time, and a departure from the true spirit
> of the above act (the 43 Elizabeth 1601), *arising frequently
> from the humane exercise* of its supposed powers, abuses
> have undoubtedly been introduced into the general admin-
> istration of the Poor Laws of England; but the Committee
> are nevertheless decidedly of opinion, that the general
> system of those laws, *interwoven as it is with the habits of
> the people*, ought, in the consideration of any measures
> to be adopted for their melioration and improvement, to be
> essentially maintained. [Italics added.]

The 1909 Majority Report also comments (p. 71) on the sub-
version of good administration by situated responsiveness (in
the context of approving the radical break of 1834):

> There is a subtle and constant influence, fostered by the
> kindly instincts of impulsive humanity, which is ever at
> work sapping and undermining restrictions upon the grant
> of public relief ... at times of stress or turmoil it is capable
> of exerting a powerful emotional force which breaks down
> the resistance of all but the firm and convinced administra-
> tor.

Of course, policy reports on social reality do not have to be
so blunt - and under modern conditions of sensitivity to public
and mass media opinion rarely are - but the passage expresses
a dialectical tension inherent to textual reality construction as
a paradigm of the rational organization of life which no amount
of public relations work, procedural humanization or architectural softening can dissolve. Indeed the strenuous proliferation
of such efforts only testifies to the irremediable presence of
the tension they seek to remedy. The search for remedy is
hopeless (though not to be despised for all that) because the
problem lies in an epistemological divide which could only disappear with the disappearance of administration itself. This, I
believe, is the import of Marx's tantalizing vision of the wither-
ing away of the state and of Weber's sobering assessment that
direct pursuit of that vision would only bind life more firmly
into a state bureaucracy.

I end with two more symptoms of administration as an
epistemological problem: the sensitivities of Dr Downes and the

answering mockery of the 1909 Minority Report. The former
represents honest confusion; the latter (and here I echo the
judgement of historians) anticipates the benevolent certainties
of the welfare state. Dr Downes signed the 1909 Majority Report
and registered his reasons in a five-page memorandum which
begins on p. 671:

> I have signed the Majority Report because I desire to sup-
> port the principle that public relief in every form should be
> administered and controlled by one local authority in each
> area. The control of assistance from public funds is a fore-
> most function of government, but it is not one which the
> people of this country would willingly surrender to a regime
> of officialdom, however this may commend itself to the ulti-
> mate aims which have inspired the Minority Report ...
> [After referring to proposals for specialized treatments of
> different classes of the poor] The breaking up of families,
> the removal of old folk from their associates and friends,
> *may outweigh many administrative advantages .... Classifi-
> cation run to an ideal entails many practical difficulties and
> even evils.* [Italics added.]

The Minority Report sees through the equivocation of
Dr Downes's balanced misgivings (breaking up the web of social
life only 'may outweigh' administrative advantage and classification; it entails practical difficulties and perhaps evils but
only so if 'run to an ideal') - and reveals it as simple-minded
sentimentality. (I define sentimentality as any expression of
the desirable which does not take responsibility for its achievement.) This is done on p. 1026 in a section titled 'Some theoretical objections answered' (a title which seizes upon the ideality
of Dr Downes's objection to classification):

> There is the objection that the breaking up of the Poor Law
> involves the breaking up of the family ... that the proposed
> scheme would lead to the harassing of the poor in their
> houses by a multiplicity of officers.

The Minority Report then refers to 'naive objectors' who imagine that if each member of a family was taken to a different
institution 'for treatment' then this would be a barrier to them
ever getting back together. Not so, p. 1027:

> In practice i.e. where this presently happens they find
> each other without difficulty when they emerge from their
> several institutions ....But in so far as any difficulty may
> arise - as, for instance, with the feeble-minded or truant
> children, or with parents wishing to evade their responsi-
> bilities - our scheme provides, for the first time, effective
> machinery for 're-uniting' the family, either voluntarily or
> compulsorily. The Registrar of Public Assistance, advised

daily of all admissions and discharges in every public
institution ... and with his Inquiry and Recovery Officers
instantly in pursuit of husbands and fathers who have run
away from their responsibilities, will, in fact, make it very
difficult for families not to re-unite.

Behind the exultant flow of this dismissive, tongue-in-cheek
response is the deep conviction that rational administration
poses no serious problem of putting together what has been
taken apart, any more than a watch or a machine for a skilled
repairer. This is seen in the fact that having spent three pages
responding in the above style to 'naive objectors' (the simple-
minded), the Minority Commissioners say, 'We pass now to what
appears to us the most *genuine* of the objections made to our
proposals' (p. 1029, italics added), and proceed to discuss the
costs of their proposals and their effects on the rates.

Setting aside stylistic exaggerations and the temptation to
caricature them as the mentality of officialdom (or some such
satirical invention), we must ask how schemes for the rational
reformation of social life are grounded such that they can be
held against the situated practices of social life as their decisive
critique. What are those accounting practices being held accountable to as a higher form of knowledge? In the next chapter I
will argue that they are being held accountable to the requirements of producing knowledge effects in reading-writing. The
problem to be taken up there is how the Reports turn their
referential content into an authoritative knowledge of problems,
causes and remedies. To borrow Louis Althusser's provocative
question:

By what mechanism does the process of knowledge, which
takes place entirely within thought [I would say within
word work], produce the cognitive appropriation of its real
object, which exists outside thought in the real world?[35]

For my purpose I will take this to mean: By what working
methods is a report representing situated practices of social
life such as to achieve knowing in reading?

CHAPTER 5

The production of knowledge effects in the Reports

Since policy reports are specifically concerned with diagnosis and remedy, the two most pertinent questions we can address to the Poor Law Reports are these:

How do they know what is wrong, distorted, confused, irrational, dangerous in the situation?

How do they know what a solution would be; how their recommended changes would be a restoration of rational order?

In both cases the answer must be the description of a writing activity and not a rehearsal of evidence, proof, methods of data collection, logical steps and so on. The procedure will be to assemble such descriptions and incorporate them into analytic themes. I talk of incorporation into themes rather than, say, testing hypotheses because this is really a matter of fashioning a textual analysis rather than a trial of theory by fact.

One theme, drawn from Kantian epistemology, is that knowledge effects are produced in an experience of rule-governed contingency, where the cognitive rules of the knower are recognized as rules out there.[1] For the knower as reader this occurs as a sense of rational legibility in an account. Legibility denotes the evident rationality of a textual representation of reality. To bring this theme to our questions, however, we must think such rules as conventions rather than philosophical absolutes. As a beginning I will consider the operation of taxonomic rules of rationality.

A great deal of that which all three reports find wrong in their minutes of evidence can be characterized, for the sake of preliminary approximation, as illegible objects revealed in taxonomic scandals. That is, denominative dark spots, confused identities and incoherent juxtapositions; in short, heterogeneous categories and categorical disconnections. Correspondingly, the dominant thrust of their recommendations is towards the creation of taxonomic integrity. I phrase this as a deliberate reminder of Jeremy Bentham's criteria for criticizing D'Alembert's map of knowledge and for constructing his own taxonomy not merely to suggest epistemic continuities between disparate writings but to note the operation of a method of rational accounting which will form any content whatsoever in the same way, including the situated content of social life.[2] In its social application, the method collapses moral propriety, administrative order and cognitive rationality into a single configuration. In so far as social policy reports are called for by unresolved tensions between moral, administrative and cognitive orderliness, it can be claimed that the method of taxonomic integrity is ideally suited to their work. Of course, this complementarity is not a matter of happening to find an appropriate methodological instrument, but arises because the method is constitutive of the society which is the source and object of reporting.

There is one more preparatory point before we go into details. Although taxonomic coding is a striking and salient feature of the reports, Foucault's work on epistemic codes alerts us to the possible presence of a second method for producing knowledge effects on paper, namely, the representation of reality as functioning systems which develop over time according to their own inner dynamics.[3] This provides us with a second way of thematizing how the reports do knowledge work (more specifically, how those arrangements of written signs might yield knowledge effects in reading). I will group the materials of the reports together so as to promote comparative analysis.

ILLEGIBLE OBJECTS AND TAXONOMIC SCANDALS

We begin with an apparent paradox in the preliminary statement. If reality is knowable in reading-writing as the recognition of rule-governed contingency, and if illegible objects, taxonomic scandals and so on are brought to view as a lack of this condition, then how could that bringing to view provide for the status of the text as knowledge? How can 'what is wrong' be known if it lacks the condition of knowability?

The nature of the paradox is the same as that remarked by Emile Durkheim in relation to moral order and deviance. Having defined a society as a moral order he argued that even a society of saints would necessarily generate deviance because a moral order can only realize itself in practical detection of that which offends it. Every order of rules seeks and discovers contraventions of itself in order to show what it is. A disciplinary order such as an army training camp necessarily seeks and discovers disobedience; a moral order seeks and discovers deviance; and an epistemological order seeks and discovers error or irrationality. When, for example, the 1834 Report says that an 'evil of settlement by apprenticeship is the influence which it allows to mere accident' (p. 88) (an apprentice was legally settled in and therefore the relief responsibility of the parish where he slept the last night of his apprenticeship, provided that he had slept there for thirty-nine nights any time previously; consequently, an apprentice seaman moored during his last night on a river between two parishes might be 'settled' in either one depending on winds and tides), it is showing itself to be governed by what is lacking in that which it criticizes, i.e. by rules rather than accident. Reality is being held against the demand of rule-government as that which it should be. It is the firm, methodical holding against the demand which is essential for producing a knowledge effect in reading-writing. This 'holding against' has a dual aspect which these reports reveal. The commissioners hold general principle against evidenced reality, recording contraventions as depart- ures from rational order, but in doing so they are holding themselves, which is to say their writing, to that same principle. 'They' (a personification of the texts) in representing what is wrong in the social order display their own constitutive features as a negative presence, a virtual order, hollowed out in the referential content of whatever substantive topics are brought to the page. Since the reality upon which knowledge work is being done is a composition of signs in writing, the rules whose recognition is the act of knowing must be rules internal to that same textual realm of reality construction. From this limitation it follows that the only things which a reality report can knowl- edgeably demonstrate as defects in reality are negations of the conditions for its own reflexive display as an orderly and rational text. The 1834 Report can and must register the situa- tion of the drifting apprentice seaman as a contravention of rational order because the accidental placement of objects in categories is incompatible with itself as knowledge in writing. Of course, a modern reader might smile at the deep concern of the report for this particular contravention of order and say, So what? But this is only to say that the definition of significant categories might change or, more importantly, as Foucault teaches us, that there might be more than one way of meeting the formal requirement of accountable placement in categories. A particular way, belonging to a particular mode of knowledge production, may become dated; yet still - precisely because of that degree of distance which makes it noticeable - permit relevant questioning of the inner dynamics and outer limits of textual practices for making sense of social reality. It is with this in mind that we examine taxonomic scandals and illegible objects in these reports.

I will begin by simply listing such objects, and then take up the very complicated question of how their illegibility is con- veyed. The 1834 Report focusses primarily on the able-bodied male pauper on out-door relief but includes two other illegible objects; the Mixed Workhouse and the Parish Work Gang. The 1909 Reports are far richer in this respect. In the Majority Report we find the Able-bodied Pauper of Working Age; the Ins-and-Outs; the Sick Pauper; the Casual Pauper; the Poor Widow; the Aged Poor; the General Mixed Workhouse; the Casual Worker; and the Vagrant. The Minority Report has, in addition to the Sick Pauper and the Aged and Infirm Pauper; the Heterogeneous Relieving Officer, the General Inspector, the Able-Bodied Woman, the Mixed Workhouse Official (also called the Master-Matron team), and the Destitution Authority.

As to the question of how these various objects are illegible and whether in different ways, this cannot be answered by simply repeating the adverse words of the commissioners because these are, for the most part, only cultural conventions

for registering an experience of illegibility and lack reflective
power to thematize the possibility of that experience. In order
to initiate reflection we must interpret their words as expressions of the possible ways in which reality can be found wanting
(i.e. disorderly, confused, inadequate) in the constitutive
realm of the text. One way, underlying the objectionability of
the Parish Work Gang, is to show that an established legisign[4]
(in this case 'work') is being applied to phenomena in which it
cannot be recognized or, worse still, which are negatives of it.
The typical activities of the gangs are said to be 'amusement',
'talking over their grievances', 'petty thefts', 'pilfering',
'poaching', 'idle work', 'nominal labour' and 'no work at all'
(1834 Report pp. 21-2 passim). From this improper application
of a proper name, the existence of a counterfeit category which
is a nominal mockery of the real thing, certain consequences
follow:
(a) The occupants of this falsely named semantic space are
beyond rule. Not only do they break the law ('universally, they
are in the habit of stealing turnips, or posts, or any little
thing that comes to hand') but they laugh at supervisors and
threaten them with violence. Practical governance is conspicuously absent.
(b) Genuine labourers who enter this space are corrupted by its
falsity: 'Whatever the previous character of a man may have
been, he is seldom able to withstand the corruption of the
roads' (1834 Report, p. 23). That is to say 'pretending to
break stones' and 'idle work' on the roads. The honest worker
no longer governed by the legisign work becomes as illegible
as the gang he joins. He loses his character, his identity and,
therefore, his identifiability.

The counterfeit category is one mode of illegibility for taxonomic knowing. Others, however, are present in the able-bodied
pauper and the mixed workhouse.

The 'Able-bodied Pauper on Outdoor Relief' is illegible because
it merges contradictory legisigns in one category. It is a heterogeneous category which bonds essential or natural differences
into a single identity. Like any unnatural union it is typically
represented as something monstrous, perverted and grotesque.
The Able-bodied Pauper 'puts on the brute' (p. 49); the 'common pauper appearance' is 'dirty, ill-fed, discontented, careless
and vicious' (p. 52); paupers are 'domesticated animals, fed,
lodged and provided for by the parish' (p. 54); the horror of
the pauper's moral debasement is as difficult to describe as 'the
horrors of a shipwreck or a pestilence', to appreciate it one
must have heard the pauper 'threaten to abandon his wife and
family unless more money is allowed him - threaten to abandon
an aged bed-ridden mother, to turn her out of his house and
lay her down at the overseer's door unless he is paid for giving
her shelter; he must hear parents threatening to follow the
same course with regard to their sick children' (p. 54).
These emotional words register an encounter with an illegible

object formed by a merging of administrative and moral legisigns which the knowledge code of the report dictated must be kept apart. We must understand the necessity of that dictation however, as the structural necessity of a sign-system in writing, not as a political, economic or psychological necessity.

The illegibility of the able-bodied pauper

The 1834 Report frequently praises the administrative clarity of Elizabethan legisigns. They clearly separated the working poor (those who obtain a mere subsistence) from the indigent (those unable to obtain even a subsistence), and strongly excluded the former from any public relief whatsoever. Within the indigent category they defined two identification categories - the able-bodied and the non-able-bodied (the impotent) - and two corresponding treatment categories: arduous work and necessary relief (such as out-door relief in money or kind). Placement according to individual characteristics was clearly defined; categories unambiguously separated and linked; contingency was properly rule-governed; 'the duty of the magistrate tolerably plain'; and in total a 'tolerably regulated society' was constituted (p. 72). Subsequent legislation, however, is a sad history of taxonomic obfuscation. Not only has it allowed out-door relief to the able-bodied, thus undermining the difference between two essentially different classes of pauper, but worse still has undermined that between indigent persons and the industrious poor (p. 72):

> The 35 Geo. III (1793) removed all these fences; it recognized as objects of relief, industrous persons, and enabled the magistrate, at his just and proper discretion, to order it to be given in a way which should not be injurious to their comfort, domestic situation and happiness.

The inherent evil of discretionary relief to the industrious poor has been institutionalized as magistrates' scales of relief drawn up for their areas. It is admitted that such 'codes' are better than 'favour or caprice' but the 'evil resides in the practice not in the scale' (p. 72). Two instances of this double undermining of differences can be given:
a) a senior magistrate, asked upon what principle he ordered relief to able-bodied labourers, said that he gave a certain sum for every child beyond the third (p. 72):

> Upon further asking him if he considered that to be the proper and legitimate construction of the statute of Elizabeth, he stated that he did so entirely, and that he thought that when a man had four children, he might fairly be considered within the meaning of the Act as 'impotent', which he further explained by saying that he considered it impossible for any labouring man to support four children.

(b) Insatiable and violent demands for relief by labourers have been let loose by 'vague terms'. Moreover (p. 29):

> those who work though receiving good wages, being called *poor*, and classed with the really indigent, think themselves entitled to a share of the 'poor funds'

Taxonomic confusion deregulates desires and expectations, contingency is no longer rule-governed, and monstrous beings no longer recognizable as members of a society are produced.

The loss of clear demarcation between the able-bodied and the impotent pauper (signified in treating one like the other) also deregulates other contingencies: the moral sentiments of punitive indignation and charity. The Elizabethan system of legisigns was a legible way of organizing the discharge of these contrary sentiments onto appropriate categories to form a rationally accountable moral order. The 1834 Report displays corruption of its categories as a dangerous moral disorder which can only be resolved by taxonomic reformation. The able-bodied pauper draws upon himself charitable sentiments which belong to the impotent; conversely, the impotent are treated punitively in a way that belongs only to the able-bodied (p. 78)

> Resistance to the demands of the bold and turbulent (by overseers) is seldom attempted, on the plea that the magistrates cannot be depended on for their support in such cases; while, on the other hand, the true objects of charity, the helpless and the impotent, are sometimes so harshly treated as to justify that interference by the magistrate on their behalf, which makes good the overseer's excuse in the former cases. By the joint operation of these two ill-assorted functions, mischief is progressing with a fearful rapidity.

In taxonomic terms we would say that the moral sentiments are out of categorical place, and anything out of place in taxonomic knowing is harmful. The impotent are persecuted (bringing discipline into disrepute) and the able-bodied have their 'moral character annihilated' (p. 49). Having no moral character to identify them, they are hardly legible as social objects.

Legibility as an integral structure of signs
Moral order is a clue to the necessary dictation of taxonomic integrity as long as one follows Durkheim's dictum that a moral order is the same as a social order and adds, (a) that a social order is an order of signs and symbols, and (b) that such an order articulates, arranges and rearranges itself through its human agents (in this we recall what theorists like Levi-Strauss Althusser and Foucault have in common). The importance of this is to resist any temptation to engage in a psychological-

motivational-purposive explanation of the 1834 Report's concern for taxonomic integrity. For example, that people experienced stresses, tensions, strains, contradictions in their environment which impelled them to take action. The inadequacy of any such formulation is that it mystifies stresses, tensions, etc. by locating them in a reified object (the society, the economy, and so on) whose externality to actors is unaccountable and can only be asserted as a methodological dogma. Against this we would insist that the crisis of 1834 belonged to a way of knowing things rather than being an objective property of things themselves. Yet it was not merely 'in the mind'; such stresses, tensions, etc. do have an experiential origin and objective meaning. Their origin (which is also a constant source) is a system of signs and they have objective meaning as the active, reactive and mutually adjustive processes of a sign-system in operation (just as Wittgenstein argues that the meaning of a word is that of a move in a language-game). The moves performed in the representation of the able-bodied pauper are certainly reactions to moral ambivalence (a positive and negative moral valence in a single category) but these occur within possibilities of meaning given by the formal characteristics of signs and must be analysed as such. For example, A.J. Greimas pursuing a structuralist analysis of sign-systems, has suggested that the 'elementary structure of signification' (let us say for our purpose the meaning of a legisign) takes the form of a set of binary contrasts called 'the semantic rectangle'.[5] According to Greimas the meaning of a sign (S) presupposes: (a) a concept of that which actively contradicts it (-S); (b) a concept of that which is simply other than itself (S); (c) a concept of that which negates the active negative and yet is still different from the original sign (-S). Typically this negative of a negation is unexplicated or enigmatic and constitutes the focal point of attempts to secure the integrity of a sign structure through new meanings.

Since the dominant theme of 1834 is the corruption of the independent labourer we may take this as the originary sign (S) which the report seeks to secure. The name itself however, stands for an identificatory attribute (industriousness) and a social response (reward) which must also be included in the rectangle. The model of legibility which the report projects onto its details can now be presented in a formal diagram:

$$S \left(\begin{array}{l} \text{Independent Labourer} \\ \text{= Industriousness} \\ \text{= Reward} \end{array} \right) \quad -S \left(\begin{array}{l} \text{Able-Bodied Pauper} \\ \text{= Idleness} \\ \text{= Punishment} \end{array} \right)$$

$$-\overline{S} \left(\begin{array}{l} \text{? Rehabilitated Pauper} \\ \text{? = Corrigibility} \\ \text{? = Reinstatement} \end{array} \right) \quad \overline{S} \left(\begin{array}{l} \text{Impotent Pauper} \\ \text{= Incapacity} \\ \text{= Charity} \end{array} \right)$$

I have placed question marks in the fourth corner to indicate that these terms have been read into the text - particularly those passages which celebrate the miraculous conversions effected in model 'dispauperised' parishes (pp. 130, 131, and 145) - rather than taken from it. The muted presence of the concept of rehabilitation in 1834, its drowning out by the dominating theme of punishing able-bodied idleness, has been used by some observers as evidence that the report was an instrument of class warfare, an act of brutal aggression against the working class. S.E. Finer has sought to modify such judgements by showing that its chief author, Edwin Chadwick, was working on proposals for 'collateral aids' (better housing, education, health care, etc.) to complement the repressive measures recommended in the deterrent workhouse test but did not finish them in time to be included in the report: 'Its non-appearance has played a large part in creating the legend of Chadwick as a black-hearted enemy of the poor.'[16]

Our interest in the production of knowledge objects suggests a completely different interpretation of this implicit presence and conspicuous non-appearance of the positively rehabilitated pauper in 1834, one which comprehends, moreover, the conspicuous presence of this figure in 1909 and the corresponding relegation of punishment for idleness to a background position. In brief, it is that the punitive concept of able-bodied idleness belongs to the episteme of taxonomic representation while the rehabilitative concept of the curable pauper belongs to that of dynamic reproduction. The latter is thought ruled by the organic idealities of function and development rather than the taxonomic idealities of identity and difference; social response categories are thought as restorations or cultivations of functional capacity rather than as desert categories matched to identification categories. Categorical connectives are thought as diagnostic insights rather than moral judgements. The problematic fourth corner in the semantic rectangle projected by the legisign 'Independent Labourer' and its active negation, 'The Able-Bodied Pauper', thus appears not as the mere completion of a binary system but as the alien intimation of an incompatible knowledge code. It has then the significance of a dialectical rather than a merely logical negation.

Our three documents can be analysed in these terms as a single text trying solutions to the problem of achieving an orderly distribution of reward, punishment, charity and rehabilitation (a standard social control response set) across a single typology of poverty and need, but resisted by the circumstance that whereas the first three belong together in the flat, exterior spatiality of a table of differences, the fourth belongs to the organic, interior spatiality of developmental entities and functioning systems. The individual and society are thoughtfully appropriated here in another fashion.

As to the solutions they attempt. The 1834 Report moves almost exclusively in the first space; it is preoccupied by punitive deterrence and the problem of contamination arising from boundary breakdowns. We have seen this in previous discussion.

The same can be seen again in its talk of categorical disconnections as evils, and reconnections as simultaneously moral and
administrative reforms. It is still haunted, however, by the
concept of rehabilitation and its non-appearance. In the very
last paragraph (p. 204) this is belatedly acknowledged:

> It will be observed that the measures which we have sug-
> gested are intended to produce rather negative than positive
> effects; rather to remove the debasing influences to which
> a large portion of the labouring population is now subject,
> than to afford new means of prosperity and virtue. We are
> perfectly aware that for the general diffusion of right
> principles and habits we are to look, not so much to any
> economic arrangements and regulations as to the influence
> of a moral and religious education ... one great advantage
> of any measure which will remove or diminish the evils of
> the present system is that it will in the same degree remove
> the obstacles which now impede the progress of instruction,
> and intercept its results ....*As the subject is not within
> our Commission, we will not dwell on it further.* [Italics
> added.]

Certainly, the subject was not named in their terms of inquiry
nor was it looked at in their report, yet, as we have indicated
in the semantic rectangle, it was present as a latent element of
the meaning structure they sought to clarify, and as a necessary,
though subversive, implication of trying to think that semantic
space in its entirety. The subject was within their Commission
even though excluded from their report.

Continuing the same terminology of comparison, the 1909
Majority Report moves through both spaces in a medley of topics
and, seeking to resolve them through a multiplication of multi-
levelled authorities, ends in administrative incoherence which
the Minority Report satirizes as an 'elaborate and mysterious
framework' and a 'swollen Poor Law'. Its own quest for clarity,
which is to say legibility, is conducted as an attempted abandonment of the reward-punishment-charity space and erasure of
the pauper as a legisign (discussed as the break-up of the Poor
Law) in order to decisively occupy a space of rehabilitative
treatment governed by diagnostic categories of functional
disorder. Its break is by no means a clean one, however. In
many respects it is still caught in the imperatives of taxonomic
rationality; moreover, the will to punish idleness still survives
though now as a residual frustration rather than an overt
intent.

The General Mixed Workhouse and the question of treatment
We must go back to what the reports know as wrong in their
realities, and to the how of this knowing as their rules of
rational order. The General Mixed Workhouse is a useful beginning. It is an illegible object in all three reports but whether

in the same way or not remains to be seen in their words.

The 1834 Report introduces the object as the 'very seldom properly denominated workhouse'. Referring to Chadwick's previously published account of maladministration in the rural workhouses of Reading, it is said (p. 29) that

> in the absence of classification, discipline, and employment ... the Reading workhouses seem to be merely fair specimens of the ordinary workhouses in thriving towns.

As an example of the latter, the ex-workhouse-master of St Pancras, London, is quoted on the same page:

> As little or no classification can take place, the younger soon acquired all the bad habits of the older, and became for the most part as vitiated. This is peculiarly the case with respect to young girls.

A concluding section on the Oxford House of Industry says (p. 31):

> It is a large almshouse in which the young are trained in idleness, ignorance, and vice; the able-bodied maintained in sluggish sensual indolence; the aged and more respectable exposed to all the misery that is incident to dwelling in such a society, without government or classification.

The object reappears in greater detail in support of a recommendation that a proposed central board be empowered to frame and enforce regulations for the government of workhouses, these to be uniform throughout the country. Again it is displayed through images of corruption and contamination as the inherent accompaniments of unregulated social intercourse and lack of classification. Captain Pringle, an Assistant Commissioner, testifies that in the workhouses he inspected classification was 'never more than nominal'; in one he learned that the boys slept 'each with one of the men' to keep them quiet, in another that one of the girls was impregnated by the brother of the workhouse contractor. A curate bemoans the 'want of a proper and extensive subdivision, so that the bad may be completely separated from the good' (p. 171). The commissioners observe (p. 172) that

> Even in the larger workhouses internal subdivisions do not afford the means of classification, where the inmates dine in the same rooms, or meet and see each other in the ordinary business of the place ... it is almost impossible to prevent the formation and extension of vicious connections.

At this point a subtle ambiguity enters the text (a reminder of the enigmatic fourth corner of the semantic rectangle) which hinges upon an unresolved hesitation between treatment as a form of social behaviour in everyday life and treatment as a form of technical intervention (e.g. medical treatment). So far the mixed workhouse has been displayed as self-evidently lacking in rational (and moral) order simply because it lacks classifications to keep the identical together and the different apart; the self-evident taxonomic defects of contingency without class rule; reality unregulated by names; or a mere heap of words without grammatical structure and syntactic connection. Now we read, however, that paupers must be divided into at least four classes - the aged and really impotent; the children; the able-bodied females; the able-bodied males - and placed in separate buildings so that each class might receive 'an appropriate treatment' (p. 172). Which meaning of treatment is intended? The classes hardly look like diagnostic categories, and our inclination towards a social understanding of 'appropriate treatment' is reinforced by an adjacent passage:

> One part of a class of adults often so closely resembles a part of another class as to make any distinction in treatment appear arbitrary and capricious to those who are placed in the inferior class, and to create discontents.

The passage speaks of rationalizing invidious distinctions of treatment, and invidious distinctions are the stuff of social (i.e. moral) behaviour. 'Appropriate' here can mean nothing more than socially proper, it has no connotation of technical efficacy. The security of understanding is disturbed, however, by a subsequent (p. 173) elaboration of what is meant by appropriate treatment:

> the old might enjoy their indulgences without torment from the boisterous; the children be educated, and the able-bodied subjected to such courses of labour and discipline as will repel the indolent and vicious.

It is the concept of education as an appropriate treatment which is troublesome in this list. Admittedly it is typically conjoined with 'moral' and 'religious', but still the final paragraph of the report refers to elevating the 'intellectual' as well as the 'moral condition' of the poor and, in any case, how could the idea of education as a treatment peculiarly appropriate to children be thought except by seeing the child as a repository of hidden forces (potentialities) which will develop through the time of its stages into a fully functional adult? Of course, it might be objected that we are reading a modern concept of education back into the text. But the text is not that far removed from us, we can decode it in literal reading without much effort, so there is no anachronistic imposition involved. The modern concept is there as a possible meaning because this is what such words have come to mean in being institutionalized.

The introduction of education as a treatment does not stand alone as a source of ambiguity. It is reinforced by references to other examples of the principle of beneficial classification; such as the establishment of specialized institutions for the lunatic, the blind, and the deaf and dumb, all managed by persons of 'appropriate qualification'. Again we are led to wonder whether the names of the categories are being dictated by the idealities of function and development rather than identity and difference. We can do no more than wonder, however, because every other part of the report concerned with the proper treatment of individuals is informed by the second, taxonomic code (which, we must continually remind ourselves, is one manifestation of how writing can be knowledge). In the report's use of the code, human beings are brought to knowledge through placement on a moral grid, structured by the names of vices and virtues, according to visible characteristics of conduct and appearance. Each place has attached to it, like a predicate attached to its subject in a sentence, an appropriate condition of pain or pleasure. This expresses the self-evidently rational form of social and moral order in taxonomic knowing.

It is an order to which any existent arrangement of conduct and condition can be held for judgement, just as any arrangement of words can be held to grammatical rules of correct structure. The judgements on categorical misconnection, disconnection and reconnection are deeply pious judgements of good and bad grammar. Consider these two samples from the 1834 Report. The first is from pp. 33-4:

> All other classes are restrained from misconduct by fear of the evils which may result to their families. Parochial legislation rejects this sanction ... if any remonstrance is made on account of the applicant's bad character, the reply of the magistrate commonly is, the children must not suffer for it ....It appears to the pauper that the Government has undertaken to repeal, in his favour, the ordinary laws of nature ... that no one shall lose the means of comfortable subsistence, whatever be his indolence, prodigality, or vice: in short, that the penalty which, after all, must be paid by some one for idleness and improvidence, is to fall, not on the guilty person or on his family, but on the proprietors of the lands and houses encumbered by his settlement.

The predicate of punishment has not only been disconnected from its proper subject but misconnected to another. The second sample is from p. 44:

> We have seen that one of the objects attempted by the present administration of the Poor Laws is to repeal *pro tanto* that law of nature by which the effects of each man's improvidence or misconduct are borne by himself and his family. The

effect of that attempt has been to repeal *pro tanto* the law
by which each man and his family enjoy the benefit of his
own prudence and virtue. In abolishing punishment, we
equally abolish reward. Under the operation of the scale
system – the system which directs the overseers to *regulate*
the incomes of the labourers according to their families –
idleness, improvidence, or extravagance occasion no loss,
and consequently diligence and economy can afford no gain.
But to say merely that these virtues afford no gain, is an
inadequate expression: they are often the causes of absolute
loss.

Anecdotal instances are then given of the many ways in which
the condition of able-bodied paupers is actually better than that
of independent labourers. This obliteration of differences and
reversal of identities is demoralizing and therefore destructive
at the individual and collective levels. Speaking of proposals to
extend the labour-rate system of compelling rate-payers to
provide work for those unable or unwilling to find it themselves,
they comment (p. 126):

The line between the pauper and the independent labourer
would be obliterated; and we do not believe that a country
in which that distinction has been completely effaced, and
every man, whatever be his conduct or his character, ensured
a comfortable subsistence, can retain its prosperity, or even
its civilization.

The significance of the line for governing the contingencies
of poverty and proper responses to them is so crucial that the
drawing of it cannot be entrusted to human rulers. Discretionary, which is to say personal, response to applicants exposes
any rule of relief to eroding sentiments. These are named
(p. 139) as 'feelings of pity, the impulse of blind benevolence
... or dread of unpopularity from the imputation of hard-
heartedness'. The fault of situated responsiveness is that it
allows for exceptions and 'Every exception, every violation of
the general rule to meet a real case of unusual hardship, lets
in a whole class of fraudulent cases by which that rule must in
time be destroyed.' (p. 146). The solution is:
1 Establish 'well-regulated workhouses' with finely determined
regimens guaranteeing (a) that they are all the same (meeting
the requirements of denominational stability and categorical
homogeneity) and (b) that the condition of life in them is 'less
eligible' than that of the independent labourer outside.
2 Absolutely forbid any relief to the able-bodied except through
entering such places. With regard to the able-bodied, the well-
regulated workhouse operates automatically to separate the
deserving from the undeserving and ensure that a person's
condition of life is appropriate to his conduct (p. 148):

By the means which we propose, the line between those who do and those who do not need relief is drawn, and drawn perfectly. If the claimant does not comply with the terms on which relief is given to the destitute, he gets nothing; and if he does comply, the compliance proves the truth of the claim - namely, his destitution.

In this we see again the principle of taxonomic knowing enunciated in Bentham's method of exhaustive bifurcation, namely, that the most secure form of classification is the either/or dichotomy. The claim to perfect classification is, however, a rhetorical excess. The 1834 Report, like any empirical knowledge production, posits a transcendental reality which cannot be completely contained in its concepts. Thus it is admitted that genuinely sick able-bodied paupers may be given 'medical attendance' outside the workhouse. Moreover 'cases of real hardship' may occur, but these must be dealt with by 'individual charity' and are beyond the scope of any 'system of relief' (p. 146). Finally, to repeat an earlier observation, there is the unresolved question of positive treatment for special categories. All these exceptions arise from the demands of the case against those of classificatory order and clear demarcation. We must now see how these conflicting demands are worked out in the 1909 Reports. (In effect this is an attempt to complete the project, taken from Foucault, of tracing epistemic breaks in the formation of these documents.) There are three related topics, already broached, which allow us to try further:
1 The critique of the general mixed workhouse.
2 The distinction between moral and technical connectives in forming treatment categories.
3 The way objects other than the general workhouse are formulated as illegible and according to what idealities of form.
In its discussion of the general workhouse, the 1909 Majority Report picks up and amplifies the latent ambiguities of 1834. It recalls the 1834 recommendation that classes of pauper be placed in separate buildings for appropriate treatment in order to criticize the subsequent practice (for financial and administrative convenience) of classifying within a single building. The criticism is introduced as a practical rather than principled objection, and in a strictly taxonomic mode. There are certain common spaces in a single building - the dining hall, the sick ward - where classification breaks down and contamination ensues. Through mixing the 'better young women' with 'the depraved', they pick up their bad habits and lose their identity; children are corrupted by coming into contact with adult paupers and beginning to take on their identity. Similarly it is wrong to mix the aged with the able-bodied since either the former are treated too severely or the latter 'too leniently' (p. 126). As Edmund Leach remarks in his analysis of cultures as sign-systems:

> The more sharply we define our boundaries, the more
> conscious we become of the dirt that has ambiguously got
> onto the wrong side of the frontier. Boundaries become
> dirty by definition [I would say by situated use] and we
> devote a great deal of effort to keeping them clean, just
> so that we can preserve confidence in our category system.[7]

Up to now the Majority commissioners are behaving like regular
boundary cleaners, which means that they are knowing reality
in a taxonomic way. But then, in recommending larger administrative areas to make separate institutions viable, the possibility of a break appears: 'Classification affords opportunities
for curative and preventative treatment.' (p. 127). The possibility is subsequently confirmed in the contorted attempts
of the report to repair the inherited legisigns of pauper administration by linking them to 'technical' as well as 'moral' courses
of action. Since, as will be shown, it was precisely the inability
of existing legisigns to govern 'technical' courses of action
which constituted the crisis in 1909, their undertaking is, to
say the least, paradoxical.

THE CONCEPT OF CURATIVE TREATMENT AS EVIDENCE OF AN EPISTEMIC BREAK

We can trace the troublesome concept of curative treatment
through three obscure objects of knowledge: the able-bodied
pauper of working age; the sick pauper; and the aged pauper.
   The chapter on the able-bodied begins confidently enough
with a review of methods of treatment since 1834 but after ten
pages this confidence is disturbed by the question of numbers.
How many able-bodied paupers are there, and are they increasing or decreasing? Suddenly, the very existence of this object
is made questionable (p. 210):

> We have in mind, of course, those who are not incapacitated
> from work by illness or physical defect. But in attempting
> to determine the number of these, we are met by the dif-
> ficulty that there is no generally accepted definition of the
> able-bodied, and that statistics are therefore difficult to
> interpret.

For example, within the workhouses the operational definition
of an able-bodied person was anyone on a No. 1 diet (the 'workhouse dietaries' issued by the central board prescribed complete
diets for each category of inmate. No. 1 was the 'plain diet'
for healthy males). Outside the workhouses the main type of
able-bodied person on relief was the normally healthy individual
suffering from 'temporary sickness'.
   After further inquiry into the composition and administration
of the category, it is concluded on p. 218:

> Broadly, speaking, what we find is a multiplicity of agencies dealing with a class which is sometimes called able-bodied, sometimes unemployed, regardless of the fact that this class is not really a class at all but a heterogeneous mass of men with no characteristic common to all of them. The honest, the criminal, the unfortunate, the strong, the weak, the industrious, the incorrigible loafer, the indifferent, all, in the prevailing confusion, are shifting about from one agency to another ... which aim more or less promiscuously at relief, deterrence, employment, training, the work of a convalescent home and of an emigration society, of a casual ward, and a labour-yard.

The solution is 'careful sifting and classification' so that 'the treatment of each class and even of individuals within each class, should be differentiated according to their antecedents, failings or needs' (p. 218).

What interests us here is not the obvious taxonomic concern with heterogeneity and classification but, first, the ability to think 'the industrious' as among the able-bodied in need of relief (something impossible in the binary coding scheme of 1834); second, the inclusion of training as an appropriate treatment for able-bodied paupers; and, third, the specification of appropriate treatment to individuals so as to take account of their 'antecedents' and 'needs' as well as failings. All three are possibilities given by the idealities of function and development; they could not be thought within the purely taxonomic idealities of identity and difference.

Regarding distress arising from want of employment, the 1834 Report certainly refers to able-bodied men who are not working but always as a sign of moral character - as idleness or vice. Neither the concept nor the word unemployment appears there. In 1909 the 'same' thing is seen in a totally different way, namely, as a sign of the operation of invisible market forces which can throw men out of work against their will. Unemployment is a concept which belongs to the presumption of a market system animated by its own inescapable motion of seasonal fluctuation and cyclical growth and decline. There is no need to quote Foucault again on the nature of this difference in knowing social reality, the reports of 1909 speak for themselves. The Majority Report is particularly explicit (p. 78):

> It [the Report of 1834] does not lay down, or proceed on, any philosophical theory of the place of poverty in the social organism, of the 'rights' to life or to work, even of the duty of the State towards its less fortunate members except in one particular that, where the State gives relief, it should make the situation of the able-bodied recipient less eligible than that of the independent labourer. It does not ask if and how far the very perfecting of the organizations by which wealth is produced leaves certain of the producers outside the

organization, and whether charity is the only or best means of dealing with these.

Before poverty can be placed in the functioning of a social organism, however, the dynamic operations of that organism must somehow be made visible. A basic descriptive device for this purpose is the arrangement of aggregate statistics in a time series. This is used by the Majority Report in its initial statistical review where pauperism is displayed as a collective phenomenon having its own 'natural cycles', and again in a section on 'distress due to unemployment' where fluctuations in pauperism are related to the operation of the national economy as manifested in aggregate statistics. The latter are more than mere head-counting, they are indicators of eufunctioning and malfunctioning, normal development and abnormal development in a life-like system. The Majority Report does not, however, understand this as a different way of knowing reality; consequently it projects its differences from 1834 onto reality itself as the objective emergence of phenomena which did not exist then (p. 359):

> Whilst the moral causes contributing to pauperism and unemployment remain much the same as before, the material influences regulating employment and industry have changed both in their character and scope. Forces have come into operation affecting employment ... which are quite beyond local control. Cyclical fluctuations are now world-wide in their effect upon industry and its employees. Changes in methods of production follow one another more rapidly than heretofore, and, as specialization becomes more marked and definite those habituated and trained to the processes that are superseded find it more and more difficult to obtain occupation elsewhere. Those who are not in the prime of life, nor in conditions of adequate physical strength or competency, are apt to fall out of an industrial system which is above their level ....These are modifications and developments in our industrial system which cannot be ignored, and their products and wreckage, when either out of employment or in distress, require a treatment more elastic and varied than the simple method which, eighty years ago, was sufficient to cope with able-bodied pauperism in agricultural districts.

The cure then is to provide for industrial training, retraining, and occupational and geographical mobility in the workforce, while retaining 'discipline' and 'moral suasion' for the causes of pauperism which remain much the same as before. In addition, since local malfunctions of the industrial system may happen (the Lancashire Cotton Famine of 1861-3 is given as an example), charity must be organized as a 'standing accessory to public relief' (p. 366). Temporary relief during emergencies was not to be the only function of organized charity, however, and its comprehensive role in the new scheme of things nicely illustrates how the change to knowing reality in a new mode of visibility transformed the fixities, the possibilities of rational order, given by taxonomic representation.

To grasp this firmly we must stress again that a constitutive principle of textual knowledge production is the effortful sub-ordination of situated contingency to trans-situational rule. Pity, being a situated response to immediate distress, an empathic identification with particular others, is, therefore, an eminently suitable topic through which a text can display itself as knowledge of social reality. We have noted that the 1834 Report calls pity 'blind benevolence', suggesting that the immediacy of the response precludes rational clarity (blindness and clarity are, of course, metaphors of ignorance and knowl-edge), and condemns its open-ended sensitivity to particular persons and hardships as destructive of any general rule. Pity is brought into taxonomic rule by, first naming it as charity (a publicly observable course of action), and, secondly, limit-ing its sphere of operation to the impotent poor. It is not fit however, to be included within an orderly 'system of relief', and must be undertaken only as a private, not as a public, form of aid. The 1909 Majority Report also comments on pity as a subversive sentiment: 'a subtle and constant influence, fostered by the kindly instincts of impulsive humanity, which is ever at work sapping and undermining restrictions upon the grant of public relief' (p. 71).

However, within the cognitive space of dynamic entities – of industrial systems, retrainable workers and curable individuals – where the logic is that of functional efficiency and transform-ational development rather than permanent classifications of sameness and difference – a place can be found for charity (if it is organized) as a complementary partner to public relief in a dual organization of preventive and remedial treatment. Through insight into the dynamics of human behaviour and the functional requirements of society, benevolence need not be blind, nor kindly instincts subversive; they can be utilized as energies and resources in social administration. It is now rationally conceivable to have public poor law institutions and charitable organizations cooperating in the same administrative space. To have in each district, for example, a Voluntary Aid Committee and a Public Assistance Committee to deal with dis-tress from unemployment: the former to handle 'the better class of workmen who may be reduced to want before the Labour Exchange can find them employment' (p. 424) and temporary distress in the same class due to 'non recurrent causes'; the latter dealing with more permanent causes such as lack of employable skills, obsolete skills and 'occasional unsteadiness in habits', in general those who 'require something more than maintenance to enable them to regain their place in the industrial world' (p. 426). Out-door relief to the able-bodied, the great evil of 1834, is now rationally conceivable as a positive aid to self-respect and self-sufficiency rather than an inevitable source of demoralization. All this is possible because individuals are being known in a different way. The significance of individual contingencies of poverty, indigence and misfortune is not now to test and verify a pre-established grid of moral identities and responses, but to call into play a carefully differentiated range of remedies and cures so as to produce or restore functional efficiency within the national economic system. The dominant question now is not how to preserve taxonomic integrity and avoid boundary contamination but how to maximize productive potential and avoid waste. (Waste is as crucial to the 1909 Report's way of knowing self-evidently what is wrong as contamination is to the 1834 Report. This is a theme which must be marked here and elaborated subsequently.)

The sick pauper as a knowledge problem

A change in thinking is marked by the fact that even though some of the moralistic distinctions of 1834 reappear in the vocabulary of both the 1909 Reports, the 'same' terms have a different meaning; they are embedded in a different 'structure of signification'. Identification labels may now stand for active interventions in social life and so have an applicative rather than contrastive significance. This point can be taken further by reviewing the Majority and Minority reports' discussion of the sick pauper.

The problem with the sick pauper as a category is that its two component terms are seen to come from separate discourses - medical science and social morality - one construing the individual as a malfunctioning physical organism, the other as a defective or wanting member of society. Their conjunction produces a particular form of illegibility in 1909 which might be called discursive double vision. The Majority Report registers this as a history of administrative difficulties and institutional confusion. The administrative principle applied after the enactment of the 1834 Report was to stress the pauper element in the mixed sign and require a person to pass the workhouse test of absolute destitution before receiving treatment for sickness. The principle could not however be applied to the numerous cases of sudden and dangerous illnesses or accidents which called for relief, so exceptions were made and a supplementary definition of destitution formulated: 'In practice ... "destitution" as applied to medical relief has come to mean no more than this, viz.: - inability to provide whatever medical treatment is necessary.' (p. 237)

As medical knowledge expanded and treatment became more sophisticated and expensive, the definition gathered greater numbers of the sick poor under its province. The poor law infirmaries (separate from the sick wards established within the workhouses, the sphere of pauperism proper) became increasingly like general hospitals in equipment, facilities, staff, etc. - even surpassing them in many cases - so that they appeared as medical rather than poor law institutions and lost the stigma of shame essential to the deterrent function of the latter. Even artisans, respectable workmen and domestic servants of the wealthy attended them. Many witnesses are quoted to the effect that the poor law infirmaries had become state hospitals for the sick poor of the nation. To complicate the situation and provide further opportunities for functional confusion and irrational anomalies, medical treatment was also provided to the poor by voluntary hospitals, local sanitary authorities (for contagious, epidemic diseases) and education authorities. The objectionable features of the situation are retrieved from such details by applying to them the familiar textual requirement of categorical connection. If a person is in identification category X (whatever the essential characteristics for being there might be), then treatment Y should follow. This conforms to the standard writing format of rule-governed contingency whereby contingency is brought into a sign-set through 'If' and disciplined through 'then'. At this point the text turns back upon itself and the double vision which has been displayed by the report as the flaw of a failed legisign - the sick pauper - recurs in its own strained argument that the priorities of 1834 should be reversed to stress 'sick' rather than 'pauper', but that both elements should be retained. Having demonstrated through its historical-administrative review how the authority of a moral legisign (pauper) has been eroded through conjunction with a technical legisign (sick), making it possible to question the rationale of their joint rule to its roots, the Majority Report abandons that possibility in order to keep the needy sick within the ethical rules of pauperism, thus risking a reverse erosion. Its equivocation appears as supplements (p. 297) to the administrative principle that all methods of prevention and cure 'generally approved by science' should be made available to everyone needing them:

> It has been argued that it is the relieving officer who gives the order for medical relief, and his tradition is to consider the economic, rather than the medical, necessity of the applicant, whereas, in the interests of the community, it is of the utmost importance that the applicant should first be treated, and the question of his economic position and his capacity to pay determined afterwards.

The supplement here is an investigation of means to pay, described as an 'unattractive but necessary corollary' of the right to recover costs from those who could have afforded to insure themselves through a provident society or the like, but had neglected to do so. Recovery of costs would then be a punishment for lack of thrift and foresight. The cures and preventions of medical science must be provided under conditions which will preserve the moral distinctions of 1834 (p. 291):

While one of the first objects of a change in the present system of medical assistance should be to render it more accessible to the working classes, it should be administered in such a way that those who contribute towards their own medical assistance should obtain it on more eligible terms than those who do not so contribute.

Of course, if the needs of the body - as defined by the availability of curative and preventive knowledge - are given primacy, then the fine tuning of treatment to match moral desert categories would be subverted. The functional imperative of necessary physical treatment and the taxonomic imperative of clear moral classification must come into conflict at the point of application to particular individuals. The conflict of imperatives surfaces in the Minority Report as the dilemmas of Medical Officers and revelations of scandalous neglect. A District Medical Officer neatly pinpoints the problem (p. 851):

The tradition of the [poor law] service is that every pauper is to be looked on as being such through his or her own fault, and the tendency is to treat the case accordingly ... he is a shade only above a criminal. Now to this tradition the Medical Officer tends, like all other officers, to become a victim, and the tendency is that the case of sickness is treated as a 'pauper' and not as a 'patient'. The Commission will, I trust, see the distinction.

For us the interest is not in asking whether the Commission can see the distinction but what its presence in the text can tell us about the production of knowledge effects in general and about this production, compared to that of 1834, in particular. It is of general interest to note that the distinction is made visible in the organization of referential detail such that the reader receives it as an objective property of a reality beyond the text (i.e. as knowledge of reality) rather than as a construction device within it. The objectivity of the pauper-patient division is accomplished by representing the particulars which its application finds as consequences of its real-world existence beyond words. However, while wishing to bear this in mind we will review the consequences with an interest primarily in comparatively describing the Minority Report's method of knowing. There are four main consequences:
(a) The intervention of the Relieving Officer, a non-medical authority, between sick bodies and doctors. He could, for example, refuse a sufferer access to a Medical Officer at his own discretion if he suspected a fraudulent claim either to destitution or illness. A rule of knowing implied here is that the inhibition of expert treatment to a moral legisign (the pauper) is self-evidently wrong.
(b) Delays of medical treatment beyond the time of effective intervention due to the success of the poor law system in deter-

ring applications for relief. The timetabling of action dictated by the developmental stages of diseases is in conflict with the reactive tardiness required in testing claims to destitution - (p. 856):

> the very great mortality from phthisis ... is to be attributed in no small degree to the fact that sufferers are not encouraged to present themselves for treatment in the early stages of the disease, when it is often curable, but when they are still capable of going to work, and are not regarded as destitute and thus not technically eligible for a Medical Order.

The same is said of cancer, ulcerated legs, varicose veins, heart diseases and so on. The pauper-patient superimposition is thematized here as a temporal disconnection whereby medical treatment is not given in time (i.e. in its appropriate time) because it is subordinate to the scheduling priorities of deterrent relief. The sick pauper is, in part, an illegible object because it is placed in the wrong time schedule. As Foucault says, in the 'modern' episteme things are presented to thought 'with a time that is proper to them'.[8]

(c) Medical treatment under the poor law tends to be unduly narrow because the Medical Officer is called upon to treat sickness only as it is brought into that administrative purview and not to undertake preventive action on individuals before or after they cross its threshold. There is no linkage of treatment, for example, with the encouragement of (p. 867):

> better methods of living among his patients, to advise as to personal and domestic hygiene, or to insist on the necessity of greater regularity of conduct. No attempt is made to follow into their homes the hundreds of phthisical and other patients discharged every week from the sick wards of the Workhouse and Poor Law Infirmaries.

The sick pauper is not treated as a functioning entity in a medically significant environment but as an administratively abstracted case for relief. Beyond the institutional boundaries of the poor laws is a great unknown darkness of unregulated life within which destitution is produced and reproduced in multiple forms. The glaring defect of the 'Destitution Authorities' is that 'they deal with these cases only during a narrowly limited period of time. Their patients come to them out of the unknown, and after the briefest period of treatment, disappear again into the unknown, having received temporary physical advantage, but the very minimum of mental or moral improvement' (p. 792). The same thing is said later (p. 1043) of able-bodied distress:

> Out of the darkness these starving men apply to the Relieving Officer; he visits their miserable abodes and leaves them

with their loaves of bread; then unless they choose to
attend the next meeting of the Board of Guardians – into
the darkness they disappear again ....What does not happen is any effective public assistance in securing employment at wages, or in providing such physically or mentally
restorative treatment as would fit the men for employment.

The existence of this dark unknown could not be brought
forward as a policy criticism if it was an authentic area of
ignorance and incapacity to intervene. It is not authentic, however, but the false darkness of a shadow cast by the poor laws
(by the legisigns 'pauper', 'destitution' and 'relief') standing
in the light of available know-how. The defect of the poor laws
is found not so much in the courses of action which they allow
for as those which they exclude. Moreover, the defect is for
the Minority Report a radical one because the exclusions are a
necessary counterpart of an inclusionary method. Its agents
have to confine, to withhold, to delay treatment in order to
make their courses of action socially visible as poor law work:
All the defects and all the shortcomings of the Poor Law Medical
Service as it presently exists are *inherent* in its association
with the Destitution Authority.' (p. 868).
    In order to show more clearly the negative face of the Poor
Law Medical Service, to show what it is as what it is not, to
show what the term 'pauper' effaces in the mixed term 'sick
pauper', the Report invokes the good example of the Public
Health Authority. Its work is not oriented to an administratively
confined relief of symptoms but to the living conditions and
individual habits of life which medical science has identified as
preventable causes of disease. The work is demonstrably
rational because it intervenes in developmental processes and
makes the inner structure of functioning entities accessible to
modification (pp. 883-5):

The one recurring note in all the statements and oral evidence of the Medical Officers of Health is the vital importance
of 'early diagnosis'. The watchword of the public health
service is 'no delay' ....Actual experience of public health
administration indicates that universal medical inspection,
hygienic advice and the appropriate institutional treatment
of those found out of health might have as bracing effect
on personal character, by imposing a new standard of
physical self-control, as it would have on corporeal health
....They would not be merely passive recipients of advice
and attention. The influence of the doctor would demand
from them habits of life and even sacrifices of personal taste
in the interest of the health of the community, their families
and themselves.

With reference to our earlier discussion of the 'semantic rectangle' and the characterization of the fourth corner as an

ambivalent, potentially disruptive area within the topical structure of the 1834 Report, it is interesting to note that the Public
Health Authority, which now designates what is lacking in the
administrative framework authorized by the report, was itself
generated within that framework. The Minority Report recalls
that the Poor Law Commissioners (and specifically Chadwick,
the main author of 1834) found preventable disease to be 'so
great a cause of unnecessary pauperism' that they carried out
extensive investigations and 'importuned the government to
give the local authorities public health powers' (p. 883). The
disruptive potentiality faintly discernible as an epistemic
incoherence in the 1834 Report was objectified in its practical
implementation and provided for critical reflection on its meaning in 1909. The important lesson here is that the textual construction of social reality and the cognitive appropriation of
that reality in reading-writing, cannot be fully analysed by
treating particular texts as isolated entities but must be considered as an ongoing process in which texts imprint themselves
on situated practice (say as administrative activities) and thus
allow themselves to be read again. In knowledge production there
is always room for revision and further writing.
(d) The final consequence attributed to the patient-pauper
distinction and the subordination of the former concept to the
latter is that Poor Law Infirmaries and workhouse sick-wards
are places which must 'simultaneously treat a congeries of
hundreds of patients of the most diverse kinds ... the expectant
mother and the senile feeble-minded ... the man knocked down
by a motor car and the charwoman with bronchitis' (p. 964).
An operational rule of the report, to which all topical details are
held accountable, is that administrative categories should be in
correspondence with scientifically and experimentally validated
courses of action. Rational administration must be undertaken
as applied science and 'The whole tendency of modern applied
science is the subdivision and the breaking-up of old categories
into newer specializations.' (p. 1023).

TECHNICAL RATIONALITY, FUNCTIONAL ILLEGIBILITY AND EFFECTIVE TREATMENT

The proper role of voluntary effort and charitable donation in
the Minority Report's scheme of things is to initiate and develop
new techniques of treatment. Novelty, risk and experimentation
name the way in which voluntary institutions can complement
public ones: 'Just as no public authority can hazard the rate-
payers' money in experimental institutions, so no public authority
can assume responsibility for the desirable unconventionality
of their daily administration.' (p. 1023).
The conventionality of public institutions is not conceived
here as a concern to preserve an established moral code, but is
more like the organized scepticism of disciplinary science which

resists new theories in order to make them prove their worth. These different meanings of conventionality mark a deeper difference between (a) knowing social reality through its own constitutive categories, where knowledge claims are advanced as an idealization of cultural sense-making formulas and redeemed as a simulation or rehearsal of societal membership, and (b) knowing it as an objective natural domain where claims are advanced through subordinating cultural codification to technical methods of cognitive appropriation, and redeemed as an assurance of masterful intervention in causal sequences.[9] The reference above to the 'subdivision and breaking up of old categories' is a way of talking about the subordination of cultural to technical concepts, and both are ways of talking about the erosion of moral (culturally given) legisigns by technical courses of action which they cannot govern or seek out. Technical rationality oriented to instrumentally effective action provides a critical place from which the Minority Report can see what is wrong and what a solution must be like. We have traced this out in the discussion of the sick pauper; it appears again in other details. For example, in the argument that the category 'pauper' is as irrelevant and harmful to the treatment of the mentally defective poor as it is to the poor sick and poor children: 'The evidence shows that the division between pauper and non-pauper is quite unreal in the case of the mentally defective' (p. 896) which means that their reality as defined by categories of mental disease and curative treatments cannot be recognized in that cultural division. The same form of knowledge brings the Aged and Infirm to view as 'the most baffling of the categories into which the non-able-bodied poor are officially classified' (p. 899). And on p. 914:

We have to report that the diverse medley of persons who are officially included within the class of the Aged and Infirm do not appear to us, in any scientific analysis, to constitute a single category ... we must distinguish (in addition to the sick and mentally defective) no fewer than five separate classes for which distinct provision has, in our judgement, necessarily to be made.

Of course, there is not yet a technology for preventing and curing old age, but there is available an array of judicious treatments and related expertise developed here and there in scattered locales through experimental trial and error, capable of optimizing the social functioning of old persons, which is waiting to be systematized. And as a break with the past it is stressed that classifications must be based 'not according to past conduct or desert, on which no human being can really be judge - but partly according to physical needs, and still more according to present characteristics and conduct' (p. 924). That is to say according to observationally verifiable characteristics suitable to objective management.

Again, this form of knowledge can be traced in the reasons given for the relatively imprecise recommendations on the able-bodied compared to the non-able-bodied. In the latter case, the inquirers say on p. 1179:

> we could take for granted the existence of an elaborate body of knowledge, worked out by specialised local Authorities, as to how to run a school, a main drainage system, an isolation hospital or an asylum ....But in the prevention and treatment of Able-bodied Destitution and Distress from Unemployment, we are, at the beginning of the twentieth century, in a position somewhat similar to that in which the prevention and treatment of sickness stood at the opening of the nineteenth century. We have still to work out by actual practice the appropriate technique.

Whereas the operation of cultural rationality requires a respectful affirmation of past categories and moral linkages (as in the 1834 Report's constant references to the intentions of the 1601 Act), technical rationality, to be recognizable as such, requires the past to be a scene of obsolescence, ignorance, error and mistake so as to affirm the actuality of progressive feed-back learning.

The Minority Report displays the same form of rationality in its identification of functionally illegible objects. That is to say objects which cannot be read as instrumentalities of technical treatment. There are functionally illegible institutions such as the Poor Law Infirmary and the Workhouse Sick Ward, already referred to, and, most prominently, the General Mixed Workhouse. We must be careful to respect the text here because in some passages it speaks of promiscuous social intercourse and moral contamination in a manner indistinguishable from the 1834 code of knowledge. Full weight must be given to these (p. 728):

> We have ourselves seen, in the larger workhouses, the male and female inmates, not only habitually dining in the same room in each other's presence, but even working, men and women together in laundries and kitchens; and enjoying in the open yards and the long corridors innumerable opportunities to make each other's acquaintance ....No less distressing has it been to discover a continuous intercourse, which we think must be injurious, between young and old, innocent and hardened ....The young servant out of place, the prostitute recovering from disease the feeble-minded woman of any age ... the senile, the paralytic, the epileptic, the respectable deserted wife, the widow to whom outdoor relief has been refused, are all herded indiscriminately together.

This is not an isolated passage dismissible as an aberration, it is replicated at the end of the report (p. 1058) in the description of an Urban Workhouse:

> Of all the spectacles of human demoralization now existing on these islands, there can scarcely be anything worse than the scene presented by the men's day ward of a large Urban Workhouse during the long hours of leisure on week-days or the whole of Sundays. Through the clouds of tobacco smoke ... the visitor gradually becomes aware of the presence of one or two hundred wholly unoccupied males of every age between fifteen and ninety - strong and vicious men; men in all stages of recovery from debauch; weedy youths of weak intellect ... men subject to fits; occasional monstrosities or dwarfs ... the sodden loafer, and the temporarily unemployed man who has found no better refuge ... all free to associate with each other, and to communicate to each other, in long hours of idleness, all the contents of their minds.

In the face of what appear to be strong affirmations of taxonomic coding, it must be asked what grounds there are for calling the Mixed Workhouse a functionally illegible object. These are found in what the report recommends positively as an establishment of rational order. It does not recommend the improvement of workhouses, say through more effective methods of separation or barriers to communication, but their complete abolition and the reassignment of all inmates to specialized treatment agencies: Residential Training Establishments, Day Training Depots, Labour Exchanges, Domestic Economy Schools, Lunatic Asylums, Asylums for the Aged, Industrial and Reformatory Schools for the young. This is the virtual order which the mixed institutions of the poor law obscure, it is not, however a reform inferred from their defects but a prior construct making possible the perception of defects in the first place. So complete is its authority that even the worst of characters, the recalcitrant 'won't works', are to be given technical treatment (p. 1078):

> Equally unsatisfactory is the provision made inside the Able-Bodied Test Workhouse for the wise treatment of such persons, even assuming that they are in some way or other worthy of punishment. No one acquainted with the administration of prisons, or reformatories ... will under-rate the difficulty of securing for such institutions officers with the requisite characteristics for making discipline curative and reformatory. The whole technique of dealing with adults who are criminal, disorderly or merely 'work-shy' is yet in the making. Boards of Guardians and their officials are not only deficient in this technique; they have not the remotest idea that any such special qualification is necessary. Any man or woman, if a disciplinarian, is good enough as a Labour Master or Labour

Mistress ....Hence the note of brutality and arbitrariness
which is so noticeable in these institutions. It is not that the
Labour Master is by nature brutal or even unkind. But the
constant association with disorderly and defective characters,
with no training either in the science or art of dealing with
them, forces him to rely exclusively on a rigorous and unbend-
ing discipline.

Corresponding to functionally illegible mixed institutions are
functionally illegible mixed officials: the Relieving Officer, whose
duties require 'an impossible combination of the training and
attitude of an accountant and an enquiry agent, a debt collector
and an Assessor of Income Tax, a Sanitary Inspector and a
Health Visitor, a School Manager and a School Attendance
Officer' (p. 759); the General Inspector whose 'technical knowledge' about destitution is described as now obsolete because
of the development of specialized knowledge which no one person
can hope to master; and the Master–Matron team (referred to
singularly as the mixed official) whose androgynous nature and
ineffective jumble of functions precisely matches the notable
features of the workhouses they manage. We should digress
briefly here to note a rare flash of sociological insight into the
dynamics of social reality construction. The Minority Report
argues that because the Master–Matron official lacks the trained
capacity (science or art) for separative treatment, it treats all
inmates as one category – the pauper – and in expecting the
one attribute of 'ready and unhesitating obedience, passing into
servility' they mould all inmates into that one character, recognizable as a 'certain trick of bearing' and a 'peculiar facial
expression' (p. 731). By this means the official secures 'a
machine-like order' (as opposed to an organic order of functional
treatments). The reporters can clearly see the constitutive
significance of typification as part of the substantive reality
they describe but not as a principle of their own work of reporting. Like any unilateral text concerned with literal representation, this one projects its own unexamined methods of achievement into its referential content as an observed reality. Textual
closure to methodological accomplishment is an essential condition for cognizing social life as a natural realm which an artful
science can comprehend and control. That is to say for factual
empirical inquiry about society.

Returning to our theme, it is significant that the social treatment of workhouse inmates (strict discipline) called for by the
moral category pauper is explicitly used to name the negation
of the treatment called for by knowledge of natural development
and inner causality. Even if strict discipline was to be universally applied this would still only be a 'superficial equality of
treatment' and not 'the deeper equality of treatment according
to ascertained need' (p. 746). The Majority Report uses the same
oppositional code when remarking (p. 599):

Of *mechanical* uniformity there is more than enough in
Poor Law administration. The repetition of routine decisions,
e.g., the indiscriminate application of a scale of outdoor
relief to case after case, without regard to individual differences, is the bane of administration. But *true* uniformity
lies rather in the general acceptance of certain definite
principles and their consistent application. Such principles
are thorough enquiry, the consideration of each case in all
its bearings with a view to ascertaining how it can best be
treated, the granting of assistance at once appropriate and
adequate, the securing of co-operation between all the
various agencies of public assistance. [Italics added.]

In the episteme predominating the 1834 Report, knowledge of
social beings was already given in conventional cultural norms,
and the task of public administration was to ensure their strict
application across all local areas. For this purpose it was sufficient to establish a Central Board of Control with adequate
powers of direction enforced by a staff of general inspectors
(1834 Report, p. 169):

We recommend, therefore, that the *same* powers of making
rules and regulations that are now exercised by upwards of
15,000 practically irresponsible authorities, liable to be
biassed by sinister interests, should be confined to the
Central Board of Control, on which responsibility is strongly
concentrated, and which will have the most extensive information.

In the episteme struggling for realization in 1909, effective
knowledge of social beings cannot be given in cultural categories
because social beings exist now in a realm of natural causality
as organic entities and developmental systems of action, it must,
therefore, be discovered through properly conducted inquiry.
Mixed officials are incapable of conducting inquiry; in part
because they know too little (Minority Report, 1909, p. 758):

The very heterogeneity of their functions, involving the
absence of expert technique and the lack of any definite
standard of professional efficiency, has a deteriorating
effect on their character. Like the Workhouse Master and
Matron, and for the same reason, this 'Mixed Officer' almost
inevitably comes to despair of the preventative and curative
side of his task.

In part also because a prior security of knowing what to do
and how to do it precludes any need for inquiry. Within that
security rational order is confidently construed as the correct
application of culturally defined and legally sanctioned rules of
treatment. The 1909 Reports can see that rational order only as
'superficial treatment' and 'mechanical uniformity'. An expression

of this superficial rationality is the General Inspector. The Minority Report says that he had only 'a single function to supervise, and a single technique to invent or acquire, namely, the relief of destitution in such a way as to render the relief deterrent' (p. 988). This required no investigation of individual needs and was adequately met by an 'elaborate machinery of Clogs and Deterrents on Relief, applied to all applicants alike'. The passage then moves from negative to positive in what is by now a familiar way:

> The very idea of having 'General Inspectors' in the abstract is, we need hardly say, diametrically at variance with the conception of an Inspectorate supplying the counsel and guidance, together with the supervision and control that can only come with specialized expert knowledge ....It is, we believe, a necessary condition of any efficient admin- istration that each kind of treatment, involving a separate technique, requires to be supervised, not by a General Inspector knowing none of the techniques, but by a profes- sionally trained specialist.

THE INDIVIDUAL IN TEXTUAL REALITY CONSTRUCTION

The 1909 Reports specifically reject the mechanical treatment of applicants in an abstract manner and recommend concrete, individualized treatment based upon full personal inquiry. This sounds like a recommendation to place the treatment of poverty and distress in the realm of situated reality construction. But, if so, does it not undermine the claim that rationally accountable knowledge of the social in writing tends inherently towards a methodical and practical negation of situated reality construc- tion?

To test the question it is necessary to see what these criticisms and recommendations actually come to in the texts. Let us take up the issue of abstract, mechanical administration first. The Minority Report criticizes it in a way which is remarkably close to the comments on bureaucratic red tape, 'leafletisis', and modern profusions of official forms, instructional pamphlets, regulatory addenda and the like, cited at the beginning of our analysis. The critical topos of the chapter on administration (ch. XI Supervision and control by the national government) consists of the 'tens of thousands of General and Special Orders from 1834 down to the present day' (p. 979) through which policy has been enacted. The Orders in all their proliferation and prolixity might well serve as an emblem of the endless task of bureaucracy in seeking to achieve a practical enclosure of situated reality within the realm of writing. Nothing must be left to chance (there was in fact an explicit prohibition against games of chance in the workhouses); diets, rising times, sleep- ing times, eating times were all strictly specified for each of seven classes of pauper on indoor relief. Exhaustive operational definitions were provided to direct the giving of outdoor relief. Even the bathing of paupers was finely regulated. Article 95 of the 1847 General Order (in R.C. Glen, 'The Poor Law Orders', 1898, p. 275):

> In preparing a bath, the cold water should always be placed in the bath before the hot water. Before any inmate enters the bath the officer ... should ascertain by a thermometer the temperature of the bath, which should not be lower than 80 degrees of Fahrenheit and not higher than 98 degrees of the same scale.

The Minority Report contrasts this 'clumsy machinery of mandatory Orders' with 'the varied difficulties, unthought by the bureaucrat at his desk, which actual administration has to face ... the new issues that the changing environment is always producing' (p. 980). The day to day administration of institutions and decisions on out-door relief (p. 980)

> is not work that can properly be prescribed in detail .... This administrative work does not consist of a series of judicial decisions as to whether a case falls within one category or another; and it is not to be accomplished by even the most minute and persistent torturing of the terms of a statute or mandatory Order. Administrators must be free to make the most of the actual material with which they have to deal and to act as seems best in all the complex circumstances of each case ... if there is to be any social progress they must be perpetually devising new ways, undreamt of before, of coping with the new needs that from time to time emerge.

This passage with its talk of freedom to make the most of the actual in complex circumstances certainly appears to be respecting the claims of what we have called situated reality construction. It seems to recommend as administrative virtues what, in ethnomethodology, are called the 'indexical properties' of situated speech - the determination of meaning by circumstance, ad hoc revision of preliminary understandings in the light of their consequences, elaborative openness of general terms to the particulars of an occasion - and to oppose the placement of closure on those properties which we claim underlies scientific as well as administrative rationality. We must say 'seems' and 'appears', however, because the positive ideal from which the passage issues is a reaffirmation of administrative enclosure but with an 'elasticity' appropriate to the practical-cognitive containment of organic entities and dynamic systems. Existing provisions for central supervision and control are found wanting only because of 'their failure to distinguish in form between peremptory laws which have to be applied judicially and inflexibly, and administrative injunctions serving as ideals and patterns which can only be carried out with such modifications as local circumstances require' (p. 979). There is no objection to peremptory laws as such – they are said to be useful for tasks like defining liable relatives – but their detailed inflex-ibility in the face of local circumstances has given rise to informal practices such as 'private letters to particular Authori-ties', the 'oral sanction' of inspectors to local modifications, and evasive circulars concerning the meaning of earlier Orders which have 'nibbled away' at them, the overall result of which has been to 'destroy the moral authority and prevent the enforce-ment of the Orders themselves' (p. 980). It is the lack of deci-sive order which is troublesome to the report and calls for reformation. The moral authority of the Orders is being destroyed, which is to say that there is a failure in the govern-ance of legisigns over the particular and the concrete. The fault is not, however, in their manufacture or their application (for example, poor drafting or illiterate officials), but in their form – in being peremptory, fixed and final instead of adaptive to circumstances; in being mechanical instead of organic forms of language. Forms which are obedient to the inner logic of writ-ing in its self-sufficiency, to semiological imperatives such as stable signifiers, contrastive differences and separative bound-aries, rather than to an outer logic of things in themselves which language must accommodate. The distinction we are try-ing to see here in the Minority Report's critique of abstract, mechanical regulation is the one marked by Foucault to make sense of the breaks between natural history and biology; general grammar and philosophy; the analysis of wealth and economics. Things are no longer 'presented to knowledge in the interstices of words or through their transparency' but are confronted as 'beings radically different from them'.[10] With reference to the break between natural history and biology, this means that precisely articulated naming is no longer ade-quate for knowing plants and animals:

> As long as classification consisted of a pattern of progres-
> sively smaller areas fitted into a visible space, it was quite
> conceivable that the delimitation and denomination of the
> resultant groups could be accomplished simultaneously
> ....But now that character can classify only by means of
> prior reference to the organic structure of individuals,
> *'distinction' can no longer be achieved in accordance with
> the same criteria, or by means of the same operations as
> 'denomination'*. In order to discover the fundamental groups
> into which natural beings can be divided, *it has become
> necessary to explore in depth* the space that lies between
> their superficial organs and their most concealed ones, and
> between these latter and the broad functions they perform
> ....*There is a fundamental distortion between the space of
> organic structure and that of nomenclature: or rather,
> instead of being exactly superimposed, they are now per-*

pendicular to one another ... designation and classification, language and nature, cease to be automatically interlocked. *The order of words and the order of beings no longer intersect except along an artificially defined line* ....There is talk of things that take place in another space than that of words. [Italics added.][11]

Of course, this is a matter of talking of things as if they were in a space other than that of words. What Foucault calls 'the space of organic structure' must be understood as another possibility of language since it is discerned as a transformation of written discourses. We can now understand the administrative recommendations of the 1909 Minority Report as an attempt to formulate the 'artificially defined line' where the classificatory order of words can intersect the 'external' order of social life. Concretely, there will be technically expert officials investigating the 'deep space' which intervenes between the visible characteristics of a needy individual and possible causes of his or her need; there will be specialized institutions run by trained staff to which individuals can be referred according to diagnostic classifications relevant to social functioning; institutions will be placed according to functional specialization under local authority committees responsible for day to day management within 'ideals and patterns' laid out by central government departments. The democratic composition of local management committees ensures a place for cultural nomenclature (named as public opinion): 'essential to successful administration is the common consent of the community, which the local representative body brings from its dependence on popular election' (p. 980). The place of technical rationality, answering to the organic structure of social life, will be assured by the professional training of its operatives and reinforced by an expertly qualified 'staff of peripatetic agents of the Department concerned, who can keep the local administration constantly under observation ... and convey to the Local Authority the advice and instructions in which the policy of the Department is from time to time embodied'.

The strong intent here is to reconstruct the unitary rule of 'peremptory laws' into a cooperative rule of moral and technical rationality. Not, however, in the interest of situated reality construction but as a deeper negation of it.

The logic of organic thinking dictates exploration in depth to know individuals effectively and reliably. The Minority Report expresses the dictates of that logic in several places. For example, the section on public health and the prevention of poverty quotes with approval the opinion of a 'distinguished doctor': 'We have pretty well removed the filth from outside the human body; what we have now to do ... is to remove the filth from the inside' (p. 884).

Inner filth is not like the dirt which accumulates at taxonomic boundary lines and can be cleaned up by stronger definitions, it is located in a place below the level of ordinary words which only specialized treatment could hope to reach and remove.

Again, speaking this time of the vagrant, it is asserted that 'he will not disappear so long as we persist in confining our treatment of him to his periods of vagrancy ....What is required is to take hold of a larger section of that man's life, in order to find out the cause and character of his distress, and to bring him under influences which may set him on his feet.' (p. 1088)

The figure of the vagrant is especially revealing in connection with our claim that textual-documentary rationality must methodically negate the essential features of situated experience. He symbolizes in pure form its open, fluid, indeterminate, ad hoc features, the negation of which constitutes objective knowledge of the social in writing. The play of legislative and investigative words around this figure provides us with a figurative confirmation of the negation principle and further evidence of epistemic differences between the reports in their manner of enacting it.

The vagrant as a knowledge object
The preambles of the old (pre -1834) poor laws represent the vagrant as a person who is out of proper place, a disorderly person dirtying boundaries, who must be physically carried back to his place of 'settlement'. Since displacement and replacement are recognized here through geographical boundaries mapping the public realm and there is reliance upon a concrete, visual organization of territorial space to represent social order, we might describe it as taxonomic knowing through primitive classification.[12] Its classificatory nomenclature consists of the names of villages, towns, hamlets, hundreds, rapes, wapentakes and parishes. Its boundaries consist of the lines between them. This epistemological primitiveness is matched by a savagery of treatment which the 1834 Report records with repugnance: 'This part of our history looks like the history of the savages in America. Almost all severities have been exercised against vagrants except scalping' (p. 190). The report itself scarcely recognizes the vagrant as a distinct knowledge object, perhaps because its taxonomic method relies upon a classificatory set consisting of culturally defined types of persons identified by characteristic motivations. In this ascriptive scheme geographical fixity has no special significance (indeed the willingness of labourers to move from one territorial place to another is interpreted as a sign of ambition and industriousness). Vagrancy is made sufficiently accountable for them as an instance of idleness, irresponsibility and improvidence. From this standpoint it is reasonable to suppose that the principle of deterrent relief nullifying such motives in the public sphere, will remove that type of person from it (p. 191):

Feeling convinced that vagrancy will cease to be a burthen if the relief given to vagrants is such as only the really destitute will accept; feeling convinced that this cannot be

effected unless the system is general; and also convinced
that no enactments to be executed by parochial officers
will in all parishes be rigidly adhered to, unless under the
influence of strict superintendence and control – We recommend that the Central Board be empowered and directed to
frame and enforce regulations as to the relief to be afforded
to vagrants and discharged prisoners.

Beyond this, the vagrant is not discussed and we must conclude that for the 1834 Report it does not serve as a significant
symbol of situated disorder: that role is served by the soft
magistrate, the lax vestry and (as in the above quote) parochial
diversity. In contrast both reports of 1909 make strong use of
the figure in their compositions, but the epistemic methods
behind the usage are not reducible to those of the old poor laws
in spite of a continuing concern to remedy the instability of the
vagrant through unambiguous classificatory placement. The
meaning of classification is not the same because the project of
establishing social order has a different definition in the spatiality of functioning systems than that of tables, maps and territorial demarcations.
    The 1909 Majority Report registers the difference in recalling
the recommendation of a Departmental Committee on Vagrancy
(1906) that the police rather than the poor law authorities should
deal with vagrancy: 'the work of control is akin to much that
already is discharged by the police in their control of the community, such as the regulation of traffic ... granting of pedlar's
licences: impounding stray cattle' (quoted on p. 574 of the
Report). The Committee's recommendation issues from the same
territorial relevance system as the old vagrancy and settlement
laws. So does its further suggestion of allocating 'way-tickets'
to the 'bone fide working man travelling in search of employment' which would bear 'proofs of identity ... be limited to a
certain period ... and be so framed as to form a record of the
man's journey' (quoted on p. 571).
    The Majority Report has no objection to this kind of device for
identificatory settlement of economically purposeful travellers
but is much more concerned with vagrancy as an offensive
life-style. Its offensiveness is that of particulars which are
resistant to collection, classification, institutionalization; in
short, to knowing. This resistance is displayed in the following:
    First, vagrants are disrespectful to the institutional places
designed to appropriate them as knowledge objects. It is said
that they treat the casual wards of workhouses as clubs or
hotels for their own convenience. They even use the walls of
their enclosures as bulletin-boards. Examples are given of
messages copied down from casual ward walls, such as: 'Saucy
Harry and his moll will be at Chester to eat their Christmas
dinner, when they hope Saucer and the fraternity will meet
them at the Union' (p. 570). Anyone wishing to celebrate the

claims of situated against textual-documentary reality construction might well identify with Saucy Harry as a resistance movement hero. He could be compared to Randle McMurphy, the joyful anarchist who undermines the authority of a mental institution in Ken Kesey's novel, 'One Flew Over the Cuckoo's Nest'. Modern plays, films, novels abound with tramps, wanderers and irrepressibles who defy or flop across the pieties of social placement. It should be added that these are sentimental celebrations in the sense that the audiences who laugh and dream along with such characters would not in their own situated activities at work and home tolerate them. None the less, the pervasiveness of the heroic vagrant as a mass culture theme can be taken as a sign of the conflict we are seeking to establish in social reality construction. The Poor Law Commissioners, being serious reality inquirers rather than sublimatory entertainers, cannot see anything heroic in casual ward characters: the wall messages are interpreted by them as 'picturesque details of degraded and criminal types'.

Secondly, the vagrant life-style is offensive because it affirms the heresy that individual contentment can be found without serving recognizably useful socio-economic functions (i.e. recognizable in public procedures for making utility a visible matter of fact): 'The modern tramp lives an unsocial and wretched sort of existence. He has no object in life, and his very contentment with his miserable surroundings renders any · improvement in his condition practically hopeless.' (p. 572). The commissioners are knowing in such a way that arranging to have Christmas dinner at Chester cannot be counted as an object in life, neither can the linkages between Harry and his moll, and Saucer and his fraternity be counted as social ones. They are negative acts within a specific vocabulary of purposes and motives for determining what is properly social behaviour.

Thirdly, the vagrant life-style is evasive: it evades official counting and recording procedures as well as the practical application of curative treatment. In its statistical review the Majority Report identifies 'a troublesome class' who go in and out of the workhouse several times a year. Anecdotal reference is made to an old woman who had done so 163 times in one year and a man who had been in-and-out 593 times since 1884. Later on (p. 513) reference is made to the alarming capacity of this class to expand and shrink:

> The casual pauper is but an incident of vagrancy, at one time swelling, at another shrinking in volume, merging into a shifting and shiftless fringe of the population in such a way as to elude definition.

Locational volatility and evasiveness to procedural accounting is made a cause for concern in terms of curative treatment (p. 138):

Under such circumstances the curative treatment of pauperism becomes, in many cases, impossible. The worst
characters may flock into the workhouse to recuperate from
the effects of their evil lives, and as soon as they have,
at ratepayers' cost, partially recovered their physical
condition, they can leave the workhouse and resume their
degenerate careers. Their period of stay is not long enough
to cure them of their evil courses, but it is long enough to
give them fresh strength to pursue them. In this way has
sprung up that crowd of prostitutes, drunkards, mendi-
cants, loafers, and the like who are now known as the
'Ins-and-Outs'.

The illegibility of the Ins-and-Outs, the nature of their
offence against rational order, is not merely taxonomic – an
elusion of definition, being on both sides of a boundary – it
consists of the lack of fixity necessary for curative treatment.
This is why the Minority Report requires means to 'take hold
of a larger section of that man's life' (including, for professional tramps and confirmed vagrants, compulsory detention in
a 'Reformatory Colony'), and what underlies the Majority Report's
contention that 'it should be part of the regulations of every
institution that each case in that institution is periodically
reconsidered ... with a view to seeing whether the existing
treatment is producing the desired results ....It is only by
treating paupers as individuals that there is any chance of
restoring them to their sense of individual responsibility for
self-maintenance.' (p. 139). The call to 'treat paupers as
individuals' cannot be understood as a resistance to the textual-
documentary mode of appropriating situated lives; on the contrary, it means that individuals must be constructed as cases
in order to make them more fully accessible to technical courses
of treatment, i.e. to appropriate them more completely.
This is made explicit in the Majority Report's endorsement
(repeated by the Minority Report) of what is called the case-
paper system. Its distinctive merits are described by contrast
with the unsystematic character of the existing 'system'
(pp. 160-1):

Under the ordinary system, no continuous record is kept
of an applicant and his family; at every application he is
entered afresh in the application and report book of the
relieving officer, and, where this book is not indexed, it
depends entirely upon the memory of the relieving officer
how much of the applicant's past history is brought before
the Guardians ....Under the case-paper system every
application is recorded on the same set of papers, which
thus constitute a running history of the case; every set of
case-papers is indexed, and can be turned up by anyone
who is dealing with the case; in whatever institution the
applicant may be sent his history goes with him.

The statement is a remarkably concise expression of two constitutive features of knowing social reality in writing which
arise directly from the general imperative of negating the
constitutive features of situated reality construction:
1 Time is taken out of passage and made an observational dimension of objective being and change. In situated interaction
(speaking-hearing-gesturing-responding), time is experienced
as practical duration and an aspect of participation; it belongs
to the flow of on going events as coordinated experiences of
beginning, continuing, halting, interrupting, sequencing and
ending. For textual-documentary reality construction concerned
with securing researchable knowledge objects, situated temporal-
ity can only signify a fleeting evanescence whose remedy is
part of the meaning of knowledge. Remedying passage is a
reflexive feature of the production of knowledge effects. In
order for an individual to be objectively known, his attributes
and actions must be abstracted from passage and reconstructed
on a permanent time-scale, i.e. one which is itself impervious
to passage. Thus each individual is to be objectified as a
'running history', retrievable by anyone at any time, which
will go with him as the essential definition of what he is.
2 In situated reality construction the identity of the individual
is negotiably embedded in particular scenes and occasions of
interaction. Typification (by age, sex, race, status, etc.) is
always provisional and merely an aid in the primary social task
of making sense of these words, these gestures, here and now.
The situated particularity of the other person, what he is in
this context and in addition to typical attributions, must be
attended to in the performance of what ethnomethodologists
call 'interpretive procedures' and 'everyday practical reasoning'. To the extent that these situated, personal particularities
are excluded from interaction then it loses its primary character
and becomes mechanical, impersonal, ritualized, phony,
inauthentic, and so on. Textual-documentary construction of
the individual as a stable knowledge object requires precisely
the remedy of contextual, situated identity, again as a reflexive
confirmation that objective knowing is being done. Thus the
1909 Report finds fault in the discontinuity of the 'ordinary
system' in the practice of starting afresh each time a person
makes a new application, in relying on the memory of the
receiving officer - and seeks to negate the dispersal of
particulars by gathering them into a standardized, continuous,
indexed record. The case-paper is a practical epistemic device
for remedying spatial dispersal, as well as temporal passage,
through a permanent, cumulative record.

The case-paper system as a knowledge device
Regarding our claim that the 1909 call for individual treatment
represents an intensified appropriation of social life compared
to 1834 (which may be interpreted as an emerging articulation
of Foucault's 'modern' episteme and the technical rationality it

dictates),. it is interesting to pursue the topic of the case-
paper method in the volumes of evidence accompanying the main
reports. Particularly relevant is the first volume of Minutes[13]
which contains transcripted testimony from several poor law
officials on the advantages of the method as well as specimen
case-papers and a sample page from an Application and Report
Book. My interest here is in how the Application and Report
Book is described as inadequate to provide knowledge of poverty
for appropriate treatment.

Dr Davy, a General Inspector, says that the book is inadequate to cover 'the whole circumstances of the case' and does
not provide enough information for the Guardians to make
decisions. Another General Inspector, Mr Lockwood, elaborates
(p. 545) on the question of adequate information:

> The advantage of the case-paper system is that you have,
> as it were, the life history of each individual accessible ...
> if you have an inquisitive guardian, and he asks a question
> about a case which has perhaps been heard three months
> before, in the ordinary course the Application and Report
> Book would not give the particular information asked for
> and ... you would have probably to get another book and
> to send to another office, and so on: whereas with the case-
> paper system the whole thing is self-contained, and every-
> thing that has happened is there on the file.

He adds later in his testimony that the case-paper will contain
every communication, every letter from other organizations the
case has come to. They are 'there immediately at hand, and
you can turn over the sheets and read them' (p. 556). A third
inspector, Mr Fleming, agrees with the suggestion that the
provision of a single column for cause of application is not
enough, adding that typically it is either left blank or filled
with a single word 'poverty' (p. 419):

> There is really no sufficient column for recording the reasons
> of the application. You have columns for the name of the
> applicant, the residence, how long resident, occupation,
> whether single or married, widow or widower etc. Among
> the other columns you have is one headed 'Present cause of
> seeking relief or nature of application'; but that is only a
> very narrow column, with no room, or, at all events, no
> invitation to fill up the particulars one would like to see.

An inspection of the samples and specimens in the appendices
of this volume shows that the 'present cause' column is indeed
narrow and uninviting in the Application and Report Book. The
case-papers are totally different in format; there are large
open spaces for inserting detailed accounts of the biography
and institutional career of the applicant. The form titled 'History
Sheet' is one suitable for compiling a diagnostic file, for

bringing the pauper to paper and hence to appropriate treatment. Through the case-paper system the individual in need
is reconstituted as a dossier which is moved in space and time,
from cabinets to tables at scheduled meetings, from institution
to institution, as a rational administrative process. The essential being of the individual is made visible and sanctionable as
check marks in boxes, notations in columns and remarks in
open spaces. For any official concerned it is enough to read
marks, notations and remarks to know the case for decisions
and revisions. In the fourth volume of evidence (Session
volume xxxi), Mr Dearden, Superintendent of Out-relief, says
that for him the main advantage of the case-paper method is
'that if an officer resign or die, the newly appointed official
can, if sufficiently energetic, start where the old officer left
off, and not have to spend years of time and experience to find
out the ins and outs of every case' (p. 237). In other words
the case-papered pauper has the objectivity of a thing which
stands indifferently the same for all competent observers.

It would be possible to interpret the case-paper system as
a merely reactive solution to the practical problem of administering relief on a large scale. Mr Bircham, Poor Law Inspector for
Wales, says as much in the first volume of Minutes arguing that
while the case-paper system might be useful in large towns,
where personal knowledge of applicants is lacking, it is unnecessary for officials in the Welsh unions because 'they have known
these people, and know more about them than any case paper
would supply ... they know exactly what they have in their
pot in the kitchen, and every sixpence they have got' (p. 259).
Undoubtedly this could be advanced, and was advanced at the
time, as a good reason for adopting an administrative innovation
like the case-paper system. It would be more efficient in keeping track of large-scale relief work. But to treat the method in
Mr Bircham's way as a matter of convenience, a reasonable
response to a monitoring and book-keeping problem in large
populations, is not, for us, enough because it glosses its
significance as a device for giving knowledge. The Reports
describe it as something more than a tracking mechanism; the
case-paper is needed to provide an insight into causes which
will allow for the selection of appropriate curative and preventive treatments. This is why its format must be so different
from that of the Application and Record Book. The Welsh Receiving Officer who knows the ingredients of the kitchen pot and
the whereabouts of every sixpence knows something relevant
to deterrent relief but nothing relevant to technically effective
treatment. In short, he really knows nothing. The case-paper
method does not signify a book-keeping invention to be used
where 'personal knowledge' is impracticable but a transformation
of what counts as genuine knowledge of poverty, need and
destitution which defines Mr Bircham's kind of knowledge as
inadequate. Ideas, like things, may become obsolete.

Summary statement

Restating what has been said in Foucault's terms, the declared concern of the 1909 Reports for treating paupers as individuals does not indicate a slackening or abandonment of the administrative project of making situated reality conform to the requirements of knowledge production in reading-writing, but a change in the definition of those requirements corresponding to a change of the 'space' in which words and things are ordered and can merge. In the 1834 Report the space is almost entirely (we have noted the ambiguity there) constructed as a taxonomic grid made up of cultural classifications of conduct, motivation, condition of life and social treatment. The requirements of rational order (of legibility, accountability, knowledge) are that the classificatory attributes actually appear only in prescribed combinations and that other logically possible combinations are ruled out. This ruling out is a basic task of public policy. Taxonomic knowing is essentially an imposition and recognition of classificatory restraint on random or logically possible combinations of attributes. It corresponds to the cybernetic definition of meaning as 'pattern' or 'redundancy'.[14] An aggregate of objects or events is said to have meaning if it can be divided by a 'slash mark' such that an observer seeing only what is on one side of the boundary can project with high probability of success what is on the other side. The 1834 Report complains constantly that observation of those on the receiving side of poor law relief (a monetary slash mark) is an insufficient base for projecting the financial condition of those on the other side (the working poor); similarly, that observation of individuals on the positive side of a moral slash mark (the industrious) does not allow for a reliable projection of the material condition of individuals on its negative side (the idle). The report's central recommendation – universal and strict application of the principle of less eligibility – can be understood then as a ruling out of possible combinations of attributes in order to make cultural dividing lines meaningful, i.e. enabling members 'to face a cut or slash in the sequence of items and to predict across that slash what items might be on the other side'.[15] In taxonomic knowing, social reality is recognized as a rational order by virtue of being a meaningfully divided aggregate.

The 1909 Reports retain a concern for culturally given demarcation lines – it appears, for example, in the Majority Report's references to contamination in the General Mixed Workhouse, in the Minority Report's recommendation that the aged poor be sorted into establishments 'of various grades of comfort and permitting of various degrees of liberty ... in accordance with their present characteristics and conduct' (p. 924), and in both reports' condemnations of indiscriminate and unconditional relief – but that concern is secondary to the task of cognizing the space in which individuals develop, function and can be changed. In this knowledge frame, appropriate treatment requires a grasp of causal connection between past and present,

person and environment, which cannot be obtained through a
narrow column inviting the single word 'pauper' (i.e. through
a form devised only for taxonomic demarcation). Interventional
grasp (technical control) requires a form like the case-paper
through which the life of an individual can well up in tangible
accessibility. Or, changing the metaphor to describe the turn
from investigation to treatment, a shaft sunk down through
the surface appearance of a person to reach those inner dynamics and springs through which treatment works. The conception of the individual as an inner-outer, depth-surface phenomenon, with an inner core separable from situated acts (from
mere contingency) is crucial to the project of remedial treatment
in 1909. It is distantly comparable to Dante's formulation of
salvable persons (the inhabitants of Purgatory) in their essential
difference from the eternally damned inhabitants of Hell. The
former have an inner core separable from the sum of their bad
actions (signified by repentance), the latter do not. Thus
gluttons who are nothing but the sum of their actions are fixed
in a Hellish circle, while those who are more than that tread
the Purgatorial terrace of Gluttony en route to salvation. I say
distinctly comparable because, first, this distinction between
types of souls in Dante was not clearly noticed, according to
Thomas Bergin,[16] until the nineteenth century (on the modern
side of Foucault's epistemic break); secondly, because the 1909
Reports do not speak primarily of moral salvation but of saving
waste material for utilization, i.e. of salvaging. The significance
of that for us is that moral salvation concerns correct placement
in a taxonomic scheme whereas salvaging concerns placement in
a functioning system (the national economy). The topic of
salvaging human waste serves, therefore, a dual purpose for
our discussion: (a) it provides further explication of the nature
of the interest which the 1909 Reports have in treating paupers
as individuals; (b) it provides for further translation between
the details of these texts and Foucault's account of the epistemic
break of our time (which we are treating as a revelation of two
epistemic possibilities of language realized through writing).
Since the Minority Report is more 'modern' in this respect attention will be confined to its wording of the topic.

THE SIGNIFICANCE OF WASTE AS AN EPISTEMIC CATEGORY

The Minority Report expresses the inner-person outer-appear-
ance theme as a distinction between pecuniary destitution and
personal destitution. The former is the concept used by the
existing 'Destitution Authority' as a warrant for taking action
(also as a legisign giving a field within which objects for knowledge and action can take shape). The official definition given
by Mr Adrian, Legal Advisor to the Local Government Board,
(which, incidentally, illustrates again the pathology of endless
provisos which afflicts administrative language as an attempt

of writing to fully replace situated social reality) is as follows
(p. 161):

> Destitution when used to describe the condition of a person
> as a subject for relief implies that he is for the time being
> without material resources: (i) directly available, and (ii)
> appropriate for satisfying his physical needs; (a) whether
> actually existing; or (b) likely to arise immediately. By
> physical needs in this definition are meant such needs as
> must be satisfied: (i) in order to maintain life; or (ii) in
> order to obviate, mitigate, or remove causes endangering
> life or likely to endanger life or impair health or bodily
> fitness for self-support.

The Minority Report finds the definition inadequate because
in referring only to material resources and physical needs,
it cannot authorize preventive and curative treatment. Effective
intervention needs a concept of personal destitution: 'the
existence *in the person* dealt with of conditions which, without
the intervention of the public Authority *would produce* consequences inimical to the common weal' (p. 1019, italics added).
The change of preposition from 'of' to 'in' a person, and the
change of tense from present indicative 'is' to the imperfect
'would' capture basic features of organic thinking. The report
goes on to reveal (p. 1019) how a cognitive shift, manifested
as a battle between legisigns, is troublesome for documentary
reality construction:

> This contradiction between the two versions of eligibility
> for Public Assistance has a large share in producing the
> confusion and overlapping that we have described between
> public authorities ... it is the maintenance of the contrary
> view by the Destitution Authorities - the insistence on
> pecuniary destitution - which has excluded them from the
> whole domain of preventive work, and has given to their
> operations, humane and philanthropic though they are,
> their characteristic barrenness.

The inadequacy of that legisign to permit treatment of degenerate
(i.e. wasteful) social lives is shown in the hypothetical case of
a boy 'running wild in low company, destitute of proper parental
control, where the presence or absence of material resources
is wholly irrelevant to the rendering of the appropriate service'
(p. 1020).
   The transformative intent behind the concept of personal
destitution, the project of salvaging individual waste in the name
of 'the common weal', comes to a full flower in the Minority
Report's discussion of the unemployed, irregularly employed
and unemployables as negations of the collective power to produce wealth; as non-contributors to the work-force of society.
The structure of signification which Foucault calls the modern

episteme, codes reality not only in terms of inner-outer and depth-surface but also fertility and barrenness. It is helpful here to recall his argument that the epistemic break can be traced in radical differences between the Classical analysis of wealth (in Malthus and Smith) and Ricardo's economics. In the former, the meaning and explanation of all economic phenomena begins and ends in their status as substitutes and tokens standing in place of one another and, ultimately, of human needs and quantifiable amounts of labour. Ricardo's economics still treats quantitative labour (labour time) as a common ground for establishing equivalences between commodities but, in addition, conceives of active labour as an originary, cumulative creation of value which transcends the circular play of things being exchanged and traded in place of one another. With Ricardo it is a question of analysing the productive power which, in historical time and social organization, underlies that surface of substitutory interchange. Whereas the taxonomic analysis of wealth is basically a semiotic explication of representing and represented elements, economics focusses upon the anthropological drama of man transforming natural infertility and barrenness into means of life, engaged in an unrelenting struggle to outrun scarcity:

> In Classical thought, scarcity comes about because men represent to themselves objects that they do not have; but there is wealth because the land produces, in some abundance, objects that are not immediately consumed and that can therefore represent others in the processes of exchange and the circulation of wealth. Ricardo inverts the terms of this analysis: the apparent generosity of the land is due, in fact, to its growing avarice; what is primary is not need and the representation of need in men's minds, it is a fundamental insufficiency ....Labour - that is, economic activity - did not make its appearance in world history until men became too numerous to be able to subsist on the spontaneous fruits of the land ....At every moment of its history, humanity is henceforth labouring under the threat of death ....Since the prospect of death becomes proportionately more fearful as the necessary means of subsistence become more difficult of access, so, inversely, labour must grow in intensity and employ all possible means to make itself more prolific.[17]

The 1909 Poor Law Reports do not speak of scarcity as death but as a danger to national prosperity or loss of civilized living standards; they are intensely concerned to make labour more prolific (through salvaging waste persons) but in a more detailed and demanding way than anxiety over mere subsistence could provide for. Our concern, however, is not with finding motives for the commissioners (whether anthropological, personal, political, social class or whatever) but in describing

how these texts formulate destitute individuals as knowledge
objects recognizable in their writing. We now return to the
words of the Minority Report.

The case of the unemployed
The chapter on the unemployed turns them into preventive,
curative courses of action by way of common place figures of
speech, coding devices of the culture, and metaphorical equations with industrial and manufacturing processes. (Jacques
Derrida's book, 'Of Grammatology', has a section on 'the turn
of writing' which prompts his translator to note that 'turn' is
the root of the word 'trope' and that 'tour' in French also means
'trick'.)[18] The trick here is to turn individual attributes and
experiences into a form of words contextually constitutive of
the social and industrial system to which they are to be returned
in administrative practice. This provides for a transitiveness
between text and context through which literal reading can
redeem metaphorical equation as a correspondence between words
and reality.
    The analysis uses a fourfold classification arranged in a
hierarchy of degeneration to provide a semantic space within
which productive workers can go to waste and forms of human
wastage can be made visible. The upper class, called 'the elite
of the unemployed', contains those who have been cast out from
a hitherto permanent situation either because of local circumstances (a bankrupt firm, a regional depression) or, more
seriously, because the skill a worker possesses has become
obsolete. Someone in the former possession is a virtually useful
worker who is only wasted in that particular locality, his remedy
therefore is relocation. The latter has a deeper problem. Since
his skill is not saleable it is, by the logic of marketplace thinking, not useful and the individual has the prospective status
of a waste product. He is savable only to the extent that he
has mental, moral and physical characteristics which can be
recycled into a saleable skill through retraining. If a worker
fails, through immobility, intransigence, lack of training facilities, etc. to enter another 'permanent' situation then three
fates await him, depending upon the nature of his personal
destitution. If physically strong he may fall to Class II, the
realm of 'discontinuous employment', exemplified by construction
workers and navvies. We might note here that the report finds
a self-evident social evil in the existence of 'a class of men ...
perpetually shifting from place to place ... without any systematic arrangement for their travelling or their accommodation'
(p. 1141).
    The report cannot help but find unsystematic shifting wrong,
because it is a contravention of its own rules of rational order;
rules dictated ultimately by the constitutive requirements of
producing knowledge objects in reading-writing. This is the
significance of the dominant obsession of the report with irregularity as a social evil. We have seen it before in the discus-

sion of vagrants, we are seeing it now in the analysis of unemployment, and it underlies every topic the report touches upon.
Local poor law authorities are condemned for displaying a 'Babel
of principles' (p. 746) in administering out-door relief; the
good work of Milk Dispensaries in making the supply of milk
'conditional on the babies being brought regularly for inspection, weighing and hygienic advice' is contrasted with the
unconditional doles given by Destitution Authorities, leaving
the mother free to neglect her infant and 'endanger its life with
irregular hours' (p. 795); the uncoordinated multiplication and
overlap of private and public relief agencies is condemned on
the grounds that it prevents regular inspection and systematic,
continuous observation of cases (e.g. the section on 'Children
under Rival Authorities', pp. 801-45); families which breed
destitution are characterized by 'an absolute lack of organization
....Existence drags along anyhow; the hours of work, leisure
and sleep are equally uncertain and irregular ....The children's
health is affected by many different evils, overcrowding, want
of sleep, dirt and general irregularity of life.' (p. 841).

The same defect appears again in Class III of the unemployed.
This is the fate of those whose destitution includes physical
weakness - the sickly, handicapped and ageing workers, those
whose bodies have been partially wasted in the course of usage.
Class III persons are ins-and-outs at the margin of the work-
force. They are engaged 'day by day, and often hour by hour,
for brief and discontinuous jobs' (p. 1145). The adverse effects
of casual employment include further physical debilitation but
'more important ... are, in our view, its demoralizing effects on
character. The perpetual discontinuity of the work, with its
intervening spells of idle loafing, is in itself deteriorating ...
wherever we have casual employment, we find drunkenness and
every irregularity of life more prevalent.' (p. 1149).

A dramatic demonstration of the real world effectuality of
irregular living is achieved through the revelation that three
sets of Special Investigators appointed to investigate the 'constant manufacture of paupers', to discover 'what it was that was
creating them' (p. 1150), had independently found casual
employment to be 'the most potent, the most certain and the
most extensive' of all causes. Low wages and high drinking
(the two most commonly cited causes) do not in themselves
reduce men to destitution 'if combined with reasonable regularity
of employment' (p. 1151). On the other hand, even high wages,
short hours and healthy working conditions, if combined with
irregularity of employment still produces 'irregularity of life,
demoralization and recruitment to the pauper army' (p. 1151).
Irregularity stands for loss of rule in the social activities of
a person (irregular hours, no fixed abode, discontinuous employment in odd jobs), demoralization for inner loss of rule in a
person's character. In combination they account for the degeneration of useful members of society into incoherent waste matter.

The third fate of a man detached from a permanent economic

position (a man who is a contravention of systematicity) is to
become a Class VI Unemployable - one of the '"Can't Works"
and "Won't Works"' - something so useless and shapeless as to
take on the aspect of undifferentiated rubbish (p. 1160):

> This flotsam and jetsam of our industrial life recalls the
> wreckage with which a foundered liner strews the ocean
> shore; material once of the most heterogeneous and sharply
> differentiated kinds, bright and clean and in active use,
> but now so battered and sodden as to appear, in bulk,
> almost homogeneous in its worthlessness.

It would be easy, perhaps instructive, to interpret these
words as a documentation of social attitudes (say the bourgeois
life-style, the capitalist ethic, the vested interests of employers)
- indeed we have noted such interpretations in the section
analysing how the reports have been read by others - but we
must refuse to take that route in order to go as far as possible
in comparatively questioning the reports as modes of knowledge
production which project certain regimes of control over their
content and the social life that content represents.
It is relevant to recall that in medieval law, able-bodied men
were recognizably out of place with reference to criteria of proper
residential settlement, and order was sufficiently re-established
by marking their bodies (with beating or branding), and returning them to their own local communities. In the 1834 Report this
is not enough because the preconception of social order is such
that it cannot be adequately operationalized through laws of
settlement on a territorial map. The displacement of able-bodied
men is now known with primary reference to a moral grid defining just deserts for types of conduct; the practical expression
of this form of knowledge - its regime of control - consists of
well regulated institutions which will guarantee the integrity of
the grid. In particular, the reformed workhouse is designed to
guarantee that no able-bodied man refusing to enter a normal
work place would be better off than one in such a place. The
1909 Reports are also sensitive to moral illegibility but this is
overlaid (especially in the Minority Report) by a constitutive
conception of the good society as a functionally efficient system
of production successfully adaptive to its environment (i.e.
good as a mechanical and biological system). This conception
provides a coding scheme through which men are brought to
account differently than before. Instead of vagabonds whose
physical movement is a violation of public territorial order,
and able-bodied paupers whose superior condition of life is a
contamination of moral boundaries, there are wasted but salvage-
able embodiments of productive capacity. The Unemployables
contain, 'if sorted out and properly treated, much that can be
made serviceable' (p. 1160).
Sorting out begins with a taxonomic task - that of separating
'won't works' from 'can't works' - but only as a preparation for

restoring functionality, not as a sufficient realization of rational social order in its own right. (The sufficiency which allowed the 1834 text to be published and read as a coherent policy report without including proposals for rehabilitation is lacking in 1909.) It is proposed that a national network of labour exchanges, devised primarily 'to obviate the present futile drifting about in search of work and the incessant "leakages" of time between jobs by which so many men are ruined' (p. 1183), would also provide 'an infallible test of willingness to work' (p. 1189). Those persistently failing the test - the 'won't works' - could then be sent to 'reformatory Detention Colonies' where 'enforced regularity of life and continuous work, of a stimulating and not monotonous kind ... opportunities of earning small luxuries by good conduct and output of work; restrictions of personal liberty; and power to those in charge to allow return to one of the ordinary Training Establishments on probation, as soon as ever it is believed that reformation has been effected' (p. 1207), would permit the will towards idleness to be broken, the individual made malleable, and a 'docile', teachable, imprintable workman formed.

Obviously, the meaning of the words on the Unemployables can be imagined in terms of social psychological processes - the eradication of old attitudes, beliefs and values in the mind of the recalcitrant individual and the substitution of new ones (the desocialization and resocialization processes described in sociological studies of slavery, prison camps, religious sects, military training camps, etc.).[19] Something of this meaning is contained in our use of the words to exemplify (with a trace of irony) the kind of interest the Minority Report has in treating paupers as individuals. We still want to understand them, however, as features of a social reality report, informed by the idealities of function and system, projecting an applicable knowledge of the reality it reports on. From this standpoint it is relevant to note another piece of circumstantial evidence sustaining Foucault's thesis of the modern episteme and its rules of knowledge: namely, the recommended provision of detector devices for making the inner attributes of a person visible matters of public fact. Thus the Labour Exchange network operates as an 'infallible test' of willingness to work. Subsequently, the theme of testing is elaborated when the report summarizes its general proposals for sorting and treating Unemployables. The stated aim is to 'solve the particular "human problem" that each man represents' (p. 1203). (Which for knowledge in writing means solving the problem of representing situated particularity in the abstract.) The solution (or resolution since what can be found as a solution is already contained in the significatory structure and conceptual set of the search) is to test each man for the strengths and weaknesses of his physical, mental and moral capacities. There would be 'what we might almost term a Human Sorting House, where each man's faculties would be tested *to see what could be made of him*' (p. 1204, italics added).

Abstraction as knowledge production
The examination sheet and test record, like the case-paper,
are knowledge devices specifically suited to the epistemic task
of signifying the inner properties and dynamics of things
exterior to language, such as the faculties of the individual.
They provide blank spaces through which faculties can take
on the shape of words, figures, marks, etc. and so become
available for educational, remedial, rehabilitative, curative and
preventive treatments. It is not, therefore, individuals as situated presences who can be appropriately treated but documentary
facsimiles which stand in their place. This is why the 1909
Reports insist again and again on professional training and
technical expertise both for public and voluntary work. The
training and expertise are in doing extractive and abstractive
work in the course of situated encounters with individuals.
Technically appropriate treatment requires the stable appropriation of that which is to be treated; a capacity for detachment
which is so alien to the situated method of putting oneself in
the place of the other (the method of mere sympathy ascribed
in the texts to the untrained 'friendly visitor', the amateur
volunteer in charity organizations and those misled by 'the
kindly instincts of impulsive humanity') that it must be cultivated
through special courses of higher education. For example, the
Minority Report, after admitting the value of 'personal service'
through home visiting, adds (p. 1022):

> But this service of visitation, to be effective, must be deli-
> berately organized, under skilled direction, in association
> with a special branch of public administration. Such special-
> ization of home visitation is the only means of keeping at
> bay the merely irresponsible amateur, and of ensuring that
> the volunteer has been sufficiently in earnest to undergo
> some sort of technical training.

The structure of effective visitation (the conceptualization of
its effectiveness) is exactly that of sorting and treating human
wreckage (the conceptualization of its serviceability); of drawing out the essential being of the individual pauper through
the case-paper method (the conceptualization of his record-
ability); of investigating observables to discover the general
patterns and principles within them (the conceptualization of
their researchability); and of writing a report on social facts
to establish the truth about them (the conceptualization of their
standing to reason). Althusser has described it as the founding
structure of empiricist knowledge. He will be quoted, however,
not for the sake of that particular label but for his eloquent
revelation of a significatory structure which the 1909 Reports
rely upon as an unexplicated resource for doing knowledge
production. Without (I assume) ever having read the reports,
Althusser describes with remarkable accuracy what they did as
inquiry and what they recommended as policy:

The whole empiricist process of knowledge lies in an operation of the subject called *abstraction*. To know is to abstract from the real object its essence, the possession of which by the subject is then called knowledge ... the essence is abstracted from real objects in the sense of an *extraction*, as one might say that gold is extracted (or abstracted, i.e. separated) from the dross of earth and sand in which it is held and contained ....Knowledge is a separation of the essence from the real which contains it and keeps it in hiding ... by special procedures whose aim is to eliminate the *inessential real* (by a whole series of sortings, sievings, scrapings and rubbings), and to leave the knowing subject only the second part of the real which is its essence, itself real ... the abstraction operation and its scouring procedures are merely procedures to purge and eliminate one part of the real in order to isolate the other ....The inessential part occupies the whole of the outside of the objects, its *visible surface*; while the essential part occupies the inside part of the real object, its *invisible* kernel.[20]

The knowledge work of the 1909 Reports then is sustained by a preconception of the actual as an objective fusion of two parts: gold and dross, kernel and husk, the essential and inessential. To produce knowledge is to do conceptual work upon the second, visible, external part of actuality (that given by sensory encounter) in order to extract the first part (the real part standing to reason). Within this dualistic coding of reality a knowledge effect occurs as the resolution of confusion arising from incomplete or faulty separation between parts. For our purpose it is necessary to add rule and contingency to Althusser's list of paired contrasts so as to stress that the dualistic structure and separative work ascribed by him to 'empiricist knowledge' is, for us, an aspect of textual reality construction. Furthermore, in the special case of knowing social objects in writing, the purgative (abstractive, separative, eliminative) procedures he describes are undertaken against situated reality construction and are correlative with certain 'rational' practices of modern social administration. All of which is added to affirm that we are interested in the structure of 'empiricist knowledge' as a feature of these policy reports, not in Althusser's usage of it to read the mature Marx as the revolutionary hero of a new, non-empiricist mode of scientific discourse. However, the distinction between science and ideology underlying Althusser's theory of knowledge is directly relevant to our inquiry and leads us to a concluding topic.

CONCLUSION: POLICY REPORTS AS A FORM OF KNOWLEDGE PRODUCTION

The conceptual base from which Althusser conducts his critique of empiricist epistemology raises an awkward question about the Poor Law Reports and the way they have been examined here. Since the examination began by 'borrowing' Althusser's question of the mechanism producing the cognitive appropriation of a real object by its thought object, it is proper to conclude by recalling the context of that question.

It is important to remember that Althusser is not asking how given knowledges have done their work or about the functioning of disciplines over time: historians of science and reviewers of the progressive displacement of mythical by rational thought have successfully addressed that kind of topic. What interests Althusser is that all such investigations, in beginning with factual records of knowledge products, silence the prior question of what it is that specifically makes these products knowledges rather than something else. This objectified conception of knowledge as something given for historical, psychological or sociological observation 'does not enable us to understand the mechanism by which the knowledge considered fulfils its function as a cognitive appropriation of the real object by means of its thought object for whoever is handling it as knowledge'.[21] The pragmatist answer that the mechanism consists of successful application in practice, while useful for ideological warfare against idealist conceptions of knowledge is still caught in the same basic error of seeking a guarantee rather than an explanation of knowledge. It cannot account for the identity as knowledge of what is applied in practice. More pertinent, however, is the further argument that since all social life is a structured arrangement of distinct practices (there is no practice in general), the appropriative activity effected as knowledge must be located among them. Althusser names it as theoretical (or scientific) practice, distinguishing it strongly from non-theoretical practices (economic, political, aesthetic, religious, ethical, technical, etc.) 'by the type of object (raw material) which it transforms; by the type of means of production it sets to work; by the type of object it produces (knowledge)'.[22] If we add to this a subsidiary distinction between scientific and ideological practice plus Althusser's 'warning' that his question of the mechanism of cognitive appropriation is most cogently addressed to the former, then two related problems arise for the present analysis:

1. What kind of practice do the Poor Law Reports (or policy reports in general) belong to? Are they scientific, ideological, political, or what?
2. If they do not belong to scientific practice can Althusser's question be appropriately addressed to them? Might it not be presumptive and misleading?

It would not be in keeping with the methodological frame of

our analysis to treat those questions as an invitation to submit
to the judgement of Althusser's 'real' meaning; they are fruitful, however, as a challenge to clarify the distinctive characteristics of policy reports. Or, as Althusser might say, to think
the particularity of policy reporting as a production practice.
To this end it is useful to move through his account of the four
dimensions in which every production practice is located. Three
of these (what is transformed, the means of production, and
the type of product) have been mentioned already; the fourth
is articulation with other practices in variable relations of
autonomy and dependence. This dimension is crucial for
Althusser's separation of scientific from ideological knowledge
production. The relative autonomy of the former can be seen as
a radical self-reliance both in the formulation of problems and
in the way demonstration, proof, verification (the establishment
of thought objects as the truth of real objects) is achieved.
A pure science has no need of other (non-theoretical) practices
either to define its problems or to judge the truth of its work;
it is pure as a completely theoretical practice:

> for theoretical practice is indeed its own criterion, and
> contains in itself definite protocols with which to validate
> the quality of its product ....No mathematician in the
> world waits until physics has verified a theorem to declare
> it proved ... the truth of his theorem is a hundred per
> cent provided by criteria purely internal to the practice of
> mathematical proof ....We can say this of the 'experimental'
> sciences: the criterion of their theory is their experiments,
> which constitute the form of their theoretical practice.[23]

Althusser says this in order to protect Marx's theory of history
from the judgement of political effectivity or of predictive adequacy and so clear a 'site' for its examination as an exemplary
form of scientific practice which does not rely upon mathematical
or experimental demonstrativity but proves itself in and as
critique of ideology. I quote it, however, for the more modest
purpose of contrastively grasping the concept of ideological
thought in order to match it with the writing of the Poor Law
Reports. Following Althusser, we can say that ideological though
has two essential characteristics: (a) it presents itself as a
rational movement of thought from problems to solutions; (b)
the claimed movement is doubly misleading: first, because the
actual direction of ideological discourse is from already secured
solutions to problems, and, secondly, because the solutions are
given to thought by extra-theoretical practices – they derive
from economic, political, moral or other practices as, for example
cultural recipes, conventional wisdom or institutional know-how.
Ideology lacks the self-sufficient inwardness of scientific (pure
theoretical) practice; it relies upon others both for its 'raw
materials' and its verification as knowledge.
Elaborating further, ideology begins with a desired solution

desired by extra-theoretical concerns) and seeks to produce a problem which reflects that solution as a rationally account-ble one. Althusser describes its mechanism of cognitive approp-iation (the ideological homologue of scientific proof) as 'mirror recognition'. Ideological thought produces a thought-mirror n which a prior product of non-theoretical practice can, with he authentic accent of discovery, recognize itself as just the solution which rational inquiry dictates.

Within the stern categories of Althusser's analysis there can be no doubt that the Poor Law Reports are ideological knowledge productions. Detailed demonstration of the point is not necessary, t is sufficient to recall that they are, like all policy reports, deeply implicated in the exigencies of political practice - in government activities and affairs of state. Since the prototypical political act is the production of effective laws - class command-ents of behaviour - from words, reports commissioned with egislation in view must, by that fact alone, have a political character and be shaped by considerations other than those of heoretical practice. Indeed, the political character of policy eports is so obvious and strong that the real analytic problem s not to demonstrate this extra-theoretic relation but to prevent policy reports from being understood as nothing but elements f political practice. The problem is that such a reductive ollapse would immediately abort the question of how any report perates as knowledge production in reading-writing. The whole f our preceding analysis can be advanced as a sufficient plea hat the question is at least worth keeping alive. If a more direct counter-argument against reduction is required, it can be pointed out that while particular reports (such as the 1834 Report) are more or less directly enacted into law, no report has political effectiveness in itself. It must undergo transforma-ion work, become 'raw material' for committee discussion, Parlia-entary debate, legal penmanship, voting procedures, etc. n order to achieve a decisively political existence. The amount f work needed marks its status as merely cognitive and not yet political appropriation of reality.

Suppose then we agree that the Poor Law reports are not nstances of either scientific (pure theoretic) or political produc-ion practices but of what Althusser calls ideological practice. Can the question of a knowledge effect be honestly addressed o them, that is to say as a question whose answer is not a oregone conclusion? If we take Althusser at his word the answer must be no. He speaks strongly of ideology as thought trapped n a 'vicious circle' of mirror recognition, a 'necessarily closed space' in which a thoughtlessly prepared solution is provided vith a 'false question' so as to mistake itself for a product of easoning about reality.[24] The falsity of ideology is intrinsic to ts identity and it would be impossible to address the question f a knowledge effect to any instance of it except as an intent o reveal a counterfeit resemblance. The question would not be onest because it would conceal the intended question of the mechanism of imposture. The term 'knowledge effect' could only be read in inverted commas as having a quasi or so-called status. Analysis of a report would consequently be confined to showing how solutions (recommendations), prescribed in advance by economic, political, ethical or other non-theoretic practices, served to dictate its descriptions, explanations and diagnoses as a circular discourse of mirror recognition.

Since the question of knowledge production can only be posed as a genuine investigative task to discourses working upon genuine cognitive problems, it follows that a methodical denial of the possibility of such problems to policy reports would preclude questioning them in that way. Only putative scientific discourses, it seems, warrant the application of Althusser's question. Fortunately for our undertaking, however (for it would be awkward to retain the question and repudiate its context), the situation is not that clear-cut. Subsequent to his strong words on ideology, Althusser speaks of it again in a quite different fashion:

> Each mode of production poses the problem of the mechanism of production of its specific 'effect', the knowledge effect for theoretical practice, the aesthetic effect for aesthetic practice etc. ... If we want to avoid pre-judging the conclusion to which the study of these different effects may lead us, we must be content with a few indications as to the effect that concerns us here, the knowledge effect .... This expression knowledge effect constitutes a generic object which includes at least two sub-objects: the ideological knowledge effect and the scientific knowledge effect. The ideological knowledge effect is distinguished by its properties (it is an effect of recognition-misrecognition in a mirror connexion) from the scientific knowledge effect: but insofar as the ideological effect, although it depends on other social functions which are dominant in it, really possesses its own knowledge effect, it falls in this respect within the general category with which we are concerned.[25]

Now the form of knowledge production which Althusser is attempting to indicate here, a form which is not scientific yet belongs with it as a sub-division of authentic theoretical practice, cannot possibly be the same as the specious similitude of knowledge production referred to previously as ideology and parenthetically recalled in the passage as 'recognition-mis-recognition'. Althusser is pointing to a third practice of cognitive appropriation, neither scientific nor ideological, yet because he has only those two names available elects the second and is forced into a misnomer. His discussion, to be clear to itself, requires a third name. I would call his unnamed category social inquiry and define its specific product as a social knowledge effect. Our entire discussion of topics like legibility as the evident rationality of textual reality construction, the

ubordination of particulars to the governance of legisigns, the
haping of legibility by trans-textual structures call epistemes,
he epistemic difference between taxonomic and functional
legibility, has been an attempt to discern the productive
echanism of the social knowledge effect at work in particular
exts. A decisive point of departure from Althusser can now
e remarked. Whereas he asks how a discourse about reality
s organized in such a way as to ensure the presence in reading
f sheer knowledge (referred to awkwardly as 'the presence of
cientificity'), we ask what is needed to ensure that the reading
f a discourse is specifically a presence of social knowledge.
ur refusal of any strict and exclusionary equation between
nowledge proper and 'scientificity' is based upon acceptance
f the proposition - advanced, for example, by Schutz and
uckmann (and again by Berger and Luckmann)[26] - that in
very collectivity there exists a diffuse social stock of knowledge
ithin which special provinces of knowledge (disciplines and
ciences) are fashioned through systematizing moments of
e-pragmatization' and detachment. These delimitations cannot,
owever, mark a distinction between knowledge and non-knowl-
dge, if only because specialized disciplines must continue to
ely upon social and subjective stocks of knowledge to maintain
hemselves as going concerns (i.e. as thought communities
ndertaking observation, conjecture, testing, refutation,
ommunication of meanings, etc). The name knowledge cannot
e withdrawn from these trans-disciplinary practices (as, for
xample, by Althusser's criterion of radical inwardness) with-
ut making disciplinary knowledge production an unthinkable
ystery.[27]
    From this observation we can move back to the question of
hat it is about policy reports that allows for their redemption
n reading as social knowledge. The beginning of an answer,
refigured in our examination of reality effects, lies in the
oncept of contextual transitivity. A social stock of knowledge
an be thought of as an array of cultural coding devices - what
thnomethodologists call sense-making practices - through which
therwise disparate events and behaviours are exhibited as
eterminate social realities. Assuming that such coding devices
orm a common ground between writing and reading we can say,
s a first approximation, that contextual transitivity is a recog-
itionary match between cultural coding devices in a text and
evices present as prior plausibility structures in the person
ho reads. More accurately (trying to escape the concrete
nagery of interlocking structures), the presence of contextual
ansitivity means that the reading of a text can be carried on
ompletely as a contexted work practice, i.e. as another enact-
ent of cultural membership, and is undisturbed by the reading
ct itself. This is synonymous with the negotiation of a non-
uplicitous text by literal reading. A complex text, one whose
uplicity turns reading back upon itself in a forced act of self-
eflection, cannot sustain a literal reading and cannot, therefore,

appropriate reality as objective social knowledge. Duplicity fills the unremarkable spaces, the unstated assumptions, holding together literally readable words with question marks and, since unstatedness or taken-for-grantedness is essential to cultural membership, makes that membership inadequate to fulfil reading. It subverts the equation between them.

Contextual transitivity (or literal readability) is necessary but not sufficient to produce a social knowledge effect. As we have already argued the presence of an authentic problem is needed to differentiate between celebratory social rhetoric (what Althusser properly calls ideological production) and an investigative text with a knowledge effect. All knowledge produc tion in writing occurs as an overcoming of tension between particulars and concepts, an effortful grasping of the former by the latter; in social knowledge production the concepts belong to cultural coding devices and the tension (the authentic prob- lem) to some incoherence, contradiction or incompleteness in their application. In these terms the posing of Althusser's ques- tion of the mechanism of cognitive appropriation to a social report must be heard to include a demand for the coding prob- lem(s) sustaining its self-declared tasks and aims. We took a first step to meeting it by describing illegibilities marked on the surface of our selected texts. These are not illegibilities of the texts in the sense of obscurities which obstruct reading and call for hermeneutic repair work, but illegibilities identified by the play of the texts themselves (their coding practices) upon referential detail. That is to say, illegibilities revealed to a literal reading, where literal reading is conceived as an enact- ment of cultural membership. Even this preliminary description, however, staying as closely as it does to what the texts say is, nonetheless, an analytic break with their self-understanding as objective inquiries. Merely naming, or recalling their accounts of poor law problems as illegibilities is a radical shift of under- standing. The shift means that the procedural statements of these or any reports as to the external location of their problems as something outside of themselves, together with their declared methods of data-collection and evidential checking, must be set aside as glosses on their actual text work and the problems sustaining it. The question of textual knowledge production can- not be touched by a rehearsal of research methods and what was done by way of inquiry; it distracts attention from what is being done by way of writing. And one thing, we claim, that is being done is the reproduction on paper of an unexplicated cultural coding problem: a reproduction accomplished through a significatory structuring of referential detail. An analytic explication of the coding problem (identifying that which under- lies a specific set of illegibilities in the content of a report) would then take the form of describing a structure of significa- tion made up of cultural concepts.

In the case of the 1834 Report the structure was described as a semantic rectangle with an enigmatic fourth corner. In

terms of the rectangle it was possible to distinguish strongly
between two types of coding problems giving work to do: (a)
those corrigible within that frame of binary contrasts as a problem of restoring spoiled distinctions (for example, between
the independent labourer and the able-bodied pauper); (b)
those arising from the fourth corner as a problem of inventing
new concepts; in particular, the concepts of curative and
preventive treatment as something different from punishment.
We have argued that the second task, discernible in 1834 as a
repressed topic, was a major problem sustaining the 1909
Reports, moreover, that it was compounded by the fact that
the new concepts belonged to a new knowledge code (we have
referred to it as the functional-organic episteme), incompatible
with the taxonomic code informing the semantic rectangle of
1834. This authentic problem of 1909 is simultaneously epistemic
and cultural. We have, however, focussed almost exclusively
on the former dimension at the expense of the latter, a neglect
which should be remedied for the sake of completion.

The cultural coding problem of 1909 can be formalized as a
disjunction between two pairs of concepts: inner-outer and
public-private. The first pair provides a spatial imagery to
encode meanings; the second pair structures rights of access
and usage. It is not claimed that the disjunction was absent
from the 1834 Report and present in 1909, but that the intent
to undertake individual treatment made the conjunction of those
concepts problematic in a new way requiring new solutions.
The difference can be understood as one between (a) using the
inner-outer distinction to give visible expression to the divide
between private and public, and (b) relying upon it to formulate
technically treatable individuals. In both situations, coding
problems arise in retaining the equation of private with inner
and public with outer, but from different sources.

Following Emile Durkheim's analysis of property rights[28] it can
be said that the force of the term private (including its social
and moral force) is that of withdrawal from common access and
use. A boundary is signified which forbids or limits intrusions
from the outer (i.e. public) realm into that which is private
(i.e. inner). It is easy to see how the mere existence of a poor
law system could pose challenges to the operation of those coding equations. For example, a poor-rate levied upon property
owners requires a public agency to collect private money from
some private persons and transfer it to others. The standard
method for warranting that intrusion by the coding equations
is to call the collected money public funds (conspicuously
distinguishing this from charitable funds accumulated through
private donations), and limit their transfer to those who have,
through appropriative rituals and ceremonies, been transformed
from private persons into public property. The transformation
devices consist of negations of privacy which open-endedly
provide for more of the same. Within this system of meanings
the potentially transgressive collection of private money is

legitimated as a contribution to public uses by persons in their public role as citizens of the state. Settlement of a cultural code is not that easily achieved, however, since the transformation work required to preserve its integrity is always liable to generate further disturbances of its own. This can be seen in the work of the Poor Law Reports.

The symbolic use of inner-outer to solve the problem of making private persons into public objects is illustrated in the device of removing them from private spaces (homes) to public spaces through institutional incarceration. This is the central recommendation of the 1834 Report. It raises a problem for the original equations, however, since people are to be placed inside buildings in order to become public objects. The adequacy of incarceration as a solution depends upon that institutional inside being a negation of the private inside of a domestic dwelling. Thus 'the House', the ideal workhouse, required by the report is in its well-regulated structure of deterrence (its precise regimentation of ordinary activities like dressing, eating, talking, visiting and sleeping) a perfect nullification of being at home. The ideal poorhouse is not one that invites but repels; its inside is the opposite of privacy and turns its name 'house' into a profound irony. Through this trope the semantic economy of the equations is kept in good repair.

Another illustration emerges from the attempts of the reports to settle the vexed question of out-door relief, where public funds are conveyed to private persons in their own homes. The 1834 Report seeks settlement by erasure; it recommends that all out-door relief be abolished. The reports of 1909 review that as a failed policy and take up the question as something to be solved within the limits and resources of the code it disturbs (i.e. by theoretical rather than political practice). Their solution is to transform the privacy of the recipient home into a public space through the devices of authoritative visiting and checking. The declared purposes of visiting and checking (expert advice, reformation of habits, prevention of fraud, etc.) are not relevant here; what matters is that the home, its occupants and their affairs are opened to access from the outside. Privacy, the effective right of withdrawal, is breached by calls, questions and commands which must be heeded. Public money must only be spent on public objects or public property. We are not talking then of unwarranted intrusions, 'snooping' and the like but a legitimate solution, in terms of an accepted cultural code, of making public assistance to private persons a rationally accountable practice.

A third, and final, illustration of how poor relief challenged the capacity of inner-outer symbolism to mediate the private-public distinction, is found in the discussions of wanderers and wayfarers: the 'homeless poor'. As we have seen, the studied objectivity of the 1909 Reports was disturbed by the 'ins-and-outs' and vagrants; as unsettled and unsettling knowledge objects they generated perplexity and anger. A clear example of the trouble they could cause for the coding equations is a section in the Minority Report on 'the sleepers of Manchester' (pp. 1083-4). This concerns a category of the poor who, being 'homeless' and 'houseless', were beyond the grasp of either of the two transformation devices described above. Only the first device (placement in the negation of a private space) was practicable on them, but its application served merely to demonstrate their recalcitrance to coding.

In 1897 the Manchester Board of Guardians opened a 'gigantic Casual Ward on the newest deterrent models, to accommodate up to a thousand inmates'. Admissions of casual paupers immediately declined from 52,872 in 1896 to 23,684. A 'Free Shelter' was opened by a charitable organization to accommodate the paupers now found crowding the streets. Its homeliness attracted such large numbers of vagrants from doss-houses and from other towns that 'public opinion' was scandalized and the shelter closed. The people of Manchester now found 'literally hundreds of homeless persons "sleeping out" in the brickfields and other sheltered places'. In a culture where sleeping is normatively marked as a private act inside the home, to voluntarily sleep out in public places is to be morally and legally out of place, i.e. an offence. The police initially approached the problem in this way, by arresting offenders, but desisted when magistrates dismissed cases on the grounds that 'their position as sleepers was due to circumstances over which they had no control'. The ensuing debate on what to do revealed the incapacity of the existing inner-outer, private-public code to cope with the situation. Manchester Town Councillors, concerned with the sleepers as a threat to public order and (through their contaminatory diseases) to public health, urged the Poor Law Guardians to relax the regimen of the Casual Ward, i.e. to make it homely enough for voluntary sleeping. The Guardians insisted that deterrence was their duty to the public. The Chief Constable of Manchester, with remarkable perspicacity, said that the real problem was 'how to house these persons'. By which we take him to mean that the problem was how to provide an inside place homely enough to want to sleep in yet clearly marked as a public and not private inside place. Hotels, hostels and guest-houses manage this through the public medium of monetary contracts, but the destitute, by definition, are excluded from that possibility. In the event, the rules of the Casual Ward were relaxed and the problem returned to its pre-1897 state of irresolution. The Minority Report comments (p. 1084):

> this oscillation of policy is typical of the history of the last three quarters of a century, in regard to the provision made by the Destitution Authority for the wayfarer and the houseless poor.

Its own solution - incarceration in Reformatory Colonies to undertake rehabilitative and curative treatments of character -

involves another usage of and challenge to the inner-outer, private-public equations.

A person's character (his identity) is inside, private and, therefore, bounded by the right of withdrawal. It is also, from a technically reformative point of view, the locus of inner springs of conduct which must be brought to public observation and record as materials for treatment to work upon. The empirical structuring of the individual as a knowledge object dictates an investigative movement inwards which threatens a transgression of privacy. This is recognized by the Minority Report (p. 1129) in discussing unemployment:

> We may note that the form and substance of the inquiries into the applicants' conduct and past life prescribed by the Local Government Board, excited resentment, and greatly limited the benefits of the Act [the 1905 Unemployed Workmen Act]. Some of the questions on the Record Paper are of such an inquisitorial character that the best class of unemployed workmen ... have refused to register ....It was, in fact, never made clear with what objects or on what principle the inquiries were prescribed ....It is, in our opinion, only ... as diagnosis for guidance in treatment that inquiries as to character ... are warranted or socially useful.

The difference between inquisition and diagnostic inquiry is that the latter is carried out within strict requirements of ethical propriety and expert competence. A right of access is established but in such a carefully delimited way as to acknowledge that movement across a normatively sacrosanct boundary is involved. Professional qualifications clear special sites within which public work upon personal-private-inner properties can be undertaken. They sanction the creation of socio-physical spaces like the interview, the dossier, the consulting room, the treatment centre, the classroom and so on, within which such work can be carried on. Medicine and education are the explicit models for the 1909 recommendations that social workers be professionally qualified, and rehabilitative institutions run by experts. They are not referred to, however, for their instrumental effectivity: the 1909 Reports cannot be read as technical treatises on behavioural reform, they are specifically social knowledge productions. Medicine and education are relevant to their task (that of cultural reparation) because the professionalization of help offered a solution to the coding problem posed by the new concept of 'personal destitution'. A concept arising, we have argued, from an epistemic break running across cultural categories and encountered within them as nomic disjunctions calling for new meanings. Since policy reports are social knowledge productions and must, therefore, observe the rule of contextual transitivity, their solutions cannot take the scientific form of radical conceptual innovation (dramatically illustrated, for example, in the history of physics), but can occur only as metaphorical and metonymical turns of a prior stock of language. This was the work undertaken in the texts of 1909 on the vocabulary of pauperism.

A further comment should be added on the sources of cultural coding problems (the 'raw materials' which social knowledge production needs as its resources). We have deliberately avoided any appeal to familiar sociological concepts of disruptive social change - urbanization, industrialization, modernization - because they attribute problems to an objectified social reality, whereas our theoretical commitment requires them to be located in constitutive practices of reality construction. Our analysis of illegibilities in the sign-system of pauperism is consistent with that requirement, but its reliance on Foucault's typology of epistemes to provide a comparative account of different forms of illegibility also risks the error of objectification if epistemes are understood as disembodied structures of thought external to production practices. To avoid that regression an episteme must be understood as a particular possibility of knowing within the constitutive practice of reading-writing. Translated into Althusser's terms, an episteme is a particular mode of knowledge production within that practice. Using this framework, cultural coding problems can be identified as difficulties within a mode or as conflicts between one mode and another, yet the question of the primary source, the essential nature of such problems, still awaits a response. Our answer, restating the central thesis of the study, is that the very same properties which endow cultural codes with rational adequacy in situated, circumstantial use appear inescapably as defects for the recognitionary rules of knowledge in writing. Garfinkel and Sacks have described these as the indexical properties of natural language. For example, that 'the definiteness of expressions resides in their consequences; definitions can be used to assure a definite collection of "considerations" without providing a boundary; the definiteness of a collection is assured by circumstantial possibilities of indefinite elaboration'.[29]

The indexicality necessary for rational orderliness in situated talk is precisely the offence (error, deviation, fault) whose correction constitutes rational order in writing. The project of making a social world rational for writing (the joint project of legislation, administration and objective social inquiry), relies upon practices of situated reality construction for work to do and unfailingly finds in them the failings it needs to exhibit its own rationality. This ethnomethodological formulation of the ultimate source of coding problems for reportage has clear affinities with dialectical oppositions familiar in other discourses - for example, Habermas's separation of communicative from instrumental rationality, itself echoing Aristotle's distinction between praxis and techne[30] - but it is analytically preferable to them in that it explicitly relates forms of rationality to the requirements of particular media of communication (speech and writing). Habermas has, it is true, been led to attend to the specifics of speech in order to develop a formal theory of how understanding is possible in communicative action,[31] but has not attended to the specifics of writing and reading as a form of communicative action, even though it is the form within which and against which 'speech' can appear as a topical problem for theorizing. His project of reconstructing 'universal conditions of possible understanding' cannot succeed by singling out speech as the privileged exemplar of communicative action and ignoring that which allows it to be singled out. Habermas, like the Poor Law Commissioners, unreflectively relies upon writing to provide problems which the work of inquiry turns into readable solutions.

At this point we have reached the limit of the particular line of inquiry initiated by our borrowing of Althusser's question of the production of knowledge effects and its application to the Poor Law Reports. In retrospect it can be claimed that progress has been made in the following respects:
1 Identifying what it is that social knowledge production in writing relies upon (a) for work to do, and (b) to display that work as a value-added increment in rationality.
2 Showing that the rules of rational accountability governing the production processes of the reports can be understood as rules of writing; more specifically, as limits which must be observed to sustain a literal reading of social referential content.
3 Demonstrating that the rules of writing knowledge are variable and that a comparative description of those variations can be undertaken through Foucault's theory of epistemic structures.

Having claimed this, however, it must be admitted that the actual mechanisms of textual knowledge production remain to be elucidated in technical detail. We have had to proceed through an eclectic importation of concepts from various discourses because no adequate theory of reading-writing is available. Lacking such a theory we have only been able to touch blindly the significatory shaping of the reports and record impressions of their features. Attempts are currently under way to fill that theoretical vacuum. Particularly promising is Kenneth Morrison's pioneering work on scientific disciplines as distinctive organizations of writing practices. For example, how pedagogic instruction, factual demonstration and controversy are done as disciplinary specific writing practices.[32] The work is still in progress, however, and its relevance to extra- or quasi-disciplinary texts like policy reports remains to be seen.

CHAPTER 6

Textual reality construction and political critique

The dominant thrust of the analysis has been towards a reconstruction of the 1834 and 1909 Poor Law Reports as written
accomplishments of reality and knowledge effects. In terms of
purely scholarly ambition, I would be more than content to
have made a contribution to a general theory of social reality
construction. It will be recalled, however, that the analysis
was from the beginning informed by 'political' interests in
capture and emancipation. More particularly, by an interest
in taken-for-granted practices of reading-writing as a significant element of procedures for ordering and controlling social
life, and a correlative interest in the possibility of emancipatory
meta-reading with regard to documents like factual social
inquiries and policy reports. The interests are related by the
proposition that since (a) the emancipatory intent of political
critique (more broadly, critical social theory) is realized through
bringing unrecognized formative processes to conscious reflection, and (b) institutionalized practices of reading-writing are
crucial formative processes in the administrative ordering of
modern society (crucial to our way of being a society), then
(c) social theory with emancipatory adequacy needs to include
a reflective theory of reading-writing practices as constitutive
(formative) accomplishments.

THE PROBLEM OF THE STATE IN CRITICAL THEORY

A voice is haunting Marxism: the voice of Max Weber prophesy-
ing the ascendancy of the bureaucratic ideal of life in all, and
especially in socialist, societies. It echoes loudly in the hollow
lack of a Marxist theory of the state and reverberates again in
acknowledgements that bureaucratic centralism is the dominant
feature of Soviet and Eastern European communism. Marxist
scholars, no less than democratic pluralists and beleaguered
citizens, feel themselves caught up in a phenomenon that
simultaneously demands and eludes conceptual grasp. Norberto
Bobbio, a prominent Italian Marxist, has expressed this in his
argument that there is no Marxist theory of the state and, as
yet, no Marxian formulation of a viable alternative to representative democracy as a model of political organization for complex
societies.[1] Similarly, Andrew Arato has remarked:

The failure of classical Marxist social theory is nowhere more clearly demonstrated than in the face of the bureaucratic centralist societies that use Marxism as their 'science' of legitimation. The project of a critical social theory demands the immanent critique of all Marxist and neo-Marxist attempts to theorize this new social formation, but this is as yet an unfulfilled task ....In no area has 19th century Marxist theory, with its evolutionist schemata and de-emphasis of culture and politics, been a heavier liability than for thought aiming at emancipation. The theory of superstructures hides from our critical view the state - the guiding centre and identity of most modern systems, especially of bureaucratic centralist societies.[2]

Of course, it would be foolish to pretend that the outlines of a theory of social reality construction offered in this study are sufficient to meet all the wants of political critique in our present situation. I would claim, however, that a theoretical reorientation in this direction is necessary to achieve the task Arato describes, and that even the sketchy propositions we have advanced can provide a much-needed rejuvenation for critical discussions of bureaucracy, democracy and the power of the state. As to demonstrating the claim, I will proceed through indicative commentary on particular discussions rather than risk getting lost in the abstractive toil of reviewing and addressing vast literatures. Also, I have confined attention to writings in the Marxian tradition: first, because it has, in spite of tendencies to degenerate into arid theological disputation and scientistic dogma, shown a dialectical capacity to regenerate itself and keep alive the emancipatory interest of reason; second, because it insistently provokes the strategic problem of how emancipation is to be achieved and what role critical theory (and theorists) can play in practice.

THE MUTUALITY OF KNOWLEDGE AND POWER

The basic propositions linking textual reality construction to political practices are these:
1 The constitutive rules of objective, matter-of-fact (i.e. unreflexive) textual reality construction methodically negate (repress, empty out) the constitutive features of situated reality construction (its inherent orderliness) and thus unfailingly generate a disorder (want, lack, failing of rational accountability) which warrants restorative work.
2 Bureaucratic administration in all spheres of conduct - medicine, law, education, social welfare, business, as well as government - is the practical ordering of social life so as to make it rationally accountable in unreflexive writing.
3 The practical ordering of social life according to norms of discursive rationality is not an act of knowledge but of power.

4 The substantive (as opposed to formal) significance of the word democracy – the secret of its liveliness as a normative ideal – lies in the resistance of situated to textual requirements of rational accountability.

Our entire discussion of 'illegible objects' in the Poor Law Reports and their recommendations for controlling and curing pauperism can be read as an explication in detail of what the propositions mean. Should further detailing be required, it can be found in Foucault's analysis of how legal punishment in France was transformed from public torture of the body, in medieval society, to disciplinary correction of the inner person through incarceral institutions in nineteenth century industrial society.[3] Foucault contrastively sketches the difference as follows. Whereas the old 'modality of judgement' moved from a determination of what had been done, what offence it was, and who had committed it, to juridically prescribed punishments in law (as medieval paupers were branded with a 'P' according to the letter of the law); the new one required extra-juridical considerations of causality, authorial responsibility, the inner potentialities of the offender, and the best rehabilitative treatment:

> A whole set of assessing, diagnostic, prognostic, normative judgements concerning the criminal have become lodged in the framework of penal judgement. Another truth has penetrated the truth that was required by the legal machinery; a truth which, entangled with the first, has turned the assertion of guilt into a strange scientifico-juridical complex.[4]

There is no longer an offender whose actions are referred back to a written body of law, but an individual who is himself turned into writing (records, documents, test results, marginal observations, progress reports) so as to be made simultaneously an object of knowledge and of corrective rehabilitation. The more humane treatment of criminals, as of paupers, has involved what Foucault calls a lowering of the threshold of individuated writing so as to include any undocile body whatsoever in need of training, education, reformation and correction:

> This turning of real lives into writing is no longer a procedure of heroization; it functions as a procedure of objectification and subjection. The carefully collated life of mental patients or delinquents belongs, as did the chronicle of kings or the adventures of the great popular bandits, to a certain political function of writing; but in a quite different technique of power.[5]

The technique combines institutional surveillance of the fine details of individual conduct and performance with discursively warranted procedures for interpreting those details as signs of success or failure, progress or regress, in a project of normalization. It is applied in schools, mental hospitals, prisons, courtrooms, factories, offices, welfare agencies - an entire 'carceral network' of social organization. The political dimension of the psycho-social sciences is not adequately conceptualized, however, by thinking of their servicing functions, useful applications, provisions of trained personnel, and so on. Such concepts presuppose a strong distinction between power and social knowledge, hiding what they have deeply in common: the construction of social reality. Just as Habermas conceives of manipulation and control as an interested activity constitutive of knowledge, not something outside it, so Foucault (though thinking the connection historically and at the 'micro-physical' level of controls engrained in bodies and everyday routines rather at the evolutionary level of universal human activities and general forms of knowledge) argues that disciplinary power 'produces reality; it produces domains of objects and rituals of truth'.[6] The mutually constitutive complicity of power and knowledge is obscured by conventional conceptions of power as a force possessed by elites and ruling classes, or as a possessive passion which is the polar opposite of the detached objectivity needed for knowledge. The institutional separation of the human science disciplines from political-economic-legal disciplines blinds us to their common origin and interdependence, i.e. to their formation of what Foucault calls a single regime of truth and power.

Foucault displays the mutuality of knowledge and power through a series of historical configurations. An early model of disciplinary surveillance is found in a seventeenth century order as to the measures to be taken when the plague entered a town (Foucault instructs us that 'the image of the plague stands for all forms of confusion and disorder'): the town must be sealed off and no one must leave; the area is to be divided into quarters, each governed by an 'intendant'; each street is the responsibility of a 'syndic' who must lock each family into its house; only intendants, syndics and guards can move about the streets; there are to be registrations, checks and daily roll-calls at each house. In total, the town is formed into an 'enclosed, segmented space, observed at every point, in which the individuals are inserted in a fixed place, in which the slightest movements are supervised, in which all events are recorded, in which an uninterrupted work of writing links the centre and periphery'.[7] In other words, a well-ordered town would have the same form and virtues as the well-ordered workhouse and Bentham's model of a good taxonomic system of classification.

Bentham, who we herald as an authentic prophet of documentary reality construction, appears also in Foucault's text as the inventor of a multi-purpose building, the Panopticon, spatially arranged to allow for constant individual surveillance by unobservable observers/guardians/inspectors/supervisors. As an instrument of control it depersonalizes power (the

operators cannot be seen by the inmates) and automates it
(awareness of being always liable to surveillance induces self-
regulation). As an instrument of knowledge it allows not only
for comparative and diagnostic observation but also feed-back
monitoring of experiments designed to alter conduct or improve
performance. Of course, the logic of this power-knowledge
apparatus was not tied to the architectural particulars of
Bentham's building:

> The Panopticon ... must be understood as a generalizable
> model of functioning; a way of defining power relations in
> terms of the everyday life of men ... it is the diagram of
> a mechanism of power reduced to its ideal form; its func-
> tioning, abstracted from any obstacle, resistance or friction,
> must be represented as a pure architectural and optical
> system: it is in fact a figure of political technology that
> may and must be detached from any specific use.[8]

THE INADEQUACY OF CONVENTIONAL POLITICAL CRITIQUE

With these associations in mind we move now to the task of
showing the value of our propositions for political critique. I
have chosen Ralph Miliband's 'The State in Capitalist Society'
as an instructive text for initiating commentary.[9] Miliband is
close to our study in that he pursues an emancipatory critique
of the expansion of state power in contemporary society. His
interest for us is redoubled by virtue of a widespread agreement
(i.e. an agreement extending beyond fellow Marxists) that his
analysis is, in large measure, successful as critique (it conforms to widespread assumptions about what a political critique
should be like): two reviews, from publications with a reputa-
tion for doctrinal independence, are quoted on the back cover
of the book, describing it as a 'sustained essay in demystification' which 'will help to dispel many myths'. These are not
merely promotional endorsements, they are representative of
the book's reception. I need to stress this because my purpose
is not specifically to challenge Miliband but a general strategy
of political critique which he enacts and his reviewers take for
granted. The strategy can be stated as an analyst's protocol
for demystifying politics (I will refer to it as the strategy of
substantive revelation):
(a) Assume that the dynamic and structural reality of political
institutions lies below the surface of public appearance, official
statement and the operative language of a political order.
(b) Bring that obscured reality into focus through an analytic
schema taken to reveal the actual properties of institutions.
(Marxian class conflict theory is one possibility, others include
psychoanalytic theory, game theory, general systems theory,
functionalist theory, exchange theory, and sociobiology.)
(c) Document that revealed, substantive reality in empirical

detail.

Thus Miliband, armed with Marxian scepticism about the real as opposed to the democratically declared functioning of the state in capitalist society, undertakes an intensive scrutiny of its powerful activities. My initial source of doubt here is whether any amount of direct staring at a social phenomenon (such as the power of the state), even staring with a penetrative aspiration, can bring its reality to view. In this respect I share the attitude expressed by Auguste Dupin, one of the first sleuths of fiction, in Edgar Allan Poe's 'The Murders in the Rue Morgue':

> Truth is not always in a well. In fact, as regards the more important knowledge, I do believe that she is invariably superficial. The depth lies in the valleys where we seek her, and not upon the mountain-tops where she is found ....To look at a star by glances - to view it in a side-long way, by turning toward it the exterior portions of the retina (more susceptible of feeble impressions of light than the interior), is to behold the star distinctly - is to have the best appreciation of its lustre - a lustre which grows dim just in proportion as we turn our vision fully upon it ....By undue profundity we perplex and enfeeble thought; and it is possible to make even Venus herself vanish from the firmament by a scrutiny too sustained, too concentrated, or too direct.[10]

Similarly, the truth of the state, the reality of its administrative effectivity, can only be known, I believe, by indirect glancing from attention directed sideways. But upon what? Upon social practices, members' methods, of producing and sustaining a rationally accountable reality. This is the way in which ethnomethodology teaches us side-long looking at social institutions (and in light of Dupin's characterization of truth it is interesting to note that it has been repeatedly accused of attending to trivial, superficial matters). Its virtue, against all forms of direct scrutiny, is that the objective properties of social reality are always construed as practical accomplishments of reality construction, i.e. taken as occasions for inquiry into members' methods: it has no need to preserve those properties as unexplicated warrants relied upon to make sense of inquiry as closer examination of substantive entities. But this is, inescapably, the need of direct scrutiny and one which compels it, however reluctantly, to reify whatever concepts are used to represent the object of inquiry. Even revelatory analysis, intending to demystify institutions by showing what really underlies ideological facades, is pulled back into that same method of reification which it aspires to dispel. The need, the resistance and the reluctant succumbing to the former are all displayed in Miliband's text with reference to the state and its power.

Miliband begins (p. 3) with a piece of hyperbolic reification to capture the reader's interest and set out his theme:

> More than ever before men now live in the shadow of the
> state. What they want to achieve, individually or in groups,
> now mainly depends on the state's sanction and support
> ....It is for the state's attention, or for its control, that
> men compete; and it is against the state that beat the waves
> of social conflict. It is to an ever greater degree the state
> which men encounter as they confront other men.

The theme is further summarized as a concern for 'the vast
inflation of the state's power and activity in the advanced
capitalist societies'. Miliband admits, however, that this is one
of the 'merest commonplaces of political analysis', thereby
posing the question of how it is to be made analytically remarkable. How can this commonplace topic be turned into a problem
capable of authorizing and sustaining a radically different analysis of state power? Rhetorical swelling of the topic will not do:
at best, it can only promote a feeling of urgency, which by no
means satisfies the cognitive requirement of thinking the topic
in a new way. For that, it must be relocated in a discursive
space which is not merely commonplace. Given Miliband's initial
references to the state and its power as a pervasive feature
of everyday life, it is imaginable that he could have proceeded
via an analysis of how the state is objectified through, and
realized in, everyday accounting procedures; how 'its' powerful
activities are normalized as obvious, natural features of our
social life in the ordinary practices of that life. Obedient,
however, to the logic of substantive revelation, Miliband can
only find and display the state as a problematic phenomenon
by presenting it as a real object whose inner essence differs
from what it is generally (mis)taken to be.

We recall here Althusser's previously quoted account of
empiricist knowledge as a process of extracting the inner reality
of an object through scouring, sifting, rubbing away its outer
appearance. In orthodox social science this is done through the
abrasive application of rigorous test procedures either to
common-sense beliefs or to existing theories within the discipline.
Since Miliband has already used common sense to ground the
reality of the state, he cannot use it again to locate mere
appearance: that significatory function falls to existing theory.
At this point a dilemma emerges that is inherent to the strategy.
As radical critique, the strategy dictates a break with 'orthodox' political theory, but as substantive revelation it is committed to the same outer-to-inner movement of empirical knowing.
Miliband must negate orthodox political theory within its own
methodological framework.

In discursive practice this means engaging in polemical warfare, i.e. a competitive struggle to evict an opponent in order
to occupy the same terrain more fully. Thus Miliband makes a
discrediting contrast between the ubiquitous presence of the

state in everyday experience and its relative absence as an object of theorizing in Western political science and sociology. This 'remarkable paradox' is interpreted polemically as symptomatic evidence of ideologically distorted vision. Specifically, political scientists cannot see the vast object before their eyes because they are looking towards the state through the same official 'theory' of political power which the state relies upon to legitimate its activities as the practices of a liberal democracy. The theory says that power is 'fragmented and diffused; everybody, directly or through organized groups, has some power and nobody has or can have too much of it' (p. 4). To the extent that students of politics conceptualize power as something fragmented and diffused in competitive pluralism, so will they have a fragmented and diffused view of the state. In effect, they will not be able to bring it into focus as a coherent thought-object and political theory itself will fragment and diffuse into diverse topics. Conversely, it follows that theoretic concentration upon the state as a coherent unitary institution requires a theory of power distribution as something concentrated, coherent and unitary. Marxism offers precisely such a theory (Miliband appeals particularly to Karl Kautsky's proposition that the capitalist class rules but does not govern, it contents itself with ruling the government), and can, therefore, claim an advantage in principle over pluralism.

Of course, this is not enough to win victory. One discourse has been championed and pitted against another, but it must prove itself superior under the judgement of some criterion for assessing the adequacy of social theories. Positivism prescribes trial by empirically accredited facts: alternatives, however, exist and choice is possible. Karl Mannheim has argued that social knowledge is of a type that arises only in situated, purposive action. Just as the moral interpretation of one's own conduct is actively invalidated if 'it does not allow for the accommodation of action and thought to a new and changed situation and in the end actually obscures and prevents this adjustment', so a social theory is wrong 'if in a given practical situation it uses concepts and categories which, if taken seriously, would prevent man from adjusting himself at that historical stage'.[11]

If Mannheim is found wanting, adequacy could be judged with reference to the moments of a dialectical process of human self-realization. Indeed, given Miliband's Marxian identification, one might expect to find him using an historical-dialectical mode of evaluation. And, to be fair, there are traces of this. For example, the concluding chapter claims that 'a pervasive sense of unfulfilled individual and collective possibilities penetrates and corrodes the climate of every advanced capitalist society',[12] and speaks of the need for theory capable of dissolving legitimation myths and translating the sense of unfulfilment into a will for socialist change. Yet passages of this kind only lie around the margins of Miliband's critique as rhetorical stress

marks; the non-empiricist criteria of theoretic adequacy which
they evoke do not effectively inform the critical work itself.
There we find empirical demonstration: demonstration of the
correctness of Kautsky's general proposition that there is a
capitalist class which rules government, demonstration that
the distribution of political power is, in measurable reality,
concentrated and not pluralistically diffused.

I take this as evidence of the constraining power of an
ontological commitment to substantive entities to rule in objecti-
vist-empiricist knowing and rule out other possibilities even
against authorial intention. That power is dramatically displayed at the opening of chapter 3, where the analysis of the
state begins in earnest. Here a break in the text occurs as
Miliband struggles belatedly to resist the spell of reification.
The startling news is given - startling in contrast to the solidity
and certainty of his first paragraph - that '"the state" is not
a thing, it does not, as such, exist'. What then of the state
as the massive object of Miliband's inquiry: the ubiquitous
presence which all men encounter in their daily lives; against
which, cliff-like, the waves of conflict beat; and under whose
vast and lengthening shadow most people now live? If the virtual
absence of that object from orthodox political theorizing is a
'remarkable paradox' marking its inadequacy, to assert now
that the state, as such, does not exist appears, to say the least,
an ironic twist. Yet it could be more than an ironic twist. It
could be a reflexive turn of the discourse against capture in
substantive ontologizing through which the entire imagery of
the state as a solid material thing will be revealed as part of a
distorted consciousness of social reality: a consciousness which
secures objective clarity at the cost of remaining obscure to
itself. This would be possible, however, only if Miliband had
another (and, I would argue, constitutive) theoretic place to
turn to. But he does not and, consequently, his discourse is
compelled to return to the same place. The break is mended,
its reflexive possibilities erased, by reintroducing 'the state'
as the nominal sum of component substantive entities (p. 46):

> What 'the state' stands for is a number of particular institu-
> tions which, together, constitute its reality, and which
> intersect as parts of what may be called the state system.

Direct scrutiny has been shifted from one reification, the
state, to a lower level set of reifications operating as a system.
Miliband has only blinked, and the way is open again for an
empirical investigation of standing objects. Thus Miliband proceeds to examine the substantive properties and systemic
interconnections of the central government, the political parties,
the civil service, the judiciary, the military, the police, parliamentary assemblies, and 'sub-central' governments as 'the
institutions in which "state power" lies'. Concretely, he uses
statistical, behavioural and circumstantial evidence to demon-

strate a biased mobilization of state activity (and inactivity) in favour of the values, norms and interests of those who own, control and manage 'private' capital (collectively called the dominant economic class). The demonstrated virtue of Marxian theory is not then that it offers a different and better way of knowing social reality (different and better than empirical political science) but that it performs the same scraping, sorting, sifting operations of empirical knowing more adequately. My criticism is that even if Marxism was to be judged the winner over all comers in such a contest, it would be a Pyrrhic victory, since the adequacy of the contest itself would, through unexamined acceptance, remain uncontested and the emancipatory potential of Marx's method of theorizing lost by default. There must be more to political critique than either empiricist challenge or oppositional rhetoric: they do not satisfy the founding interest of that form of thought.

THE BURDEN OF REALISM

To search further, I would like to return briefly to Miliband's question of whether or not the admittedly diverse groups of 'economic dominants' in advanced capitalist society (corporate executives, large shareholders, successful entrepreneurs, the propertied rich, independent businessmen and so on) actually constitute a coherent, solidary social class. I am not so much interested in the question or its resolution as in Miliband's declared need to answer it affirmatively (p. 23):

> The first requirement, therefore, is not to determine whether an economically dominant class does wield decisive economic power in these societies. It is rather to determine whether such a class exists at all. *Only after this has been decided does it become possible to discuss its political weight.* [Italics added.]

Considered purely as a declaration of discursive need, the passage can be read as a methodological insight into the imperatives of substantialist, ontological thinking. The same insight is retrievable from Jeremy Bentham's dictum, that

> Of nothing that has place, or passes, in our minds can we give any account, any otherwise than by speaking of it as if it were a portion of space, with portions of matter, some of them at rest, others moving in it ... otherwise than in the way of fiction.[13]

In Bentham's terms, 'political weight' is a property, a second-order fiction, which cannot be discussed except by investment in a first-order fictitious aggregate (like 'a dominant class') spoken of as if it had a material existence in (social) space.

Which is to say, by phenomenal reification. Miliband's positing of a dominant class as something out there in reality may be understood then as a way of speaking and a confession of what is needed to continue in that way, not merely as an empirical hypothesis open to testing. It is his commitment to speaking substantively and ontologically (in the 'as if' mode described by Bentham) which demands the objective existence of some such class as a 'first requirement'. There are two features of the commitment especially pertinent to our question of how political critique might be done differently and better than by substantive revelation. Both were noted previously (under the names objectivism and objectivity) as limits on existing readings of the Poor Law Reports; they reappear now as latent inhibitors of critical discourse, ensured by the innocent intent to do hard, honest, straightforward scrutiny of what is really going on in society. An intent which in blithely ignoring epistemoligical reflection of the possible grounds of knowing confines knowing to its own single, powerfully anti-reflective ground.

The commitment binds the inquirer (at least in our society) to a mode of knowledge production, conventionally called positivism, in which discursive truth claims must be validated by reference to an independent, external reality standing outside of discourse. Thus Miliband feels himself bound to respectfully consult reality as to the existence there of a dominant class in order to obtain permission to discuss it further. I do not wish to make an issue of being respectful or obtaining a discussion permit (when so much of our political language is already under the arbitrary dictation of passion, will to power, vested interest and ulterior motive, it would be gratuitous folly to recommend more disrespect). What does need to be made an issue is how to be properly respectful in social theorizing, and to what. The problem can be extended and sharpened by introducing the second feature, which is that the ontological concept of reality operates in the practice of inquiry to rule out the concept of reality as something actively constituted. The latter functions only as a negative sign placing a truth claim on the far side of knowledge; for example Miliband's criticism of the pluralist theory of power distribution as an ideological construct in which subjective commitment 'turns observation into myth'.[14] Given that 'reality' is the sole conceivable basis for genuine disputation, a substantialist positing of Reality as an absolute presence makes it seem that there is only one rational ground and one rational procedure for checking truth claims. The positivist mode of knowledge production is monopolistic and monological. An inquiry conducted in that mode cannot stop to seriously question Reality without threatening to undermine itself (cutting the ground from beneath its feet) because there is nowhere else for it to go. Thus Miliband inserts a startling break in his text through his declaration that the state does not exist but is compelled to erase it in order to proceed. The issue here is whether other grounds (places, venues, arenas, frameworks) of genuine disputation exist, and, if so, which is the appropriate one for political critique. We need to challenge Bentham's assertion that knowledge production is impossible except in the 'as if' fashion of substantialist ontology.

BREAKING THE SPELL OF REALISM

The issue of mistaken respect for reality is raised by Kant in the Preface to the Second Edition of the 'Critique of Pure Reason', where it is identified as one of two obstacles to learning from experience (the other being the removal of reason beyond experience so that it circles emptily in metaphysical play with mere concepts). Kant relates, in quasi-legendary manner, how the first man to demonstrate the properties of the isosceles triangle (perhaps Thales) introduced mankind to the secret of knowledge, namely, that to know the properties of any object it is not enough to scrutinize its physical features nor, at the other extreme, meditate upon metaphysical idea or concept,

> but that he had to produce (by construction) what he had himself, according to concepts *a priori*, placed into that figure and represented in it, so that, in order to know anything with certainty *a priori*, he must not attribute to that figure anything beyond what necessarily follows from what he has himself placed into it, in accordance with the concept.[15]

Reasoning about nature did not enter the certain path of knowledge signposted by geometry until seventeenth century experimenters also comprehended that

> reason has insight into that only which she herself produces on her own plan, and that she must move forward with the principles of her judgements, according to fixed law, and compel nature to answer her questions, but not let herself be led by nature, as it were in leading strings ....Reason must approach nature, in order to be taught by it: but not in the character of a pupil, who agrees with everything the master likes, but as an appointed judge, who compels the witnesses to answer the questions which he himself proposes.[16]

In these passages the ground of knowledge shifts dramatically from reality in itself to reality formed by a priori concepts of the knower, while the learning process depends upon a firm and by no means empirically subservient questioning of nature. Kant then reopens the question of reality yet, as Habermas has shown, not decisively enough to resist the monopolistic claim of natural science methodology to be the only valid court of witnessing and judgement (the claim of positivism). A mono-

polistic claim was possible, even invited, by Kant's restriction
of a priori concepts to a single mode of experience: the appre-
hension of objects in spatial-temporal intuition. From this it
follows that only one form of certain knowledge is possible, and
that form, for Kant, is manifested in the natural sciences. To
reveal his uniform concept of knowledge as an arbitrary closure
on other possibilities, allowing reality to be mistaken in a new
respect (for example, undertaking political critique as substantive revelation), we will follow Habermas's rethinking of the
principle[17] that the attribution of properties to reality be limited
to what the knower has placed into it 'in accordance with the
concept'. The concept Kant refers to is the intuition of object
(of sheer standing against consciousness), transcendent to all
actual objects and given in the universal structure of the human
mind. Habermas retains the idea of sub-cognitive 'standing
against' as the source and limit of knowledge but relocates it
in universal structures of human activity. Three structures
are identified, yielding three constitutive frameworks of knowledge; three places of genuine discourse (ways of posing questions, receiving answers and judging them) where learning
from experience can occur:
1 Instrumental activity towards successful means-ends manipulation and control giving a concept a priori of something
there in space-time. The world constituted by instrumental
activity (originally by 'work') comes to knowledge as the feed-
back-controlled learning of behavioural rules for handling
things. This is the formative framework of natural science and
technology.
2 Communicative activity towards mutual understanding in which
there is a concept a priori of a meaning there in the words,
gestures, actions of others. The world thus constituted comes
to knowledge as a recognition of 'grammatical' rules linking
words, gestures, actions into coherent meaning structures
through which an intersubjective sharing of experience can
occur. This is the formative framework of everyday interaction
which cultural-hermeneutic science amplifies, extends and relies
upon in doing interpretive studies. The knower must still proceed in accordance with properties he has himself placed in
objects of inquiry but now they are the interpretive schemata,
the sense-making practices of the culture to which he belongs
rather than the kind of properties Kant distilled from the
apperception of phenomenal objects. What Kant reconstructed
were not the constitutive features of all possible knowing but
those of knowing within instrumental-technical activity.
3 Self-realizing activity, conceived as a dialectical pulling
towards autonomy, informed by the concept a priori of a virtual
identity there. The 'concept' operates at individual and collective
levels in species behaviours variously analysed as the development of ego identity, maturation, evolution of moral consciousness, life-stage crises, the history of oppressed classes, liberation movements, freedom struggles, and so on. Their common

feature is resistance against arbitrary rule which is, dialectically, a movement drawn towards rational rule, i.e. the self-
determined rule of rational beings acting in unforced consensus.
This is a teleological destiny anticipated in the presuppositions
sustaining linguistic communication,[18] towards which consciousness fitfully moves. Crucial to such movement is critical reflection on whatever systematically obstructs and distorts it. All
critique, whether of pure reason, political economy, capitalism,
positivism, religion, the state, or (as in psychoanalysis) a life-
history, belongs to the activity of developmental release and
human self-realization. Knowledge occurs here as a recognition
of repressed, dislocated, displaced, distorted features of self
which is simultaneously a freeing toward self-rule.

For Habermas, rational self-rule or mature autonomy is the
ultimate human interest of knowledge, and critical reflection the
form of knowledge to which all others must be held answerable.
That this is not presently the case is obvious from the continuing power of natural science methodology to hold both hermeneutic and critical knowledge claims to its demands. For our purpose
there is no need to follow Habermas's further development of
critical theory as the supreme court of inquiry, it is sufficient
to accept that natural science, cultural-hermeneutic science and
critical theory (lately termed 'reconstructive science') are three
distinct places of genuine discourse, each with an experientially·
grounded sphere of authority. Also, that critical reflection,
as long as it lacks its own methodological principles and analytic
procedures, is always liable to fall unreflectively back into
those of natural and cultural-hermeneutic science. (Habermas
has shown, for example, how Marx and Freud came to misunder-
stand and misplace their reconstructive critiques in the natural
science framework.) We can now state more precisely and
extensively how Miliband (his strategy of critique) is unduly
respectful. He is so in two ways, both of them echoing methods
for preserving constitutive innocence noted previously in the
Poor Law Reports.

First, when Miliband objectifies state institutions and their
powerful activities as spatial-temporal entities and processes,
he is (mis)placing symbolically constituted meaning structures
(properly the domain of interpretive inquiry) under the jurisdiction of natural science investigation. He is analysing the
state in an undue respect as well as with undue respect in
Kant's sense of waiting to be taught by the facts. Secondly,
Miliband produces knowledge through unreflectively recognizing
his own a priori cognitive categories as explanations.
Primarily the explanations consist of attributing immediately
transparent motives to reified 'actors', and especially the most
transparent of all motives in our society: instrumentally rational
self-interest. For example, Miliband assembles the following
reasons to explain why societies ruled by capitalist class interests in private property display increasing public intervention
in the production and distribution of wealth:[19]

(a) The ruling class accepts limitations on specific property
rights as a 'ransom' grudgingly (but rationally) paid 'for the
purpose of maintaining the rights of property in general'.
(b) Governments prudentially intervene in the market economy
'as a result of popular pressure'.
(c) Big business accepts the 'welfare state' because 'there are
no more persistent and successful applicants for public assistance than the proud giants of the private enterprise system'.
(d) The ruling class realizes that there are 'imperative requirements of modern life' which cannot be met by the private enterprise system and must, therefore, be satisfied by the state.

Any competent member of our society, accustomed in everyday
life to using such a vocabulary of motives to make behaviour
accountable, would immediately recognize Miliband's reasons as
having the form of an adequate explanation, giving a content
which can be checked, tested, contested, amended, confirmed,
refuted and further worked upon. He could, recalling Kant,
'produce (by construction) what he had himself, according to
concepts *a priori*' placed into the text. It must be added though
that members' methods possess aprioristic force only within
cultural bounds. Beyond those bounds, from the standpoint of
analytic reflection on members' methods, they are revealed as
conventional habits lacking universal necessity. (It is precisely
this difference between culturally given and universally inescapable grounds of discourse which is addressed anxiously by
Mannheim in his sociology of knowledge and boldly by Habermas
in his theory of emancipatory movement toward the ideal speech
situation.)

To the extent that social inquiry relies upon the prior plausibility structures of cultural membership to provide a point of
start and return for interpretive validation, it cannot critically
question them, and is, therefore, caught by them in undue
respect. Adapting Harold Garfinkel's phraseology, it can be said
that in respectful hermeneutic explanation what social reality
can come to is what the ethnomethods of the interpreter's culture
can come to. Thus Miliband represents the political reality of
our society as the conduct of familiarly motivated actors whose
behaviours are understandable in the 'of course' mode of everyday practical reasoning: of course 'bourgeois politicians' will
act in defence of private property; of course 'new governments
of the left', faced with crises of business confidence will try to
reassure economic elites they have nothing to fear; of course
top civil servants, recruited from professional, middle-class,
wealthy, establishment backgrounds, will be biased in favour
of the status quo; of course those same civil servants, motivated to keep their jobs, will cooperate with 'socialist masters';
and of course there will be no great difficulty given the typical
bourgeois attitudes of the latter plus the calculative matrix of
electoral politics.

The strategy of substantive revelation is arrested in varying
combinations of this interpretive form of analysis with the

empiricist representation of elites, classes, groups, organizations and so on as if they were spatial-temporal objects in a
system of causal forces. In short, it unreflectively reproduces
the constitutive substructure of the social order it describes,
including methods of reality construction crucial to policy-
making and public administration. The emancipatory intent to
reconstruct that order is thereby thwarted at the methodological,
which is to say the deepest level. The intent does not, however,
disappear in Miliband's text but turns into something else; a
supplemental appeal to non-discursive action:

> Sooner or later, and despite all the immense obstacles in the
> way, the working class and its allies in other classes will
> acquire that faculty [of ruling the nation]. When they do,
> the socialist society they will create will not require the
> establishment of an all-powerful state on the ruins of the
> old. On the contrary, their 'faculty of ruling the nation'
> will, for the first time in history, enable them to bring into
> being an authentically democratic social order, a truly free
> society of self-governing men and women, in which, as Marx
> also put it the state will be converted 'from an organ super-
> imposed upon society into one completely subordinated to
> it.'[20]

THE WORK OF GOVERNING

Of particular interest to us here is the undefined phrase 'faculty
of ruling'. It is redolent with Benthamite associations of the
legislator's power of classifying, declassifying, aggregating,
disaggregating; and may be placed alongside 'the state's power'
and 'administration by technocrats' as proper glosses (Garfinkel's term) on the work of governing. Garfinkel also refers
to such formulating statements as 'accountable texts', and
poses the ingeniously provocative question, 'What is the work
for which (X) is that work's accountable text?'[21] Applying it to
Miliband's glosses, I would answer that the work consists of
displacing situated by textual reality and knowledge production
so as to achieve commandment of conduct by categories. If this
is so, then the meaning of 'an authentically democratic social
order' where 'the state is subordinated to society' would be an
assertion of the authority of situated over textual reality construction. Such an overturning would require, however, a
disintegration of the established 'faculty of ruling' and not
merely its acquisition by the working class. At best this would
involve nothing more than a change of agents, a replacement
of topdogs by underdogs, and events of modern times do not
even allow us to hope for the best. 'Revolutionary' governments,
regimes of former underdogs, have not merely acquired the
faculty of ruling, they have become members of it, appropriated
it and vastly improved its efficiency. The totalitarian state

(meaning total bureaucratization) is the projected perfection
of textual-documentary reality construction.

I do not say this to accuse Miliband of selective blindness to
the fate of self-government in 'socialist' societies founded in
Marxism. The issue raised here is not the distortion of critical
analysis by ideological bias but its inhibition by a substantive,
ontological set of thought, and its consequent inability to
strongly question political reality in the Kantian posture of an
appointed judge. My argument is that a critically effective
renewal of old questions concerning the state and society cannot begin until there is an adequate concept of the essential
work of the state: the work it does and cannot help but do.
The suggestion advanced here is that state activity is essentially
the ordering of social life in conformity with the rationalities
of reality and knowledge production in writing. Within those
rationalities social order is fashioned abstractly, semiotically
and trans-situationally rather than accomplished for the time
being and present purposes in concrete situations.[22] Further,
the improvisatory, ad hoc features of situated reality construction are, for legible order, problems which incessantly provoke
extensions and revisions of that same state activity which compels their recognition as problems.

The reconstruction of political analysis in these terms is, of
course, a formidable project which cannot be pursued here. I
would, however, add two points to avoid unnecessary mis-
understanding. First, the negating tension of textual against
situated reality construction is at source a structural, methodological feature of language: a function of the difference between
the written and spoken word. It should not be confused with
the group conflicts through which it is played out in particular
historical and institutional configurations. Reduction of the
tension to the wishes, wills, desires, ambitions of individual
and collective actors (for example, technocrats, bureaucrats,
central authorities and those who oppose them), would be a
regression to the form of theorizing we are trying to escape.

Second, the overburdened term 'repression' which we have
used to formulate the relationship of textual to situated reality
construction, carries with it connotations of coercive imposition.
Our formula might then be interpreted as a call to simply revolt
against textual-documentary reality construction, or even a
recommendation to abolish writing! Objectors could, quite cor-
rectly, cite overwhelming evidence of the benevolent aspects
of state intervention and public administration, they could also
point to popular demands for it. There is no need, however,
for evidential argument. The interpretation is ruled out by
our assumption that writing is an inherent potentiality of language and therefore of human being. Indeed it is only through
writing that the concept of emancipatory movement towards
virtual human identity has arisen. Any recommendation to
abolish it could only be heard as an arbitrary utopian closure
on human being, requiring tremendous repression (in the

ordinary sense) to sustain it. I use the word as a theoretical concept to refer to the way reality reporting sustains constitutive innocence by limiting reflection on its origins. It is this closure against reflection that we seek to resist.

TURNING THEORY INTO PRACTICE

I will conclude with some comments on the question of how the theory of social reality construction is to enter political practice. This cannot be set aside as an issue separate from that of conceptual adequacy, an additional matter of strategic and tactical planning, because critical theory depends upon practical enactment to test the validity of its concepts. This being so, the determination of when, where, how and by whom enactment is to be done should arise strictly from the theory itself and not involve recourse to extra-theoretical criteria. A quote from Habermas will allow us to open the topic further:

> By anticipating the context of its own application, critique differs from what Horkheimer has called 'traditional theory'. Critique understands that its claims to validity can be verified only in the successful process of enlightenment, and that means: in the practical discourse of those concerned.[23]

A characteristic feature of 'traditional theory' (which I take to be theory based upon a substantive, ontological concept of social reality), is that it separates the discursive testing of propositions by logical and empirical procedures from the application of those propositions after they have been validated. Social practice as the context of validation is strongly isolated from social practice as the object or arena of application; the former being a special place (called research, inquiry, scientific method, scholarship or something of the kind) from which the latter can be contemplatively known, and made available, if anyone so wishes, for rational action. This withdrawal of social theorizing from everyday social practice, enjoined by methodological norms of disciplined knowing, means that it has to undertake a subsequent and separate movement of return to achieve practical effectivity. 'Traditional theory' does not have effectivity simply in the course of being done; moreover, its concept of practical application as social engineering (piecemeal or otherwise), authorized by a model of analogical equivalences between natural and social science, has proven incapable of settling the matter. Indeed, the concept itself, through provoking humanistic and radical repugnance, has fuelled critiques of the analogical model behind it (critiques of positivism, scientism and the hegemony of instrumental reason in modern society) and thus contributed significantly to further unsettlement.[24] The problem is particularly acute where political practice is involved, for reasons that can be gleaned from Karl

Mannheim's questioning of whether a science of politics is possible.[25]

Mannheim questions the possibility of a science of politics so
as to assert a dogged (yet ambivalent) resistance to the law-
like enclosure of human behaviour which it implies. Rule and
contingency, closure and openness, determinacy and richness
are thematically elaborated, and a positive stress given to the
second term of each pair; not, however, in order to reject the
first term but to maintain a suitably human point of balance
between them. Mannheim writes here as a dialectician, not a
polemicist. He writes as though in accordance with Georg
Simmel's dictum, given in the context of a dialectical meditation
on the opposition between form and life, that 'Man's position
in the world is defined by the fact that in every dimension of
his being and his behaviour he stands at every moment between
two boundaries'.[26] Emancipation is not then to be found through
an opposition between boundary and absence of boundary (this
can lead only to the cul de sac of Utopian anarchist-libertarian
dreaming) but in, first, the dualistic relativization of particular
boundaries allowing, second, for stepping beyond such boundaries while recognizing, third, that being between boundaries
is the inescapable human condition so that every act of stepping
beyond 'finds or creates a new boundary'.[27]

The meaning of politics, for Mannheim, lies in acts of stepping
beyond 'routine affairs of state' or, more generally, the 'rationalized', 'stereotyped' structures of repetitive action in a society.
A political act involves choice and decision in the face of oncom-
ing events for which there are no sure prescriptions. It belongs
to the sphere of what Mannheim chooses to call 'conduct', and
conduct 'does not begin until we reach the area where rationalization has not yet penetrated, and where we are forced to
make decisions in situations which have as yet not been sub-
jected to regulation'.[28] From this preliminary formula, it is not
difficult to adduce difficulties for a science of politics and its
standing between theory and practice:
1 Science discovers law, regularity, pattern; therefore its
sphere of knowledge stops where 'conduct' begins. There could
be a science of administration (the routine affairs of state), a
science of what used to be politics, of what is no longer politics,
but not of politics itself.
2 Applied science rationalizes behaviour, consequently the
application of a science of politics would be in practice a contribution towards the elimination of politics. We have then the
strange spectacle of a science which (a) relies upon the negation of its ostensive sphere of interest to provide for its
theoretical work, and (b) contributes to that negation in the
course of being practically applied.

Mannheim does not raise difficulties to justify an abandonment
of what seems a hopeless project, leaving us with nothing better
than conventional wisdom to the effect that politics is an intuitive skill, or an art, beyond the scope of science. He is too

respectful of the achievements of science in bringing the
inscrutable and the irrational within the grasp of conscious
decision, and too fearful of the dark irrationalities of self
entwined with politics to accept their separation that easily.
A resolution is possible, he argues, if we extend our concept
of scientific knowledge beyond the positivist idealization of the
exact, mathematical sciences of nature to include knowledge
arising in, and only within, interested participation in social
practice:

> There is a type of knowledge which can never be conceived
> within the categories of a purely contemplative consciousness-
> as-such, and whose first assumption is the fact that we come
> to know our associates only in living and acting with them
> ... there are certain phenomena the perception of which
> depends upon the presence of certain collective purposes
> which reflect the interests of specific social strata. It appears
> then that clear-cut and readily objectifiable knowledge is
> possible in so far as it is a question of grasping those ele-
> ments in social reality which, to begin with, we described
> as settled and routinized components of social life ....When,
> however, we enter the realm of politics, in which every-
> thing is in process of becoming and where the collective
> element in us, as knowing subjects, helps to shape the pro-
> cess of becoming, where thought is not contemplation from
> the point of view of a spectator, but rather the active
> participation in and reshaping of the process itself, a new
> type of knowledge seems to emerge, namely, that in which
> decisions and standpoint are inseparably bound up together.
> In these realms there is no such thing as a purely theoretical
> outlook on the part of the observer.[29]

The relationship of theory to practice is now completely transformed but does not cease to be problematic. Whereas for a
positivistic science of politics the problem is how to achieve an
effective return of theory to political practice without further
nullifying its specifically political (let us say volitional, purposive, interested and collectively responsible) character, the
new problem is how to see theory as something within yet more
than practice so that it could make a reconstructive difference
to politics.

Mannheim admits that the limitation of political knowledge to
knowledge gained through interested collective action authorizes
the development of 'party theories' articulating the local truths
of partisan involvement, in which case the initial effect of his
theory of political knowledge would be to legitimate a sharpen-
ing of the antagonisms and separations of current political practice. This is conceived, however, as bringing the modern
problem of political life (the problem of relativism) to a critical
turning point; a point at which both the need and the possibility
of a 'true synthesis', a 'dynamic intellectual mediation' between

partisan knowledges, will become evident, allowing the entry of Mannheim's broader theory, the sociology of knowledge, into political life as an educative comprehension of the social rooting of all knowledge, that of others and one's own. It is in the form of 'critical self-reflection' that theory can be something within yet more than practice; a catalyst through which practice can immanently transcend particular, that is to say historically and culturally given limits to collective self-rule. It can be that but always with difficulty. Critical theorizing is not in itself a political activity and is always subject to confinement in intellectual circles of discourse. Mannheim warns that 'the theorizing subject is liable to be misled in the study of politics because his own contemplative attitude tends to subordinate his politically active attitude', consequently, 'the fact that sciences are cultivated in academic surroundings constitutes a danger in that the attitudes adequate to the understanding of an actual sector of human experience are suppressed in the contemplative atmosphere which prevails in academic institutions'.[30]

The force of the warning is evident in the hard words which activists have flung at Habermas, the most thoughtful, comprehensive and influential enunciator of critical theory in contemporary scholarship. For example, Rolf Ahlers has asked, How critical is critical theory? Recalling that in 1968, at the peak of the student radical movement, Habermas publicly disowned direct revolutionary action, thus joining 'the clever and safe intellectuals who may appear to be rather "red" in the conservative public press, but who are in reality very much part of the "system"'.[31] Similarly, though less violently, Murray Bookchin complains that 'the old Marxist vocabulary has been replaced by a more enervated one in which socially neutral concepts pirouette around each other in an intellectual ballet that imparts to them an almost dream-like transcendental quality ... theoretical critique has been notable for its absence of radical reconstruction'.[32] In Mannheimean fashion he links the practical irrelevance of theory to 'a retreat from the factory to the academy' and to a disengagement of the academy from society.

Mannheim's theory does not, however, require hard words or fearful metaphors of impotence to drive it from the contemplative groves of academe, it is already forbidden to take up residence there by its own precept that political knowledge is gained only by committed participants pursuing interests generated by their location in society. If then a dynamic mediation or synthesis between partisan perspectives is to be achieved, the new science of politics to be developed, it must be through a group which simultaneously embodies such perspectives yet recognizes and needs to sublate their partiality – a group whose particular cognitive interest is universal comprehension, a group which is of society but not firmly located in any part of it; which is, as it were, socially rooted and socially homeless at the same time. Mannheim claims the real existence of such a group and uses Alfred Weber's term, the 'socially unattached intelligentsia', to name it.

The claim cannot, of course, be accepted at face value. Even a cursory inspection of its required characteristics is enough to display its purely imaginary, hopeful and utopian character. Mannheim comes close to acknowledging as much when he says that, historically, the biographies of individual intellectuals do not typically show them undertaking the synthesizing function; teaching men to see the socially conditioned limits of their own thinking and its commonality with that of opponents. Rather, they have chosen to affiliate with this or that contending group, using their plasticity to efface themselves, like impressionists, in a borrowed voice and character. The notion of betrayal comes close to surfacing here but Mannheim resists it, saying: 'Such social dereliction and transgression may be regarded as no more than a negative misuse of a peculiar social position.'[33] He means that there is no need of moral exhortation to bring intellectuals to their tutelary mission; the distrust, the rejection, the rebuffs received from their adopted groups 'must lead eventually to a clearer conception on the part of intellectuals of the meaning and value of their own position in the social order'.[34] So much then for the interested need of the 'socially unattached intelligentsia' to undertake the work of dynamic synthesis: it will be taken up as a last resort when all else has failed! Clearly, the missionary group Mannheim describes does not exist and has never existed except in the demands of his text. As such it is one of a long line of fabulous agents invented by practically oriented theorists to bridge a gap between aspirational reach and analytic grasp. Such agents belong to what might be called a rhetoric of excess and deficiency, a troping of the anxiety of impotence virtually present in every strong project to change the world by theory.[35]

Karl Marx's completely dehumanized Proletariat, the blind, implacable agent of his theory of history (and so incongruent with those 'working men' who could be reasonably addressed in manifestos and speeches), is another example. A more complete case of the syndrome (which we take to be symptomatic of inadequate conceptualization) is that of Jeremy Bentham. Bentham once exulted,

> I have formed a plan of universal conquest. I intend to govern all the nations in the habitable globe after my death – With what weapons? With rhetoric? With fine speeches? With prohibitive and irritant clauses? – No: but with reasons, with a chain of ... articulate and connected reasons, all depending upon one principle.[36]

The practical application of the chain, however, demanded a man of knowledge and action, a superman, the 'Moses of England':

He must be the nation's supreme metaphysician-lexicographer, logician and deontologist[37] - moralist, endowed with both a sharp analytic mind and a fervent, sensitive, moral imagination, a creator of new values as well as language ... he will be a Statesman. And he will bring about the necessary synthesis of is and ought by sympathetic insight into the Utilitarian logic of the will.[38]

When no Statesman, or even a passable approximation, called at his door, Bentham fell back to the rhetoric of despair and deficiency:

He pipes but they do not dance - he makes advances but they do not follow ... I have done nothing, but I could do something - I am of some value - there are materials in me, if anybody would but find out. As it is I am ashamed of an unrecognized existence.[39]

There, fully displayed, are the three elements of the syndrome of conceptual inadequacy:rhetorical excess, rhetorical despair and a fabulous agent of mediation and synthesis.

I would note finally with regard to Mannheim, and to draw one more lesson from him about the demands of adequate political critique, that even if the problem of agency were to be set aside, his theory would still not be able to specify the circumstances of its application because it is paralysed by an inner ambivalence of intent. This stems in turn from Mannheim's unresolved ambivalence between relativism and objectivism, analysed previously. It returns here as an unreflective vacillation between the values of forcing back the boundaries of decision (reducing the sphere of 'conduct'), and the value of conduct itself. Positive and negative signs are attached to each reciprocal. The positive value of forcing back decisions is to gain rational mastery and control over irrational forces. Its negative value is the Weberean spectre of a disenchanted, completely rule-governed social world. The negative and positive evaluations of conduct are given by obversion.

Two quotations will make the point (and it is interesting to note that they are placed in adjacent but separately titled essays in Mannheim's text, as if compartmentalization was being used as a self-publicizing defence against ambivalence):

This much may be safely asserted: politics as politics is possible only as long as the realm of the irrational still exists (where it disappears 'administration' takes its place) ....In politics the rational element is inherently intertwined with the irrational; and, finally, there is a tendency to eliminate the irrational from the realm of the social, and in close connection therewith, there results a heightened awareness of factors which have hitherto dominated us unconsciously ....At this point the ethical principle of responsibility begins

to dawn ... Max Weber has furnished the first acceptable
formulation of this conception of politics. His ideas and
researches reflect the stage in ethics and politics in which
blind fate seems to be at least partially in the course of
disappearance in the social process, and the knowledge
of everything knowable becomes the obligation of the acting person.[40]

'Obligation' derives from the Latin ligo, meaning to bind and,
therefore, make inactive. In the second quotation, following, it
appears that knowledge might deliver us from irrational 'blind
fate' but only into a rational replacement where we are bound
by rules instead of unconscious forces:

We could change the whole of society to-morrow if everybody
could agree. The real obstacle is that every individual is
bound into a system of established relationships which to a
large extent hamper his will. But these 'established relationships' in the last analysis rest again upon uncontrolled decisions of individuals. The task, therefore, is to remove that
source of difficulty by unveiling the hidden motives behind
the individual's decisions, thus putting him in a position
really to choose. Then, and only then would his decisions
really lie with him ....It is possible, therefore, that in the
future, in a world in which there is never anything new ...
there can exist a condition in which thought will be utterly
devoid of all ideological and utopian elements. But the complete elimination of reality-transcending elements from our
world would lead us to a 'matter-of-factness' which ultimately
would mean the decay of the human will ....The disappearance of utopia brings about a static state of affairs in which
man himself becomes no more than a thing. We would be
faced then with the greatest paradox imaginable, namely,
that man, who has achieved the highest degree of rational
mastery of existence, left without any ideals, becomes a
mere creature of impulses.[41]

It would be wrong to attribute these ambivalent contradictions
to Mannheim personally, as though he suffered from dyslexia.
We must understand them as the cracks and stresses of an
established theoretical language no longer capable of sustaining
emancipatory reflection on political experience. There could be
no clearer demonstration that political critique is hopelessly
hampered by its conventional terms of discourse and the rejuvenation will depend upon the invention of a radically different
system of signification.

From Mannheim we can now see better how it is that the entry
of critical theory into political practice is particularly problematic.

First, the idea of politics (even allowing for its disentangle-
ment from 'routine affairs of state') is torn between two contra-

dictory concepts: the democratic concept of dialogic communication between equal participants, open to one another in the interest of their future together, where matters are settled exclusively by the force of the best argument; and the Machiavellian concept of politics as the coolly calculative maximization of strategic advantage in power games. Critical theory must make a commitment one way or the other in the course of anticipating its context of application. The familiar tactic of reluctantly accepting the latter as a necessary but temporary means of achieving the former (for example, in notions of the dictatorship of the proletariat and the acquisition by underdogs of the 'faculty of rule'), has turned out in practice to be a binding commitment. On this issue I accept Habermas's argument that the proper context of application for critical theory consists of activities capable of validating or refuting it, and these are limited to 'the organization of enlightenment' (emancipatory reflection to dissolve false consciousness). The 'organization of action' is explicitly placed beyond its sphere of authority:

> The practical consequences of self-reflection are changes in attitude which result from insight into the causalities *in the past*, and indeed result of themselves. In contrast, strategic action oriented toward the future, which is prepared for in the internal discussions of groups, who (as the avant-garde) presuppose for themselves already successfully completed processes of enlightenment, cannot be justified in the same manner by reflective knowledge.[42]

More generally (and still tracking Habermas), politics represents a peculiarly sensitive configuration of technical and practical 'interests' (where 'interest' designates a pre-theoretical unity of thought and action, a constitutive context of knowledge which is relied upon by reflective reasoning to provide a sphere of validatory application). They are: environmental mastery; mutual understanding within a cultural tradition; and dialogical openness on the future. These are all constrained, however, by the eminently practical imperative of decisional closure for the time being on what to do next in the face of problems constituted as pressing for a collectivity. This is the organizing principle of political practice to which the other 'interests' and the knowledges they provide for are subservient; and the juncture at which theory is sublated into something, a decision, which is simultaneously more and less than itself. More, because thought now returns to 'the unity of the life context'[43] from which it has been abstracted; less, because it must, in that decisive moment, give up its questioning cultivation of alternatives for the sake of settlement. This is true of all theory but is especially problematic for critique, whose work it is to question apparent parameters of settlement (the causality of nature, the causality of fate, the ineluctable hold of habit) in the emancipatory interest of willed choice. Critique, to be true to itself, must always be approaching and stopping short at the threshold of decision, baulking at that for the sake of which it claims to talk, leaving itself open to charges of cowardice, obstructionism or worse, depending upon the political degrees of freedom and emotional structuring of urgency in particular situations. I wish, however, to stress the inherent difficulties of critique in entering the political process, those arising from its need to become part of decision-making while maintaining question marks against any particular grounds of decisional closure, rather than contingencies of censorship and sanction. My concern here is with methodological problems of 'free speech', presuming that the right has been institutionalized.

To the problem of questioning while participating in decisional closure we must add that of questioning the limits while not denying the legitimacy of the technical and hermeneutic forms of knowledge in political practice. Such denial would be indefensible since it would be an arbitrary denial of the pre-reflective experiences (the 'interests') grounding them, which belong to the totality of collective life. Critical theory must resist excessive claims; i.e. claims transgressing the possibilities of validation contained in their experiential origins, without itself falling into hubris. In particular, critical theory 'must guard against overburdening the concepts of the philosophy of reflection',[44] as in anticipations of world revolution and universal human emancipation. Its vital task, as political critique, is the more modest one of inducing critical reflection in situated occasions of decision-making: a task for which the conceptual capacity to reveal hidden mechanisms of reality production is the crucial and distinctive requirement.

The context of application anticipated by critical theory can be ascertained through the following question: In what circumstances would the performance of that theory be effective as an emancipatory activity simply in being done? In ethnomethodological terms the question would be: What kind of context would be required to make that theory's performance an indexical expression of emancipatory interest in autonomy and responsibility? In the case of our own theory, whose enactment consists of an emancipatory reading directed against the constitutive innocence of reports, texts, documents and the like (that is to say, their hidden power to construct social reality in determinate ways), the general answer is: All decision-making occasions strongly ruled by the rationalities of textual reality construction. These would include all kinds of documentary transform scenes: the 'turning of real lives into writing' (Foucault's phrase), whereby individuals are brought under the normative rule of behavioural sciences and technologies; the mobilization of reports, plans, surveys, etc. (in committee deliberations, public hearings and legislative debates) to formulate options and warrant choices; and the bureaucratic implementation of central directives at local levels. If these, rather than factory floors, picket lines and street corners, are the anticipated contexts of application; if, moreover, occasioned performance of the theory is the practical action, and the only one, it authorizes, then the question of how social theorists can have practical efficacy can be heard as a call for adequate theorizing rather than an ethical challenge to descend from theory to practice, or as a sarcastic slur.

I would note, finally, that there is no need to make special strategic provision for lines of action linking the academic places where theory is cultivated to institutional contexts of application elsewhere. The elements of a transmissional network have already been provided by two frequently discussed changes in our society which have gained significant impetus since the Second World War:

1 The extension of rights of access to decision-making so that its objects can, and occasionally do, become participants. (For example, workers in industry, students and parents in schools, patients in hospitals, consumers in the regulation of commerce, residents in the planning of communities.)[45]

2 The increasing centrality of properly certified knowledge for the decisional ordering of society.[46] To elaborate the point, it is helpful to recall Foucault's concept of truth as 'a system of ordered procedures for the production, regulation, distribution and circulation of statements',[47] this being constitutively linked with systems of power to form a 'regime of truth'. In these terms our society is characterized not only by the specifically scientific basis of its regime but by the pivotal role of this structural element (every society has a regime of truth) in its total organization; that is, in our way of being a society. Universities, merely through their responsibilities for developing, passing on and certifying knowledge cannot help but be crucially involved in the entire institutional order. Ivory tower isolation is in our time an impossibility:

> The lecturer and the university emerge, not perhaps as principal elements, but as 'exchangers', privileged points of intersection ....And what is called the crisis in the universities [Foucault is probably thinking of student radicalism and its consequences] should not be interpreted as a loss of power, but on the contrary as a multiplication and reinforcement of their power-effects at the centre of a multiform ensemble of intellectuals who practically all pass through and relate themselves to it.[48]

The intellectuals referred to by Foucault are nothing like Mannheim's socially unattached intelligentsia, whose prototype is the philosopher writing on behalf of humanity and its universal ideals; they are 'specific' intellectuals occupationally lodged in government, public administration, welfare work, the legal system, the economy, corrective and curative institutions, etc.: that is to say in the anticipated contexts of application for a critical theory of social reality construction.

Effective utilization of the available network depends ultimately on the conceptual adequacy of theory to induce emancipatory reflection, but it would also require curricular arrangements to ensure that the education of 'specific' intellectuals
includes this form of knowledge. For us that would mean new
courses oriented to the constitutive power of writing practices,
which would begin with the assumption that we do not yet
know how to read. Moreover, if critical theory, to have practical validation, must be performed live in concrete situations
of decision-making, then it follows that the critical theorist
must have some art as a performer, for which an appropriate
pedagogy would have to be designed. I do not mean rhetorical
skill to sway audiences - Socrates' critique of oratory as bad
speech in 'Gorgias', and again in 'Phaedrus', is sufficient to
dispel that idea[49] - but something like an ability to restore a
reflexive movement to language in the face of legislative writing (i.e. writing which unreflectively holds social life to its
own rules of rational order). In this way we might hope to
ensure that decisions are chosen by participants and not simply
made by unexamined rules of reason.

NOTES

INTRODUCTION

1 'Report from His Majesty's Commissioners for Inquiry into the Administration and Practical Operation of the Poor Laws', Session 1834, vol. XXVII, p. 1.
2 'Report of the Royal Commission on the Poor Laws and the Relief of Distress', Session 1909, vol. XXXVII, Terms of Reference.
3 Maurice Bruce, 'The Coming of the Welfare State', London: Batsford, 1968, p. 16.
4 There was an initial attempt to formulate types of reading (or what might better be called meta-readings) from pertinent literatures: to derive, for example, a structuralist reading, a hermeneutic reading, and so on. The overwhelming disadvantage of this procedure was the constant temptation to shift from using terms as convenient labels to an ideal-type distillation of methods corresponding to each type of reading. Not only does this raise the problem of typifying authors, especially creative pioneers who by nature are adverse to settlement and often disclaim the names visited upon them, but it holds the classifier accountable for the propriety of his categories and the representative adequacy of those he has nominated to them. Not wishing to be held accountable in that way – being faithful/unfaithful, fair/unfair, complete/incomplete, etc. – I have for the most part preferred to avoid typification in favour of triangular interplays between particular authors, the texts and my projected model of meta-reading.
5 I am indebted to Beng Haut-Chua for introducing me to this concept in the work of Dorothy Smith.
6 S.E. Finer, 'The Life and Times of Sir Edwin Chadwick', London: Methuen, 1952, p. 39.
7 From a comparative-historical viewpoint it is interesting to note that the report (for 1975), after stating that the central concern of the Supplementary Benefits Commission is with poverty, defines that condition in terms of living conditions relative to 'the average citizen' and as lack of means to 'participate in the social system'. A far cry indeed from previous constructions of poverty in terms of threats to minimal subsistence standards.
8 David Galloway, 'The Public Prodigals', London: Temple Smith, 1976.
9 An instructive analysis of graphetic, lexical and grammatical differences between popular and 'quality' newspaper styles is contained in David Crystal and Derek Davy, 'Investigating English Style', Bloomington: Indiana University Press, 1969, ch. 7.
10 V. Palic, 'Government Publications: A Guide to Bibliographic Tools', Washington: Library of Congress, 1975.
11 Comparable labours on the British scene are: J.G. Olle, 'An Introduction to British Government Publications', London: Association of Assistant Librarians, 1973; J. Pemberton, 'British Official Publications', Oxford: Pergamon Press, 1973.
   Her Majesty's Stationery Office publishes a 'Daily List of Government Publications', consolidated into Monthly and Annual Catalogues.
12 Stanton Wheeler (ed.), 'On Record: Files and Dossiers in American Life', New York: Russell Sage Foundation, 1969.

13 Ibid., p. 5.
14 Ibid., p. 6.
15 Ibid., p. 9.
16 Ibid., p. 25.
17 David A. Goslin and Nancy Bordier, Record-keeping in elementary and secondary schools, in Wheeler, op. cit., ch. 2.
18 Kenneth C. Leiter, Ad hocing in the schools, in A. Cicourel et al., 'Language Use and School Performance', New York: Academic Press, 1974, ch. 2.
19 Ibid., p. 17.
20 The nature of these contributions is reviewed in Hugh M. Clokie and J. William Robinson, 'Royal Commissions of Inquiry', Stanford University Press, 1937. See also T.J. Cartwright, 'Royal Commissions and Departmental Committees in Britain', Hodder and Stoughton, 1975.
21 Clokie and Robinson, op. cit., p. 121.

CHAPTER 1 THE CONCEPT OF TEXTUAL REALITY CONSTRUCTION

1 Richard J. Bernstein, 'The Restructuring of Social and Political Theory', Oxford: Blackwell, 1976.
2 The arguments have been thoroughly rehearsed, and scarcely require elaboration. See, for example, Peter McHugh, The failure of positivism, in J. Douglas (ed.), 'Understanding Everyday Life', Chicago: Aldine, 1970. See, also, contributions in Anthony Giddens (ed.), 'Positivism and Sociology', London: Heinemann, 1974.
3 This rather awkward formulation of Kant's problem is derived from M. Heidegger, 'What is a Thing?' Chicago: Henry Regnery, 1967.
4 A good account of psychologistic misunderstandings of Kant is provided in G. Bird, 'Kant's Theory of Knowledge', London: Routledge and Kegan Paul, 1962, ch. 1.
5 An especially stimulating review and renewal of Kantian critique is given in J. Habermas, 'Knowledge and Human Interests', Boston: Beacon Hill, 1971.
6 Dorothy Smith, The social construction of documentary reality, 'Sociological Inquiry' 44(4), 1974: 257-68.
7 H. Garfinkel, Aspects of the problem of common sense knowledge of social structures, 'Transactions of the Fourth World Congress of Sociology', Belgium: International Sociology Association, 1959, p. 55.
8 D. Zimmerman, Record-keeping and the intake process in a public welfare agency, in S. Wheeler (ed.), 'On Record: Files and Dossiers in American Life', New York: Russell Sage Foundation, 1969, pp. 319-54.
9 Ibid., pp. 330-1.
10 H. Garfinkel, 'Good' organizational reasons for 'bad' clinical records, in R. Turner (ed.), 'Ethnomethodology', London: Penguin Books, 1974, pp. 109-27.
11 Ibid., p. 122.
12 Ibid., p. 121.
13 Ibid., p. 122.
14 Smith, Social construction of documentary reality, op. cit., p. 260.
15 Ibid., p. 267.
16 See, for example, James Heap, What are sense-making practices?, 'Sociological Inquiry', 46(2), 1976: 107-15.
17 Brian Lee, Letter from Haltwhistle, 'Encounter', Feb. 1978: 25-35.
18 Ibid., p. 27.
19 Ibid., p. 35.
20 For examples see: Severyn Bruyn, 'The Humanistic Perspective in Sociology', Englewood Cliffs, N.J.: Prentice-Hall, 1966; Norman K. Denzin, 'The Research Act', Chicago: Aldine, 1970; Phillip Hammond (ed.), 'Sociologists at Work', New York: Basic Books, 1964.
21 Georges Gurvitch, 'The Social Frameworks of Knowledge', Oxford,

Blackwell, 1971, p. xxv.

22 The idea of applying rhetorical analysis to science writing is not, of course, a new one. See, for example, J. Gusfield, The literary rhetoric of science: comedy and pathos in drinking driver research, 'American Sociological Review', Feb. 1976, 16-34.

23 Harold Bloom, 'A Map of Misreading', New York: Oxford University Press, 1975.

24 Ibid., p. 93.

25 Ibid., p. 74.

26 Ibid., p. 72.

27 Ibid., p. 98.

28 Ibid., p. 73.

29 The Poor Law Report of 1834, p. 56. Of these evils, the greatest is profusion, stemming from contagious moral sentiments like pity which are inherent to situated, personal interaction.

30 Bloom, op. cit., p. 101.

31 Ibid., p. 74.

32 Ibid., p. 74.

33 Ibid., p. 94.

34 A similar conclusion is drawn by John O'Neill in a critical commentary on the Gusfield paper cited previously: J. O'Neill, The literary production of natural and social science inquiry, Unpublished manuscript, York University, Toronto, 1979.

CHAPTER 2 HOW THE REPORTS HAVE BEEN READ: A CRITIQUE OF READING METHODS

1 J. Habermas, 'Knowledge and Human Interests', Boston, Beacon Hill, 1971, p. 68.

2 S.G. and E.O.A. Checkland (eds), 'The Poor Law Report of 1834', London: Penguin Books, 1974, pp. 30, 31.

3 James Taylor, The mythology of the old poor law, 'Journal of Economic History', 1969, pp. 292-7.

4 J. Habermas, History and evolution, 'Telos', Spring 1979, p. 6.

5 Sidney and Beatrice Webb, 'English Poor Law History', (vols vii-ix of 'English Local Government'), London, 1927; J.R. Poynter, 'Society and Pauperism', London: Routledge and Kegan Paul, 1969; J.D. Marshall, 'The Old Poor Law 1795-1834', London: Macmillan, 1968; Michael E. Rose, 'The Relief of Poverty 1834-1914', London: Macmillan, 1972.

6 Maurice Bruce, 'The Coming of the Welfare State', London: Batsford, 1968; Oliver MacDonagh, 'Early Victorian Government, 1830-1870', London: Weidenfeld and Nicholson, 1977.

7 E.P. Thompson, 'The Making of the English Working Class', London: Victor Gollancz, 1963.

8 Bruce, op. cit., p. 7.

9 Rose, op. cit., p. 6.

10 J. Habermas, History and evolution, op. cit., p. 8.

11 Ibid., p. 43.

12 In letters written during 1865-7 when Marx was striving simultaneously to get 'Das Kapital' ready for publication and organize the International Workingmen's Association, he repeatedly refers to the former as 'my work' and the latter as an interruption, a distraction, taking up his scarce time and energy. Apologizing to Sigfrid Meyer for not writing sooner, Marx explains, 'I had to utilize every possible moment when I was capable of working, in order to complete my work, for which I have sacrificed health, happiness and family ... I would really have considered myself *impractical* if I had croaked without having finished my book.' (See P. Padover (tr. ed.), 'The Letters of Karl Marx', New Jersey: Prentice-Hall, 1979, pp. 228-9. Also, letters to Engels, pp. 197, 198, and Kugelmann, p. 219, ibid.)

13 The distinction between the expressive and the documentary meaning of a cultural product - the former relating the product (which includes gestures, actions, utterances) to subjective intent on the part of the producer, the latter to some objective code, 'grammar' or structural rules of composition embodied in the product - is taken from Karl Mannheim's essay, On the interpretation of Weltanschauung, in K. Wolff (ed.), 'From Karl Mannheim', New York: Oxford University Press, 1971, pp. 8-58.

14 For a detailed account see D. Reid, The decline of Saint Monday 1766-1876, 'Past and Present', May 1976, pp. 76-102.

15 S.E. Finer, 'The Life and Times of Sir Edwin Chadwick', London: Methuen, 1952.

16 Ibid., p. 82.

17 K. Mannheim, The problem of the sociology of knowledge, in Wolff, 'From Karl Mannheim', op. cit., pp. 59-115.

18 Ibid., p. 65.

19 Ibid., p. 65.

20 Ibid., p. 66.

21 A brief suggestion of what other language-games might be involved is offered by Jurgen Habermas in a footnote to his essay What is universal pragmatics? (see, J. Habermas, 'Communication and the Evolution of Society', Boston: Beacon Press, 1979, pp. 208-10), as a typology of social action based on a primary distinction between communicative and strategic action. Discourse is a type within the former category: the latter includes both manipulation and 'systematically distorted communication' (ideological warfare and unwitting capture in false consciousness). In terms of Habermas's model, unmasking would proceed by showing that one or more of the validity claims essential to communicative action (in addition to referential validity that is) have not been met. The honest intent of the speaker - his truthfulness - is one such claim.

22 Mannheim, op. cit., pp. 70-1, passim.

23 K. Mannheim, 'Ideology and Utopia', London: Routledge & Kegan Paul, 1936, p. 3.

24 Ibid., p. 95.

25 Ibid., p. 76.

26 Ibid., p. 78.

27 Mannheim, The problem of the sociology of knowledge, op. cit., p. 62.

28 Mannheim, 'Ideology and Utopia', op. cit., p. 88.

29 Ibid., p. 5.

30 Mannheim, The problem of the sociology of knowledge, op. cit., p. 97.

31 Mannheim, 'Ideology and Utopia', op. cit., pp. 87-9, passim.

32 Mannheim, Conservative thought, in 'From Karl Mannheim', op. cit., pp. 132-222.

33 Ibid., pp. 153-4.

34 Mannheim, 'Ideology and Utopia', op. cit., p. 79.

35 See, Mannheim, The problem of a sociology of knowledge, op. cit., p. 105.

36 Mannheim, The ideological and the sociological interpretation of intellectual phenomena, in 'From Karl Mannheim', op. cit., p. 119.

37 Ibid., p. 117.

38 The problem of a sociology of knowledge, op. cit., p. 63.

39 Ibid., pp. 107-9, passim.

40 Walter Benjamin, The author as producer, in 'Reflections', New York: Harcourt, Brace, Jovanovich, 1978, p. 222.

41 Mannheim, On the interpretation of Weltanschauung, 'From Karl Mannheim', op. cit., p. 26.

42 The ideological and sociological interpretation of intellectual phenomena, op. cit., pp. 126-7.

43 J. Habermas, 'Knowledge and Human Interests', op. cit.

44 Mannheim, 'Ideology and Utopia', op. cit., p. 169.

45 Ibid., p. 230.

CHAPTER 3 READING AND REALITY EFFECTS

1 See, M. Brodbeck (ed.), 'Readings in the Philosophy of Social Science', New York: Macmillan, 1968; also, S. Lukes, Methodological individualism reconsidered, in D. Emmet and A. MacIntyre (eds), 'Sociological Theory and Philosophical Analysis', London: Macmillan, 1970, pp. 76-88 (Footnote 12 of the article provides extensive bibliographic references on the topic.)
2 Mortimer, J. Adler and Charles Van Doren, 'How to Read a Book', New York: Simon and Schuster, 1972.
3 Ibid., p. 8.
4 E.D. Hirsch, Jr., 'Validity in Interpretation', New York: Yale University Press, 1967, p. 5.
5 Ibid., p. 23.
6 J.B. Kerfoot, 'How to Read', New York: Houghton Mifflin, 1916.
7 Ibid., p. 21.
8 Ibid., pp. 225, 237 and 248.
9 J. Habermas, 'Knowledge and Human Interests', Boston: Beacon Hill, 1971, elaborates the point in reviewing Dilthey's theory of understanding.
10 F. Nietzsche, 'On the Genealogy of Morals', New York: Random House, 1969, p. 45.
11 Peter J. Rabinowitz, Truth in fiction: a reexamination of audiences, 'Critical Inquiry', Autumn 1977: 121-41.
12 Ibid., p. 126.
13 Ibid., p. 128.
14 George Herbert Mead, 'The Philosophy of the Act', University of Chicago Press, 1938, p. 3.
15 Ibid., pp. 24-5.
16 Ibid., p. 7.
17 Ibid., p. 109.
18 Ibid., p. 445.
19 E.D. Hirsch, 'Validity in Interpretation', op. cit., ch. 3.
20 Ibid., p. 93.
21 Rabinowitz, op. cit., p. 131.
22 David Goldknopf, 'The Life of the Novel', University of Chicago Press, 1972, p. 1.
23 Ibid., p. 43.
24 Robert Scholes, Toward a semiotics of literature, 'Critical Inquiry', Autumn 1977, pp. 105-20.
25 Ibid., p. 109.
26 J. Rex, 'Sociology and the Demystification of the Modern World', London: Routledge & Kegan Paul, 1974, p. 17.
27 Ibid., p. 17.
28 On the connection between piety and strong style see Kenneth Burke, 'Permanence and Change', Indianapolis: Bobbs-Merrill, 1954.
29 Scholes, op. cit., p. 109.
30 Mark Blaug, The myth of the Old Poor Law and the making of the New, 'Journal of Economic History', June 1963, p. 177.
31 Barbara Rosenblum, Style as social process, 'American Sociological Review', June 1978: pp. 422-38.

CHAPTER 4 REALITY EFFECTS IN THE POOR LAW REPORTS

1 S.G. and E.O.A. Checkland (eds), 'The Poor Law Report of 1834', London: Penguin Books, 1974, p. 9.
2 Ibid., p. 31.
3 I am thinking here of Max Weber, Science as a vocation, in H. Gerth and C.W. Mills, 'From Max Weber', Oxford 1946.
4 M. Blaug, The Poor Law reexamined, 'Journal of Economic History', June 1964, 229-45.

5 D. Goldknopf, 'The Life of the Novel', University of Chicago Press, 1972, p. 31.
6 Schutz and Luckmann, 'The Structure of the Life World', London, Heinemann, 1974, p. 28.
7 Ibid., p. 28.
8 M. Heidegger, 'What is a Thing?' Chicago: Henry Regnery, 1967, p. 137.
9 Ibid., p. 139.
10 Ibid., pp. 139-40.
11 George Simpson (ed.), 'Emile Durkheim (Selections from his Work)', New York: Thomas Crowell, 1963, pp. 26-8 passim.
12 Ibid., pp. 29-30.
13 Ibid., p. 27.
14 Ibid., p. 27.
15 Ibid., p. 25.
16 Ibid., p. 93.
17 Ibid., pp. 95-7 passim.
18 Steven Lukes, 'Emile Durkheim: His Life and Work', London: Penguin Books, 1973, pp. 435-7.
19 Quoted by Lukes, ibid., p. 492.
20 Quoted by Lukes, ibid., p. 494.
21 'The Effect of Outdoor Relief on Wages and the Conditions of Employment', Reports, Commissioners, 1909, XLIII, Cd. 4690, p. 65.
22 Philip Wiener (ed.), 'Charles S. Peirce: Selected Writings', New York: Dover Publications, 1966, p. 107. On scholastic realism see Peirce's Critical review of Berkeley's idealism, ibid., pp. 73-88.
23 Sir George Nicholls, 'A History of the English Poor Law', (3 vols.) London: King & Son, 1898.
24 Schutz and Luckmann, op. cit., pp. 59-60.
25 Ibid., p. 60.
26 Ibid., pp. 75-7 passim.
27 Ibid., p. 80.
28 Ibid., p. 249.
29 Ibid., p. 281.
30 In referrring to the 'grammar' of a text I am thinking of the regular ways in which motive words, expressive words, labelling words, action words, etc. are organized as properly formed descriptions, explanations, qualifications, elaborations, criticisms and so on rather than rules of proper sentence construction. Habermas displays a similar usage in reviewing Dilthey's account of hermeneutic methodology. From this it appears that a text is a symbolic articulation of names, actions and expressive signs the meaning of which can be grasped as the structured orderliness of their interplay. See, J. Habermas, 'Knowledge and Human Interests', Boston: Beacon Hill, 1971, ch. 8.
31 Murray G. Murphey, 'Our Knowledge of the Historical Past', New York: Bobbs-Merrill, 1973, p. 123.
32 D. Zimmerman, Fact as a practical accomplishment, in R. Turner (ed.), 'Ethnomethodology', London: Penguin Books, 1974, p. 135.
33 Harold Garfinkel, Suicide, for all practical purposes, in R. Turner (ed.), 'Ethnomethodology', op. cit., p. 100.
34 Ibid., p. 100.
35 Louis Althusser, 'Reading Capital', London: NLB, 1970, p. 56.

CHAPTER 5:   THE PRODUCTION OF KNOWLEDGE EFFECTS IN THE REPORTS

1 Kant directly expresses the principle that rule-government of contingency is the essence of knowledge in these passages from the 'Critique of Pure Reason': 'From whence should experience take its certainty, if all the rules were always again and again empirical, and therefore contingent?' (T. Greene, 'Kant Selections', New York: Scribner's, 1957, p. 29). And again: 'We have before given various definitions of the understanding,

by calling it the spontaneity of knowledge, or the faculty of thinking ....
We may now characterize it as the faculty of rules. This characteristic
is more significant, and approaches nearer to the essence of understanding' (p. 90).

The indispensability of contingency for knowing is variously revealed
by Kant. For example, in the argument that 'Mathematical concepts, by
themselves, are not yet knowledge' (ibid., p. 96) because they are
'pure'. They do not become knowledge until applied to empirical intuitions
of phenomena, i.e. until recognized as rules in and of contingency.
Similarly, the product of Kant's subtraction of everything empirically
contingent from our representation of things is a perfectly complete
account of the limits of knowledge: a tribunal to which all knowledge claims
are subordinate and from which there is no appeal. Rules beyond contingency are also beyond the process of knowledge. They are fixed and
finished 'as a capital that can never be added to' (p. 18). Kant had to
remove contingency in order to arrive at the bounds of knowledge; in
doing so he demonstrates the necessity of contingency for knowledge to
proceed.

Charles Peirce, probably Kant's most dedicated reader, revised the
question of knowledge by asking how cumulatively valid learning from
experience is possible (again with the progress of natural science in
mind). His answer confirms the joint role of contingency and rule. Want
of knowledge arises as a privation of habit, 'a condition of erratic
activity that in some way must get superseded by a habit'. (P. Wiener,
'Charles S. Peirce: Selected Writings', New York: Dover, 1966, p. 181.)
Contingency provides for genuine doubt or surprise, the settlement of
which through conjectural hypothesis, deductive amplification and induc-
tive checking is a knowledge effect. When Peirce goes on to argue that a
pure chance world would be unknowable because it could not engender
privation of habit, I take him to be affirming again that knowledge effects
are produced only in conjunctions of rule and contingency.

2 Bentham's critique of D'Alembert occurs in his proposal to found a
Chrestomathic School (the neologism means conducive to useful learning)
based upon new teaching methods. (See, Chrestomathia, in J. Bowring,
'The Works of Jeremy Bentham', New York: Russell and Russell, 1962,
vol. VIII.) To plan the curriculum he found it necessary to undertake a
complete codification of human knowledge, using his privileged method
of species and genera classification constructed by exhaustive bifurcation.
Thus pure knowledge of Being is Ontology. This splits into 'Coenoscopic'
knowledge of what is common to all existent being and 'Ideoscopic' knowledge of what is peculiar to particular classes of being. The latter bifurcates
into 'Somotology' and 'Pneumatology'; Somotology into 'Posology' and
'Piology'; Pneumatology into 'Noology' and 'Pathology', etc. The finished
table lays out the whole field of human knowledge to the interested eye.
Each label (for those knowing Greek roots) telling what a category contains,
and the interconnections telling the relationships between branches of
knowledge. Bentham says of such an exhaustive classification system with
a proper nomenclature that there are 'No parts in it, from which through
the medium of these appropriate denominations ... ideas, more or less
clear, correct and complete are not radiated to the surveying eye: in a
word, no absolutely dark spots' (ibid., p. 101).

Contrastively, D'Alembert's encyclopedic map of knowledge shows the
defects of an improperly constructed taxonomy: vague labels which do
not properly define (or appropriate) what is intended; the use of three
fold, four fold and other irregular divisions departing from the certainty
of either-or bifurcation; mere nominal distinctions ungrounded in a
demonstration of significant difference; the appearance of an object in
more than one category; and, finally, a lack of propositional connectives
to join the categories into a coherent discourse.

My point is that what Bentham saw as self-evident deficiencies in
D'Alembert's map (its illegibilities) is what the Commissioners could see

as self-evidently wrong in the operation of the Poor Laws, and this
because all were seeing (knowing) within the same taxonomic mode of
evident rationality.
3 M. Foucault ('The Order of Things', London: Tavistock Publications,
1970) identifies three modes of knowledge production in his archeological
history of Western European thought. Each is organized around a
distinct rule of evident rationality and displays characteristic ways of
making word-thing connections.

The first, corresponding to pre-seventeenth century Renaissance
thought, conceives the world as a divinely authored text whose meaning
has been obscured by the fragmentation of the single original language in
which it was composed into the diverse languages of men. However, the
visible marks of things, their relationships of proximal connection and
similitude, provide decipherable clues to their place in the unitary chain
of being. Knowing proceeds as an interpretive search for essential
qualities and linkages readable in indicative marks and iconic signs
(Charles Peirce defined an icon as that which signifies through resemblance). Knowledge is the elaboration of exegetical commentary on the world
as text. There is no problem here of accurately representing objects in
language because no essential separation between things and words is
acknowledged.

The second knowledge code, the 'Classical episteme', appearing abruptly
at the end of the seventeenth century, construes the world as things
existing in determinate sets of adjacency and separation, identity and
difference: a subdivided region to be represented in a taxonomic order
of signs overlaying it. Bentham knew whatever topic he turned to in this
way.

In the third, the modern, episteme appearing in the early nineteenth
century, the world is thought differently again. Now things cohere into
systems with their own functional unities and developmental rules which
knowers strive to reproduce in models of structural maintenance, functional process, evolutionary transformation, and sequential emergence.
Foucault characterizes it comparatively in these passages from 'The Order
of Things':

> the general area of knowledge is no longer that of identities and
> differences ... of a general taxinomia ... but an area made up of
> organic structures, that is, of internal functions between elements
> whose totality performs a function; it (archeological analysis) will
> show that these organic structures are discontinuous, that they
> do not, therefore, form a table of unbroken simultaneities, but that
> certain of them are on the same level whereas others form series of
> linear sequences [p. 218].

> The space or order, which served as a *common place* for represent-
> ation and for things, for empirical visibility and for the essential
> rules, which united the regularities of nature and the resemblances
> of imagination in the grid of identities and differences, which displayed
> the empirical sequence of representations in a simultaneous table,
> and made it possible to scan step by step, in accordance with a logi-
> cal sequence, the totality of nature's elements thus rendered contemp-
> oraneous with one another - this space or order is from now on shat-
> tered: there will be things, with their own organic structures ... the
> space that articulates them, the time that produces them; and then
> representation, a purely temporal succession, in which those things
> address themselves (always partially) to a subjectivity, a conscious-
> ness, a singular effort of cognition [p. 239].

I would add that in applying Foucault to the Poor Law Reports I have
deliberately resisted the temptation to read him as a philosopher of history
chopping a horizontal time continuum into epistemic segments. Certainly

such a reading could be justified by his fine dating references to complete 'ruptures' and 'breaks'. One would then be led into the potentially absurd procedure of hypothesizing particular break dates and examining documents as tests of such hypotheses. This, however, would ignore Foucault's repeated insistence that he is doing an archeology of knowledge and not a history of ideas. Whereas 'history' locates things on a continuum receding horizontally back from the present, 'archeology' locates them in vertical layers extending downward in a work site. Thus a document like the 1834 Report would have to be treated not as a periodized object but as an excavation site in which more than one knowledge code might be uncovered. For the purpose of exploring knowledge effects I will treat Foucault's epistemes as three distinct ways of recognizing legibility and illegibility in a textually formulated reality.

4 The concept of a legisign is taken from Charles Peirce's semiotic. It defines one of three ways in which a sign exists as something in itself ready for use. A sign can exist as unembodied quality, say redness, (a Qualisign); an embodied collection of qualities, say an individual piece of cloth, (a Sinsign); or as a general type projecting endless replicas of itself, for example the word 'pauper' as a class name. This is a Legisign.

The concept can be developed by recalling Garfinkel's analysis of the knowledge work performed by Suicide Center inquirers for the Coroner's Office in Los Angeles. They begin with an array of possible death titles and seek to affix one to each case as it comes. That is, they begin with a set of legisigns and search through the remnants of a death - the 'whatsoever bits and pieces' - to see if they can be recognized as replicas of one general type over the others. An authoritative finding on type of death brings the particulars of a case under the governance of a legisign. In this we observe the epistemological function of the legisign as a search device which precedes research, helping to guarantee a rational order for inquiry to discover. A legisign has something of the active constitutive powers of scanning devices: sonar equipment finding objects in the echoes of the ultrasonic waves it transmits, radar sets picking up whatever is and can be reflected in their radio waves. It is in this sense that a legisign 'seeks' and 'finds' its own replicative reflections as objects in the world.

To this must be added the political connotations of saying that legisigns have an active ordering power. These are strongly displayed in Bentham's linguistic theory of good government. The primary instrument for achieving the greatest good of the greatest number was to be a reformed language of legislation obedient to the rules of a universal grammar of practical discourse which Bentham called the logic of will. Mary Mack ('Jeremy Bentham: An Odyssey of Ideas', London: Heinemann, 1962) observes, 'the logic of the will is a class logic ....Its prerequisite dictionary is occupied in distributing groups of people into logical not social classes. It has subjects and objects, it commands someone to do something - to himself (self-regarding law); to other individuals (private law); to groups (semi-public law); to his fellow citizens in general (public or constitutional law)' (p. 181). Since Bentham says that the strength of government consists in being able to make people act by class and the power of the legislator is that of aggregation and disaggregation, then, as the name of a class is a legisign, there is an overtly political meaning to the notion of legisign governance. A legisign is simultaneously a device for knowing and controlling conduct. It is the core of rational administration.

5 The following account is based upon Jameson, 'The Prison-House of Language', Princeton University Press, 1972, pp. 163-8.
6 S. Finer, 'The Life and Times of Sir Edwin Chadwick', London: Methuen, 1952, p. 69.
7 E. Leach, 'Culture and Communication', Cambridge University Press, 1976, p. 61.
8 Foucault, op. cit., p. 335.
9 These different possibilities of knowing social life are, of course, familiar

in academic sociology as an unresolved methodological debate concerning the very purpose and nature of the discipline. It appears particularly in critiques of scientistic or positivistic sociology, i.e. rejections of the second method of knowing as inappropriate to this subject matter. Given the tendency of such critiques to romanticize the concepts of membership and community, two comments are in order concerning my own use of the distinction. First, I see it as a difference between two forms of textual reality construction and not between a method continuous with members' situated practices (faithful to real social life) and a method radically discontinuous with them. The method of idealized membership (using their own categories of meaning) is not continuous with situated reality construction, on the contrary it stands in place of it as a written substitute. Consequently, even if there was 'metaphysical pathos' attached to the concept of actual, personal community it could not legitimate a preference for that method. Second, there are no connotations of kindness and cruelty, humanity or inhumanity attached to the distinction. Idealized membership could authorize the branding of paupers as well as charity for the impotent; similarly, masterful intervention could authorize programmes of education, physical care and occupational training as well as incarceration under regimes of expert authority.

10 Foucault, 'The Order of Things', op. cit., p. 217.
11 Ibid., pp. 229-30 passim.
12 I have in mind here the book 'Primitive Classification' by Emile Durkheim and Marcel Mauss, University of Chicago Press, 1963 (First published as an article in L'Année Sociologique, 1903).
13 House of Commons, 1909, vol. xxxlx.
14 See, for example, Gregory Bateson, 'Steps to an Ecology of Mind', New York: Chandler, 1972, pp. 128-52 and 405-16.
15 Ibid., p. 413.
16 Thomas G. Bergin, 'An Approach to Dante', London: The Bodley Head, 1965, pp. 269-70.
17 Foucault, 'The Order of Things', op. cit., p. 256.
18 J. Derrida (tr. Gayatri Spivak), of 'Grammatology', Johns Hopkins Press, 1976, p. 216.
19 On desocialization-resocialization practices see, for example, E. Goffman, 'Asylums', New York: Doubleday, 1961: pp. 127-69; B. Bettelheim, 'Symbolic Wounds', London: Thames and Hudson, 1955; E. Schein, Brainwashing, in W. Bennis et al., 'Inter-Personal Dynamics', Homewood Ill.: Dorsey, 1964.
20 L. Althusser, 'Reading Capital', London: NLB, 1970, pp. 35-7, passim.
21 Ibid., p. 61.
22 Ibid., p. 59.
23 Ibid., p. 59.
24 Ibid., pp. 51-3, passim.
25 Ibid., pp. 66-7.
26 A. Schutz and T. Luckmann, 'The Structures of the Life World', London: Heinemann, 1974; also P. Berger and T. Luckmann, 'The Social Construction of Reality', New York: Doubleday, 1966.
27 Berger and Luckmann, ibid., make this argument strongly in their Introduction, pp. 1-18.
28 E. Durkheim, 'Professional Ethics and Civic Morals', London: Routledge & Kegan Paul, 1957, pp. 155 ff.
29 H. Garfinkel and H. Sacks, On formal structures of practical actions, in J. McKinney and E. Tiryakian, 'Theoretical Sociology', New York: Appleton-Century Crofts, 1970, p. 338.
30 The separation is traced out in various works of Habermas. For example, 'Knowledge and Human Interests', Boston: Beacon Hill, 1971; 'Theory and Practice', Heinemann, 1974; Rationalism divided in two, in Giddens (ed.), 'Positivism and Sociology', London, Heinemann, 1974, pp. 195-224.
31 J. Habermas, What is universal pragmatics? in 'Communication and the Evolution of Society', Boston: Beacon Press, 1979, pp. 1-68.

32 Much of Morrison's work is not presently available in published form. This includes his doctoral dissertation (cited in the Preface). Also, Social objects and their rendered specificity, paper presented at the Ethnomethodology Session, 9th World Congress of Sociology, Uppsala, Sweden, 1978; and Some researchable recurrences in social science and natural science inquiry, paper presented at the International Conference on Practical Reasoning and Discourse Practices, St. Hugh's College, Oxford, 1979.
   One article in publication is, Some properties of 'telling-order designs' in dialectical inquiry, 'Philosophy of the Social Sciences', June 1981.

CHAPTER 6 TEXTUAL REALITY CONSTRUCTION AND POLITICAL CRITIQUE

 1 N. Bobbio, Is there a marxist theory of the state?, 'Telos', Spring 1978, pp. 5-16. Also, Are there alternatives to representative democracy, pp. 17-30.
 2 A. Arato, Understanding bureaucratic centralism, 'Telos', Spring 1978, pp. 73, 74.
 3 M. Foucault, 'Discipline and Punish', New York: Pantheon Books, 1977.
 4 Ibid., p. 19.
 5 Ibid., p. 192.
 6 Ibid., p. 194.
 7 Ibid., p. 197.
 8 Ibid., p. 205.
 9 Ralph Miliband, 'The State in Capitalist Society', London: Quartet Books, 1973.
10 Edgar Allan Poe, 'Tales and The Raven and Other Poems', Columbus, Ohio: Charles E. Merrill, 1969, pp. 131-2.
11 K. Mannheim, 'Ideology and Utopia', London: Routledge & Kegan Paul, p. 85. See also pp. 38-43, 146-53, 253-75 for elaborations of the activist, purposive, situated concept of truth and validity.
12 Miliband, op. cit., p. 241.
13 Bentham, A fragment on ontology, in J. Bowring, 'The Works of Jeremy Bentham', vol. VIII, New York: Russell and Russell, 1962, p. 199.
14 Miliband, op. cit., p. 131.
15 T. Greene (ed.), 'Kant Selections', New York: Scribner's, 1957, p. 11.
16 Ibid., p. 12.
17 The following account is taken from J. Habermas, 'Knowledge and Human Interests', Boston: Beacon Hill, 1971.
18 Habermas has attempted to specify the universal properties of communicative action in his essay What is universal pragmatics?, in 'Communication and the Evolution of Society', Boston: Beacon Press, 1979, pp. 1-68.
19 Miliband, op. cit., p. 72, passim.
20 Ibid., p. 247.
21 H. Garfinkel and H. Sacks, On formal structures of practical actions, in McKinney and Tiryakian, 'Theoretical Sociology', p. 352.
22 The contrast, harking back to Scholes's discussion of writing, also bears resemblances to Garfinkel's distinction between scientific and common-sense rationality. See, H. Garfinkel, The rational properties of scientific and common-sense activities in A. Giddens (ed.), 'Positivism and Sociology', London: Heinemann, 1974, pp. 53-74.
23 J. Habermas, 'Theory and Practice', London: Heinemann, 1974, p. 2.
24 For a concise review of these issues, see, Brian Fay, 'Social Theory and Political Practice', London: Allen and Unwin, 1975.
25 Mannheim, 'Ideology and Utopia', op. cit., ch. 3.
26 D. Levine (ed.), 'Georg Simmel on Individuality and Social Form', University of Chicago, 1971, p. 353.
27 Ibid., p. 354.
28 Mannheim, 'Ideology and Utopia', op. cit., p. 102.
29 Ibid., pp. 150-2, passim.
30 Ibid., p. 154.

31 R. Ahlers, How critical is critical theory?, 'Cultural Hermeneutics', August 1975; 119-36, p. 133.
32 M. Bookchin, Beyond neo-marxism, 'Telos', Summer 1978: 5-28, p. 5.
33 Mannheim, 'Ideology and Utopia', op. cit., p. 141.
34 Ibid., p. 142.
35 The root of the problem of anxiety may be in the nature of language itself. Frederic Jameson, tracing out the implications of structuralism says, 'language can never really express any *thing*: only relationships (Saussurean linguistics) or sheer absence (Mallarme). Thus language has of necessity recourse to indirection, to substitution: itself a substitute, it must replace that empty centre of content with something else, and it does so either by saying what the content is like (metaphor), or describing its context and the contours of its absence, listing the things that border around it (metonymy).' ('The Prison-House of Language', Princeton University Press, 1972, pp. 122-3.) Small wonder that theory might suspect itself of impotence to really change things (assuming that this is what reality consists of).
36 Quoted by Mary Mack, 'Jeremy Bentham: An Odyssey of Ideas', London: Heinemann, 1962, pp. 273-4.
37 Deontology was defined by Bentham as the art-and-science of what is fitting and proper to be done in particular situations; very close to Mannheim's concept of politics as an active science.
38 Quoted by Mack, ibid., p. 291.
39 Ibid., pp. 4, 9.
40 Mannheim, 'Ideology and Utopia', op. cit., pp. 170-1.
41 Ibid., pp. 234-6, passim.
42 Habermas, 'Theory and Practice', op. cit., p. 39.
43 Ibid., p. 9.
44 Ibid., p. 13.
45 For illustratory discussions of the process see, T. Cook and P. Morgan, 'Participatory Democracy', San Francisco: Canfield Press, 1971; C. Pateman, 'Participation and Democratic Theory', Cambridge University Press, 1970; M. Kotler, 'Neighbourhood-Government', New York: Bobbs-Merrill, 1969.
46 See, for example, B. Holzner and J. Marx, 'Knowledge Application', Boston: Allyn and Bacon, 1979; D. Price, 'The Scientific Estate', Cambridge, Mass.: Belknap Press, 1967; H. Wilensky, 'Organizational Intelligence', New York: Basic Books, 1967.
47 M. Foucault, The political function of the intellectual, in 'Radical Philosophy', Summer 1977: 12-14, p. 14.
48 Ibid., p. 12.
49 The 'Phaedrus' dialogue resonates with themes close to our concerns. Not only does it dwell on the negative tension between writing and speech (the occasion of the dialogue is a speech written by Lysias, 'the best writer living', for anyone to use who wishes to obtain the favour of a boy who is not in love with him), but Socrates' artfully ironic performance serves as a kind of mirror-play in which the badness of legislative writing (in this case, technical instruction on turning a non-lover into a lover) is critically reflected so as to dissolve its hold on the enthusiastic Phaedrus. In this dialogue, as in 'Gorgias', Socrates seeks to show that knowledge of technically effective rules of communication is foolish and misleading when divorced from concern with the good of speaking and writing. Socrates is a distantly close model of the practically skilled critical theorist.

Routledge Social Science Series

Routledge & Kegan Paul   London, Henley and Boston

39 Store Street,
London WC1E 7DD
Broadway House,
Newtown Road,
Henley-on-Thames,
Oxon RG9 1EN
9 Park Street,
Boston, Mass. 02108

Contents

*Authors wishing to submit manuscripts for any series
in this catalogue should send them to the Social Science Editor,
Routledge & Kegan Paul Ltd, 39 Store Street,
London WC1E 7DD.*
● *Books so marked are available in paperback.*
○ *Books so marked are available in paperback only.*
*All books are in metric Demy 8vo format (216 × 138mm approx.)
unless otherwise stated.*

2

International Library of Sociology
General Editor   John Rex

GENERAL SOCIOLOGY

Barnsley, J. H. The Social Reality of Ethics. *464 pp.*
Brown, Robert. Explanation in Social Science. *208 pp.*
● Rules and Laws in Sociology. *192 pp.*
Bruford, W. H. Chekhov and His Russia. *A Sociological Study. 244 pp.*
Burton, F. and **Carlen, P.** Official Discourse. *On Discourse Analysis, Government Publications, Ideology. About 140 pp.*
Cain, Maureen E. Society and the Policeman's Role. *326 pp.*
● **Fletcher, Colin.** Beneath the Surface. *An Account of Three Styles of Sociological Research. 221 pp.*
Gibson, Quentin. The Logic of Social Enquiry. *240 pp.*
Glassner, B. Essential Interactionism. *208 pp.*
Glucksmann, M. Structuralist Analysis in Contemporary Social Thought. *212 pp.*
Gurvitch, Georges. Sociology of Law. *Foreword by Roscoe Pound. 264 pp.*
Hinkle, R. Founding Theory of American Sociology 1881–1913. *About 350 pp.*
Homans, George C. Sentiments and Activities. *336 pp.*
Johnson, Harry M. Sociology: *A Systematic Introduction. Foreword by Robert K. Merton. 710 pp.*
● **Keat, Russell** and **Urry, John.** Social Theory as Science. *278 pp.*
Mannheim, Karl. Essays on Sociology and Social Psychology. *Edited by Paul Kecskemeti. With Editorial Note by Adolph Lowe. 344 pp.*
Martindale, Don. The Nature and Types of Sociological Theory. *292 pp.*
● **Maus, Heinz.** A Short History of Sociology. *234 pp.*
Myrdal, Gunnar. Value in Social Theory: *A Collection of Essays on Methodology. Edited by Paul Streeten. 332 pp.*
Ogburn, William F. and **Nimkoff, Meyer F.** A Handbook of Sociology. *Preface by Karl Mannheim. 656 pp. 46 figures. 35 tables.*
Parsons, Talcott and **Smelser, Neil J.** Economy and Society: *A Study in the Integration of Economic and Social Theory. 362 pp.*
Payne, G., Dingwall, R., Payne, J. and **Carter, M.** Sociology and Social Research. *About 250 pp.*
Podgórecki, A. Practical Social Sciences. *About 200 pp.*
Podgorecki, A. and **Łos, M.** Multidimensional Sociology. *268 pp.*
Raffel, S. Matters of Fact. *A Sociological Inquiry. 152 pp.*
● **Rex, John.** Key Problems of Sociological Theory. *220 pp.*
Sociology and the Demystification of the Modern World. *282 pp.*
● **Rex, John.** (Ed.) Approaches to Sociology. *Contributions by Peter Abell, Frank Bechhofer, Basil Bernstein, Ronald Fletcher, David Frisby, Miriam Glucksmann, Peter Lassman, Herminio Martins, John Rex, Roland Robertson, John Westergaard and Jock Young. 302 pp.*
Rigby, A. Alternative Realities. *352 pp.*
Roche, M. Phenomenology, Language and the Social Sciences. *374 pp.*
Sahay, A. Sociological Analysis. *220 pp.*
Strasser, Hermann. The Normative Structure of Sociology. *Conservative and Emancipatory Themes in Social Thought. About 340 pp.*
Strong, P. Ceremonial Order of the Clinic. *267 pp.*
Urry, John. Reference Groups and the Theory of Revolution. *244 pp.*
Weinberg, E. Development of Sociology in the Soviet Union. *173 pp.*

FOREIGN CLASSICS OF SOCIOLOGY

● **Gerth, H. H.** and **Mills, C. Wright.** From Max Weber: *Essays in Sociology. 502 pp.*

● **Tönnies, Ferdinand.** Community and Association *(Gemeinschaft und Gesell-schaft).\Translated and Supplemented by Charles P. Loomis. Foreword by Pitirim A. Sorokin. 334 pp.*

SOCIAL STRUCTURE

Andreski, Stanislav. Military Organization and Society. *Foreword by Professor A. R. Radcliffe-Brown. 226 pp. 1 folder.*

Broom, L., Lancaster Jones, F., McDonnell, P. and **Williams, T.** The Inheritance of Inequality. *About 180 pp.*

Carlton, Eric. Ideology and Social Order. *Foreword by Professor Philip Abrahams. About 320 pp.*

Clegg, S. and **Dunkerley, D.** Organization, Class and Control. *614 pp.*

Coontz, Sydney H. Population Theories and the Economic Interpretation. *202 pp.*

Coser, Lewis. The Functions of Social Conflict. *204 pp.*

Crook, I. and **D.** The First Years of the Yangyi Commune. *304 pp., illustrated.*

Dickie-Clark, H. F. Marginal Situation: *A Sociological Study of a Coloured Group. 240 pp. 11 tables.*

Giner, S. and **Archer, M. S.** (Eds) Contemporary Europe: *Social Structures and Cultural Patterns, 336 pp.*

● **Glaser, Barney** and **Strauss, Anselm L.** Status Passage: *A Formal Theory. 212 pp.*

Glass, D. V. (Ed.) Social Mobility in Britain. *Contributions by J. Berent, T. Bottomore, R. C. Chambers, J. Floud, D. V. Glass, J. R. Hall, H. T. Himmelweit, R. K. Kelsall, F. M. Martin, C. A. Moser, R. Mukherjee and W. Ziegel. 420 pp.*

Kelsall, R. K. Higher Civil Servants in Britain: *From 1870 to the Present Day. 268 pp. 31 tables.*

● **Lawton, Denis.** Social Class, Language and Education. *192 pp.*

McLeish, John. The Theory of Social Change: *Four Views Considered. 128 pp.*

● **Marsh, David C.** The Changing Social Structure of England and Wales, 1871–1961. *Revised edition. 288 pp.*

Menzies, Ken. Talcott Parsons and the Social Image of Man. *About 208 pp.*

● **Mouzelis, Nicos.** Organization and Bureaucracy. *An Analysis of Modern Theories. 240 pp.*

● **Ossowski, Stanislaw.** Class Structure in the Social Consciousness. *210 pp.*

● **Podgórecki, Adam.** Law and Society. *302 pp.*

Renner, Karl. Institutions of Private Law and Their Social Functions. *Edited, with an Introduction and Notes, by O. Kahn-Freud. Translated by Agnes Schwarzschild. 316 pp.*

Rex, J. and **Tomlinson, S.** Colonial Immigrants in a British City. *A Class Analysis. 368 pp.*

Smooha, S. Israel: Pluralism and Conflict. *472 pp.*

Wesolowski, W. Class, Strata and Power. *Trans. and with Introduction by G. Kolankiewicz. 160 pp.*

Zureik, E. Palestinians in Israel. *A Study in Internal Colonialism. 264 pp.*

SOCIOLOGY AND POLITICS

Acton, T. A. Gypsy Politics and Social Change. *316 pp.*

Burton, F. Politics of Legitimacy. *Struggles in a Belfast Community. 250 pp.*

Crook, I. and **D.** Revolution in a Chinese Village. *Ten Mile Inn. 216 pp., illustrated.*

Etzioni-Halevy, E. Political Manipulation and Administrative Power. *A Comparative Study. About 200 pp.*

Fielding, N. The National Front. *About 250 pp.*

● **Hechter, Michael.** Internal Colonialism. *The Celtic Fringe in British National Development, 1536–1966. 380 pp.*

Kornhauser, William. The Politics of Mass Society. *272 pp. 20 tables.*

Korpi, W. The Working Class in Welfare Capitalism. *Work, Unions and Politics in Sweden. 472 pp.*

Kroes, R. Soldiers and Students. *A Study of Right- and Left-wing Students. 174 pp.*

Martin, Roderick. Sociology of Power. *About 272 pp.*

Merquior, J. G. Rousseau and Weber. *A Study in the Theory of Legitimacy. About 288 pp.*

Myrdal, Gunnar. The Political Element in the Development of Economic Theory. *Translated from the German by Paul Streeten. 282 pp.*

Varma, B. N. The Sociology and Politics of Development. *A Theoretical Study. 236 pp.*

Wong, S.-L. Sociology and Socialism in Contemporary China. *160 pp.*

Wootton, Graham. Workers, Unions and the State. *188 pp.*

CRIMINOLOGY

Ancel, Marc. Social Defence: *A Modern Approach to Criminal Problems. Foreword by Leon Radzinowicz. 240 pp.*

Athens, L. Violent Criminal Acts and Actors. *104 pp.*

Cain, Maureen E. Society and the Policeman's Role. *326 pp.*

Cloward, Richard A. and **Ohlin, Lloyd E.** Delinquency and Opportunity: *A Theory of Delinquent Gangs. 248 pp.*

Downes, David M. The Delinquent Solution. *A Study in Subcultural Theory. 296 pp.*

Friedlander, Kate. The Psycho-Analytical Approach to Juvenile Delinquency: *Theory, Case Studies, Treatment. 320 pp.*

Gleuck, Sheldon and **Eleanor.** Family Environment and Delinquency. *With the statistical assistance of Rose W. Kneznek. 340 pp.*

Lopez-Rey, Manuel. Crime. *An Analytical Appraisal. 288 pp.*

Mannheim, Hermann. Comparative Criminology: *A Text Book. Two volumes. 442 pp. and 380 pp.*

Morris, Terence. The Criminal Area: *A Study in Social Ecology. Foreword by Hermann Mannheim. 232 pp. 25 tables. 4 maps.*

Rock, Paul. Making People Pay. *338 pp.*

● **Taylor, Ian, Walton, Paul** and **Young, Jock.** The New Criminology. *For a Social Theory of Deviance. 325 pp.*

● **Taylor, Ian, Walton, Paul** and **Young, Jock.** (Eds) Critical Criminology. *268 pp.*

SOCIAL PSYCHOLOGY

Bagley, Christopher. The Social Psychology of the Epileptic Child. *320 pp.*

Brittan, Arthur. Meanings and Situations. *224 pp.*

Carroll, J. Break-Out from the Crystal Palace. *200 pp.*

● **Fleming, C. M.** Adolescence: Its Social Psychology. *With an Introduction to recent findings from the fields of Anthropology, Physiology, Medicine, Psychometrics and Sociometry. 288 pp.*

● The Social Psychology of Education: *An Introduction and Guide to Its Study. 136 pp.*

Linton, Ralph. The Cultural Background of Personality. *132 pp.*

● **Mayo, Elton.** The Social Problems of an Industrial Civilization. *With an Appendix on the Political Problem. 180 pp.*

Ottaway, A. K. C. Learning Through Group Experience. *176 pp.*

Plummer, Ken. Sexual Stigma. *An Interactionist Account. 254 pp.*

● **Rose, Arnold M.** (Ed.) Human Behaviour and Social Processes: *an Interactionist Approach. Contributions by Arnold M. Rose, Ralph H. Turner, Anselm Strauss, Everett C. Hughes, E. Franklin Frazier, Howard S. Becker et al. 696 pp.*

Smelser, Neil J. Theory of Collective Behaviour. *448 pp.*

Stephenson, Geoffrey M. The Development of Conscience. *128 pp.*

Young, Kimball. Handbook of Social Psychology. *658 pp. 16 figures. 10 tables.*

SOCIOLOGY OF THE FAMILY

Bell, Colin R. Middle Class Families: *Social and Geographical Mobility. 224 pp.*
Burton, Lindy. Vulnerable Children. *272 pp.*
Gavron, Hannah. The Captive Wife: *Conflicts of Household Mothers. 190 pp.*
George, Victor and **Wilding, Paul.** Motherless Families. *248 pp.*
Klein, Josephine. Samples from English Cultures.
    1. Three Preliminary Studies and Aspects of Adult Life in England. *447 pp.*
    2. Child-Rearing Practices and Index. *247 pp.*
Klein, Viola. The Feminine Character. *History of an Ideology. 244 pp.*
McWhinnie, Alexina M. Adopted Children. *How They Grow Up. 304 pp.*
● **Morgan, D. H. J.** Social Theory and the Family. *About 320 pp.*
● **Myrdal, Alva** and **Klein, Viola.** Women's Two Roles: *Home and Work. 238 pp.
27 tables.*
Parsons, Talcott and **Bales, Robert F.** Family: Socialization and Interaction Process. *In collaboration with James Olds, Morris Zelditch and Philip E. Slater. 456 pp.
50 figures and tables.*

SOCIAL SERVICES

Bastide, Roger. The Sociology of Mental Disorder. *Translated from the French by Jean McNeil. 260 pp.*
Carlebach, Julius. Caring For Children in Trouble. *266 pp.*
George, Victor. Foster Care. *Theory and Practice. 234 pp.*
    Social Security: *Beveridge and After. 258 pp.*
George, V. and **Wilding, P.** Motherless Families. *248 pp.*
● **Goetschius, George W.** Working with Community Groups. *256 pp.*
Goetschius, George W. and **Tash, Joan.** Working with Unattached Youth. *416 pp.*
Heywood, Jean S. Children in Care. *The Development of the Service for the Deprived Child. Third revised edition. 284 pp.*
King, Roy D., Ranes, Norma V. and **Tizard, Jack.** Patterns of Residential Care. *356 pp.*
Leigh, John. Young People and Leisure. *256 pp.*
● **Mays, John.** (Ed.) Penelope Hall's Social Services of England and Wales. *368 pp.*
Morris, Mary. Voluntary Work and the Welfare State. *300 pp.*
Nokes, P. L. The Professional Task in Welfare Practice. *152 pp.*
Timms, Noel. Psychiatric Social Work in Great Britain (1939–1962). *280 pp.*
●   Social Casework: *Principles and Practice. 256 pp.*

SOCIOLOGY OF EDUCATION

Banks, Olive. Parity and Prestige in English Secondary Education: a Study in Educational Sociology. *272 pp.*
● **Blyth, W. A. L.** English Primary Education. *A Sociological Description.*
    2. Background. *168 pp.*
Collier, K. G. The Social Purposes of Education: *Personal and Social Values in Education. 268 pp.*
Evans, K. M. Sociometry and Education. *158 pp.*
● **Ford, Julienne.** Social Class and the Comprehensive School. *192 pp.*
Foster, P. J. Education and Social Change in Ghana. *336 pp. 3 maps.*
Fraser, W. R. Education and Society in Modern France. *150 pp.*
Grace, Gerald R. Role Conflict and the Teacher. *150 pp.*
Hans, Nicholas. New Trends in Education in the Eighteenth Century. *278 pp.
19 tables.*
●   Comparative Education: *A Study of Educational Factors and Traditions. 360 pp.*
● **Hargreaves, David.** Interpersonal Relations and Education. *432 pp.*
●   Social Relations in a Secondary School. *240 pp.*
    School Organization and Pupil Involvement. *A Study of Secondary Schools.*

6

- **Mannheim, Karl** and **Stewart, W. A. C.** An Introduction to the Sociology of Education. *206 pp.*
- **Musgrove, F.** Youth and the Social Order. *176 pp.*
- **Ottaway, A. K. C.** Education and Society: An Introduction to the Sociology of Education. *With an Introduction by W. O. Lester Smith. 212 pp.*

  Peers, Robert. Adult Education: *A Comparative Study. Revised edition. 398 pp.*

  Stratta, Erica. The Education of Borstal Boys. *A Study of their Educational Experiences prior to, and during, Borstal Training. 256 pp.*
- **Taylor, P. H., Reid, W. A.** and **Holley, B. J.** The English Sixth Form. *A Case Study in Curriculum Research. 198 pp.*

SOCIOLOGY OF CULTURE

Eppel, E. M. and **M.** Adolescents and Morality: *A Study of some Moral Values and Dilemmas of Working Adolescents in the Context of a changing Climate of Opinion. Foreword by W. J. H. Sprott. 268 pp. 39 tables.*
- **Fromm, Erich.** The Fear of Freedom. *286 pp.*
- The Sane Society. *400 pp.*

  Johnson, L. The Cultural Critics. *From Matthew Arnold to Raymond Williams. 233 pp.*

  Mannheim, Karl. Essays on the Sociology of Culture. *Edited by Ernst Mannheim in co-operation with Paul Kecskemeti. Editorial Note by Adolph Lowe. 280 pp.*

  Merquior, J. G. The Veil and the Mask. *Essays on Culture and Ideology. Foreword by Ernest Gellner. 140 pp.*

  Zijderfeld, A. C. On Clichés. *The Supersedure of Meaning by Function in Modernity. 150 pp.*

SOCIOLOGY OF RELIGION

Argyle, Michael and **Beit-Hallahmi, Benjamin.** The Social Psychology of Religion. *256 pp.*

Glasner, Peter E. The Sociology of Secularisation. *A Critique of a Concept. 146 pp.*

Hall, J. R. The Ways Out. *Utopian Communal Groups in an Age of Babylon. 280 pp.*

Ranson, S., Hinings, B. and **Bryman, A.** Clergy, Ministers and Priests. *216 pp.*

Stark, Werner. The Sociology of Religion. *A Study of Christendom.*

   Volume II. *Sectarian Religion. 368 pp.*

   Volume III. *The Universal Church. 464 pp.*

   Volume IV. *Types of Religious Man. 352 pp.*

   Volume V. *Types of Religious Culture. 464 pp.*

Turner, B. S. Weber and Islam. *216 pp.*

Watt, W. Montgomery. Islam and the Integration of Society. *320 pp.*

SOCIOLOGY OF ART AND LITERATURE

Jarvie, Ian C. Towards a Sociology of the Cinema. *A Comparative Essay on the Structure and Functioning of a Major Entertainment Industry. 405 pp.*

Rust, Frances S. Dance in Society. *An Analysis of the Relationships between the Social Dance and Society in England from the Middle Ages to the Present Day. 256 pp. 8 pp. of plates.*

Schücking, L. L. The Sociology of Literary Taste. *112 pp.*

Wolff, Janet. Hermeneutic Philosophy and the Sociology of Art. *150 pp.*

SOCIOLOGY OF KNOWLEDGE

Diesing, P. Patterns of Discovery in the Social Sciences. *262 pp.*

● Douglas, J. D. (Ed.) Understanding Everyday Life. *370 pp.*
● Hamilton, P. Knowledge and Social Structure. *174 pp.*
  Jarvie, I. C. Concepts and Society. *232 pp.*
  Mannheim, Karl. Essays on the Sociology of Knowledge. *Edited by Paul Kecskemeti. Editorial Note by Adolph Lowe. 353 pp.*
  Remmling, Gunter W. The Sociology of Karl Mannheim. *With a Bibliographical Guide to the Sociology of Knowledge, Ideological Analysis, and Social Planning. 255 pp.*
  Remmling, Gunter W. (Ed.) Towards the Sociology of Knowledge. *Origin and Development of a Sociological Thought Style. 463 pp.*
  Scheler, M. Problems of a Sociology of Knowledge. *Trans. by M. S. Frings. Edited and with an Introduction by K. Stikkers. 232 pp.*

URBAN SOCIOLOGY

  Aldridge, M. The British New Towns. *A Programme Without a Policy. 232 pp.*
  Ashworth, William. The Genesis of Modern British Town Planning: *A Study in Economic and Social History of the Nineteenth and Twentieth Centuries. 288 pp.*
  Brittan, A. The Privatised World. *196 pp.*
  Cullingworth, J. B. Housing Needs and Planning Policy: *A Restatement of the Problems of Housing Need and 'Overspill' in England and Wales. 232 pp. 44 tables. 8 maps.*
  Dickinson, Robert E. City and Region: *A Geographical Interpretation. 608 pp. 125 figures.*
    The West European City: *A Geographical Interpretation. 600 pp. 129 maps. 29 plates.*
  Humphreys, Alexander J. New Dubliners: *Urbanization and the Irish Family. Foreword by George C. Homans. 304 pp.*
  Jackson, Brian. Working Class Community: *Some General Notions raised by a Series of Studies in Northern England. 192 pp.*
● Mann, P. H. An Approach to Urban Sociology. *240 pp.*
  Mellor, J. R. Urban Sociology in an Urbanized Society. *326 pp.*
  Morris, R. N. and Mogey, J. The Sociology of Housing. *Studies at Berinsfield. 232 pp. 4 pp. plates.*
  Mullan, R. Stevenage Ltd. *About 250 pp.*
  Rex, J. and Tomlinson, S. Colonial Immigrants in a British City. *A Class Analysis. 368 pp.*
  Rosser, C. and Harris, C. The Family and Social Change. *A Study of Family and Kinship in a South Wales Town. 352 pp. 8 maps.*
● Stacey, Margaret, Batsone, Eric, Bell, Colin and Thurcott, Anne. Power, Persistence and Change. *A Second Study of Banbury. 196 pp.*

RURAL SOCIOLOGY

  Mayer, Adrian C. Peasants in the Pacific. *A Study of Fiji Indian Rural Society. 248 pp. 20 plates.*
  Williams, W. M. The Sociology of an English Village: *Gosforth. 272 pp. 12 figures. 13 tables.*

SOCIOLOGY OF INDUSTRY AND DISTRIBUTION

  Dunkerley, David. The Foreman. *Aspects of Task and Structure. 192 pp.*
  Eldridge, J. E. T. Industrial Disputes. *Essays in the Sociology of Industrial Relations. 288 pp.*
  Hollowell, Peter G. The Lorry Driver. *272 pp.*
● Oxaal, I., Barnett, T. and Booth, D. (Eds) Beyond the Sociology of Development.

Economy and Society in Latin America and Africa. 295 pp.

Smelser, Neil J. Social Change in the Industrial Revolution: *An Application of Theory to the Lancashire Cotton Industry, 1770–1840. 468 pp. 12 figures. 14 tables.*

Watson, T. J. The Personnel Managers. *A Study in the Sociology of Work and Employment, 262 pp.*

ANTHROPOLOGY

Brandel-Syrier, Mia. Reeftown Elite. *A Study of Social Mobility in a Modern African Community on the Reef. 376 pp.*

Dickie-Clark, H. F. The Marginal Situation. *A Sociological Study of a Coloured Group. 236 pp.*

Dube, S. C. Indian Village. *Foreword by Morris Edward Opler. 276 pp. 4 plates.*
India's Changing Villages: *Human Factors in Community Development. 260 pp. 8 plates. 1 map.*

Fei, H.-T. Peasant Life in China. *A Field Study of Country Life in the Yangtze Valley. With a foreword by Bronislaw Malinowski. 328 pp. 16 pp. plates.*

Firth, Raymond. Malay Fishermen. *Their Peasant Economy. 420 pp. 17 pp. plates.*

Gulliver, P. H. Social Control in an African Society: a Study of the Arusha, Agricultural Masai of Northern Tanganyika. *320 pp. 8 plates. 10 figures.*
Family Herds. *288 pp.*

Jarvie, Ian C. The Revolution in Anthropology. *268 pp.*

Little, Kenneth L. Mende of Sierra Leone. *308 pp. and folder.*
Negroes in Britain. *With a New Introduction and Contemporary Study by Leonard Bloom. 320 pp.*

Tambs-Lyche, H. London Patidars. *About 180 pp.*

Madan, G. R. Western Sociologists on Indian Society. *Marx, Spencer, Weber, Durkheim, Pareto. 384 pp.*

Mayer, A. C. Peasants in the Pacific. *A Study of Fiji Indian Rural Society. 248 pp.*

Meer, Fatima. Race and Suicide in South Africa. *325 pp.*

Smith, Raymond T. The Negro Family in British Guiana: *Family Structure and Social Status in the Villages. With a Foreword by Meyer Fortes. 314 pp. 8 plates. 1 figure. 4 maps.*

SOCIOLOGY AND PHILOSOPHY

Adriaansens, H. Talcott Parsons and the Conceptual Dilemma. *About 224 pp.*

Barnsley, John H. The Social Reality of Ethics. *A Comparative Analysis of Moral Codes. 448 pp.*

Diesing, Paul. Patterns of Discovery in the Social Sciences. *362 pp.*

● **Douglas, Jack D.** (Ed.) Understanding Everyday Life. *Toward the Reconstruction of Sociological Knowledge. Contributions by Alan F. Blum, Aaron W. Cicourel, Norman K. Denzin, Jack D. Douglas, John Heeren, Peter McHugh, Peter K. Manning, Melvin Power, Matthew Speier, Roy Turner. D. Lawrence Wieder, Thomas P. Wilson and Don H. Zimmerman. 370 pp.*

Gorman, Robert A. The Dual Vision. *Alfred Schutz and the Myth of Phenomenological Social Science. 240 pp.*

Jarvie, Ian C. Concepts and Society. *216 pp.*

Kilminster, R. Praxis and Method. *A Sociological Dialogue with Lukács, Gramsci and the Early Frankfurt School. 334 pp.*

● **Pelz, Werner.** The Scope of Understanding in Sociology. *Towards a More Radical Reorientation in the Social Humanistic Sciences. 283 pp.*

Roche, Maurice. Phenomenology, Language and the Social Sciences. *371 pp.*

Sahay, Arun. Sociological Analysis. *212 pp.*

● **Slater, P.** Origin and Significance of the Frankfurt School. *A Marxist Perspective. 185 pp.*

Butler, J. R. Family Doctors and Public Policy. *208 pp.*
Davies, Martin. Prisoners of Society. *Attitudes and Aftercare. 204 pp.*
Gittus, Elizabeth. Flats, Families and the Under-Fives. *285 pp.*
Holman, Robert. Trading in Children. *A Study of Private Fostering. 355 pp.*
Jeffs, A. Young People and the Youth Service. *160 pp.*
Jones, Howard and Cornes, Paul. Open Prisons. *288 pp.*
Jones, Kathleen. History of the Mental Health Service. *428 pp.*
Jones, Kathleen with **Brown, John, Cunningham, W. J., Roberts, Julian** and
    Williams, Peter. Opening the Door. *A Study of New Policies for the Mentally
    Handicapped. 278 pp.*
Karn, Valerie. Retiring to the Seaside. *400 pp. 2 maps. Numerous tables.*
King, R. D. and **Elliot, K. W.** Albany: Birth of a Prison—End of an Era. *394 pp.*
Thomas, J. E. The English Prison Officer since 1850: *A Study in Conflict. 258 pp.*
Walton, R. G. Women in Social Work. *303 pp.*
● **Woodward, J.** To Do the Sick No Harm. *A Study of the British Voluntary Hospital
    System to 1875. 234 pp.*

International Library of Welfare and Philosophy
General Editors   Noel Timms and David Watson

● **McDermott, F. E.** (Ed.) Self-Determination in Social Work. *A Collection of Essays
    on Self-determination and Related Concepts by Philosophers and Social Work
    Theorists.* Contributors: *F. P. Biestek, S. Bernstein, A. Keith-Lucas, D. Sayer,
    H. H. Perelman, C. Whittington, R. F. Stalley, F. E. McDermott, I. Berlin, H. J.
    McCloskey, H. L. A. Hart, J. Wilson, A. I. Melden, S. I. Benn. 254 pp.*
● **Plant, Raymond.** Community and Ideology. *104 pp.*
Ragg, Nicholas M. People Not Cases. *A Philosophical Approach to Social Work.
    168 pp.*
● **Timms, Noel** and **Watson, David.** (Eds) Talking About Welfare. *Readings in
    Philosophy and Social Policy.* Contributors: *T. H. Marshall, R. B. Brandt, G. H.
    von Wright, K. Nielsen, M. Cranston, R. M. Titmuss, R. S. Downie, E. Telfer, D.
    Donnison, J. Benson, P. Leonard, A. Keith-Lucas, D. Walsh, I. T. Ramsey.
    320 pp.*
● Philosophy in Social Work. *250 pp.*
● **Weale, A.** Equality and Social Policy. *164 pp.*

Library of Social Work
General Editor   Noel Timms

● **Baldock, Peter.** Community Work and Social Work. *140 pp.*
○ **Beedell, Christopher.** Residential Life with Children. *210 pp. Crown 8vo.*
● **Berry, Juliet.** Daily Experience in Residential Life. *A Study of Children and their
    Care-givers. 202 pp.*
○ Social Work with Children. *190 pp. Crown 8vo.*
● **Brearley, C. Paul.** Residential Work with the Elderly. *116 pp.*
● Social Work, Ageing and Society. *126 pp.*
● **Cheetham, Juliet.** Social Work with Immigrants. *240 pp. Crown 8vo.*
● **Cross, Crispin P.** (Ed.) Interviewing and Communication in Social Work.
    *Contributions by C. P. Cross, D. Laurenson, B. Strutt, S. Raven. 192 pp. Crown
    8vo.*

● **Curnock, Kathleen** and **Hardiker, Pauline.** Towards Practice Theory. *Skills and Methods in Social Assessments. 208 pp.*

● **Davies, Bernard.** The Use of Groups in Social Work Practice. *158 pp.*

● **Davies, Martin.** Support Systems in Social Work. *144 pp.*

Ellis, June. (Ed.) West African Families in Britain. *A Meeting of Two Cultures. Contributions by Pat Stapleton, Vivien Biggs. 150 pp. 1 Map.*

● **Hart, John.** Social Work and Sexual Conduct. *230 pp.*

● **Hutten, Joan M.** Short-Term Contracts in Social Work. *Contributions by Stella M. Hall, Elsie Osborne, Mannie Sher, Eva Sternberg, Elizabeth Tuters. 134 pp.*

Jackson, Michael P. and **Valencia, B. Michael.** Financial Aid Through Social Work. *140 pp.*

● **Jones, Howard.** The Residential Community. *A Setting for Social Work. 150 pp.*

● (Ed.) Towards a New Social Work. *Contributions by Howard Jones, D. A. Fowler, J. R. Cypher, R. G. Walton, Geoffrey Mungham, Philip Priestley, Ian Shaw, M. Bartley, R. Deacon, Irwin Epstein, Geoffrey Pearson. 184 pp.*

Jones, Ray and **Pritchard, Colin.** (Eds) Social Work With Adolescents. *Contributions by Ray Jones, Colin Pritchard, Jack Dunham, Florence Rossetti, Andrew Kerslake, John Burns, William Gregory, Graham Templeman, Kenneth E. Reid, Audrey Taylor. About 170 pp.*

○ **Jordon, William.** The Social Worker in Family Situations. *160 pp. Crown 8vo.*

● **Laycock, A. L.** Adolescents and Social Work. *128 pp. Crown 8vo.*

● **Lees, Ray.** Politics and Social Work. *128 pp. Crown 8vo.*

● Research Strategies for Social Welfare. *112 pp. Tables.*

○ **McCullough, M. K.** and **Ely, Peter J.** Social Work with Groups. *127 pp. Crown 8vo.*

● **Moffett, Jonathan.** Concepts in Casework Treatment. *128 pp. Crown 8vo.*

Parsloe, Phyllida. Juvenile Justice in Britain and the United States. *The Balance of Needs and Rights. 336 pp.*

● **Plant, Raymond.** Social and Moral Theory in Casework. *112 pp. Crown 8vo.*

Priestley, Philip, Fears, Denise and **Fuller, Roger.** Justice for Juveniles. *The 1969 Children and Young Persons Act: A Case for Reform? 128 pp.*

● **Pritchard, Colin** and **Taylor, Richard.** Social Work: Reform or Revolution? *170 pp.*

○ **Pugh, Elisabeth.** Social Work in Child Care. *128 pp. Crown 8vo.*

● **Robinson, Margaret.** Schools and Social Work. *282 pp.*

○ **Ruddock, Ralph.** Roles and Relationships. *128 pp. Crown 8vo.*

● **Sainsbury, Eric.** Social Diagnosis in Casework. *118 pp. Crown 8vo.*

● Social Work with Families. *Perceptions of Social Casework among Clients of a Family Service. 188 pp.*

Seed, Philip. The Expansion of Social Work in Britain. *128 pp. Crown 8vo.*

● **Shaw, John.** The Self in Social Work. *124 pp.*

Smale, Gerald G. Prophecy, Behaviour and Change. *An Examination of Self-fulfilling Prophecies in Helping Relationships. 116 pp. Crown 8vo.*

Smith, Gilbert. Social Need. *Policy, Practice and Research. 155 pp.*

● Social Work and the Sociology of Organisations. *124 pp. Revised edition.*

● **Sutton, Carole.** Psychology for Social Workers and Counsellors. *An Introduction. 248 pp.*

● **Timms, Noel.** Language of Social Casework. *122 pp. Crown 8vo.*

● Recording in Social Work. *124 pp. Crown 8vo.*

● **Todd, F. Joan.** Social Work with the Mentally Subnormal. *96 pp. Crown 8vo.*

● **Walrond-Skinner, Sue.** Family Therapy. *The Treatment of Natural Systems. 172 pp.*

● **Warham, Joyce.** An Introduction to Administration for Social Workers. *Revised edition. 112 pp.*

● An Open Case. *The Organisational Context of Social Work. 172 pp.*

○ **Wittenberg, Isca Salzberger.** Psycho-Analytic Insight and Relationships. *A Kleinian Approach. 196 pp. Crown 8vo.*

12

Primary Socialization, Language and Education
General Editor   Basil Bernstein

Adlam, Diana S., *with the assistance of Geoffrey Turner and Lesley Lineker*. Code in Context. *272 pp.*
Bernstein, Basil. Class, Codes and Control. *3 volumes.*
●   1. *Theoretical Studies Towards a Sociology of Language. 254 pp.*
   2. *Applied Studies Towards a Sociology of Language. 377 pp.*
●   3. *Towards a Theory of Educational Transmission. 167 pp.*
Brandis, W. and **Bernstein, B.** Selection and Control. *176 pp.*
Brandis, Walter and **Henderson, Dorothy.** Social Class, Language and Communication. *288 pp.*
Cook-Gumperz, Jenny. Social Control and Socialization. *A Study of Class Differences in the Language of Maternal Control. 290 pp.*
● **Gahagan, D. M.** and **G. A.** Talk Reform. *Exploration in Language for Infant School Children. 160 pp.*
Hawkins, P. R. Social Class, the Nominal Group and Verbal Strategies. *About 220 pp.*
Robinson, W. P. and **Rackstraw, Susan D. A.** A Question of Answers. *2 volumes. 192 pp. and 180 pp.*
Turner, Geoffrey J. and **Mohan, Bernard A.** A Linguistic Description and Computer Programme for Children's Speech. *208 pp.*

Reports of the Institute of Community Studies

Baker, J. The Neighbourhood Advice Centre. A Community Project in Camden. *320 pp.*
● **Cartwright, Ann.** Patients and their Doctors. *A Study of General Practice. 304 pp.*
Dench, Geoff. Maltese in London. *A Case-study in the Erosion of Ethnic Consciousness. 302 pp.*
Jackson, Brian and **Marsden, Dennis.** Education and the Working Class: *Some General Themes Raised by a Study of 88 Working-class Children in a Northern Industrial City. 268 pp. 2 folders.*
Marris, Peter. The Experience of Higher Education. *232 pp. 27 tables.*
●   Loss and Change. *192 pp.*
Marris, Peter and **Rein, Martin.** Dilemmas of Social Reform. *Poverty and Community Action in the United States. 256 pp.*
Marris, Peter and **Somerset, Anthony.** African Businessmen. *A Study of Entrepreneurship and Development in Kenya. 256 pp.*
Mills, Richard. Young Outsiders: *a Study in Alternative Communities. 216 pp.*
Runciman, W. G. Relative Deprivation and Social Justice. *A Study of Attitudes to Social Inequality in Twentieth-Century England. 352 pp.*
Willmott, Peter. Adolescent Boys in East London. *230 pp.*
Willmott, Peter and **Young, Michael.** Family and Class in a London Suburb. *202 pp. 47 tables.*
Young, Michael and **McGeeney, Patrick.** Learning Begins at Home. *A Study of a Junior School and its Parents. 128 pp.*
Young, Michael and **Willmott, Peter.** Family and Kinship in East London. *Foreword by Richard M. Titmuss. 252 pp. 39 tables.*
  The Symmetrical Family. *410 pp.*

13

Reports of the Institute for Social Studies in Medical Care

Cartwright, Ann, Hockey, Lisbeth and **Anderson, John J.** Life Before Death. *310 pp.*
Dunnell, Karen and **Cartwright, Ann.** Medicine Takers, Prescribers and Hoarders. *190 pp.*
Farrell, C. My Mother Said. . . *A Study of the Way Young People Learned About Sex and Birth Control. 288 pp.*

Medicine, Illness and Society
General Editor W. M. Williams

Hall, David J. Social Relations & Innovation. *Changing the State of Play in Hospitals. 232 pp.*
Hall, David J. and **Stacey, M.** (Eds) Beyond Separation. *234 pp.*
Robinson, David. The Process of Becoming Ill. *142 pp.*
Stacey, Margaret *et al.* Hospitals, Children and Their Families. *The Report of a Pilot Study. 202 pp.*
Stimson, G. V. and **Webb, B.** Going to See the Doctor. *The Consultation Process in General Practice. 155 pp.*

Monographs in Social Theory
General Editor Arthur Brittan

● **Barnes, B.** Scientific Knowledge and Sociological Theory. *192 pp.*
Bauman, Zygmunt. Culture as Praxis. *204 pp.*
● **Dixon, Keith.** Sociological Theory. *Pretence and Possibility. 142 pp.*
The Sociology of Belief. *Fallacy and Foundation. About 160 pp.*
Goff, T. W. Marx and Mead. *Contributions to a Sociology of Knowledge. 176 pp.*
Meltzer, B. N., Petras, J. W. and **Reynolds, L. T.** Symbolic Interactionism. *Genesis, Varieties and Criticisms. 144 pp.*
● **Smith, Anthony D.** The Concept of Social Change. *A Critique of the Functionalist Theory of Social Change. 208 pp.*

Routledge Social Science Journals

The British Journal of Sociology. *Editor – Angus Stewart; Associate Editor – Leslie Sklair. Vol. 1, No. 1 – March 1950 and Quarterly. Roy. 8vo. All back issues available. An international journal publishing original papers in the field of sociology and related areas.*
Community Work. *Edited by David Jones and Marjorie Mayo. 1973. Published annually.*
Economy and Society. *Vol. 1, No. 1. February 1972 and Quarterly. Metric Roy. 8vo. A journal for all social scientists covering sociology, philosophy, anthropology, economics and history. All back numbers available.*

14

Ethnic and Racial Studies. *Editor – John Stone. Vol. 1 – 1978. Published quarterly.*
Religion. Journal of Religion and Religions. *Chairman of Editorial Board, Ninian Smart. Vol. 1, No. 1, Spring 1971. A journal with an inter-disciplinary approach to the study of the phenomena of religion. All back numbers available.*
Sociology of Health and Illness. *A Journal of Medical Sociology. Editor – Alan Davies; Associate Editor – Ray Jobling. Vol. 1, Spring 1979. Published 3 times per annum.*
Year Book of Social Policy in Britain. *Edited by Kathleen Jones. 1971. Published annually.*

Social and Psychological Aspects of Medical Practice
Editor   Trevor Silverstone

Lader, Malcolm. Psychophysiology of Mental Illness. *280 pp.*
● Silverstone, Trevor and Turner, Paul. Drug Treatment in Psychiatry. *Revised edition. 256 pp.*
Whiteley, J. S. and Gordon, J. Group Approaches in Psychiatry. *240 pp.*